JOHN

Vive la Cuisine!

# Rover's

THE CHEF IN THE HAT!!!

# Rover's

*Recipes from Seattle's Chef in the Hat*

THIERRY RAUTUREAU and CYNTHIA NIMS

photographs by FRANCE RUFFENACH

TEN SPEED PRESS
Berkeley | Toronto

TEN SPEED PRESS
P.O. Box 7123
Berkeley, California
94707
www.tenspeed.com

Distributed in Australia by Simon and Schuster Australia,
in Canada by Ten Speed Press Canada, in New Zealand by
Southern Publishers Group, in South Africa by Real Books,
and in the United Kingdom and Europe by Airlift Book Co.

Design by Catherine Jacobes for The Book Kitchen
Food Styling by Pouké
Project Management by Annie Nelson

Library of Congress Cataloging-in-Publication Data

Rautureau, Thierry.
  Rover's : recipes from Seattle's chef in the hat / Thierry
Rautureau and Cynthia Nims.
      p. cm.
  Includes index.
  ISBN 1-58008-479-6
  1. Cookery, American. 2. Cookery--Washington--Seattle. I.
Nims, Cynthia C. II. Rover's (Restaurant) III. Title.
  TX715.R238 2005
  641.5'09797'772--dc22
                              2005014669

First printing, 2005

Printed in China
1 2 3 4 5 6 7 8 9 10 — 09 08 07 06 05

*To Kathy, Ryan, and Adrian.*

*To my mother, Jeanette,*
*and in loving memory of*
*my father, Luc.*

# TABLE *of* CONTENTS

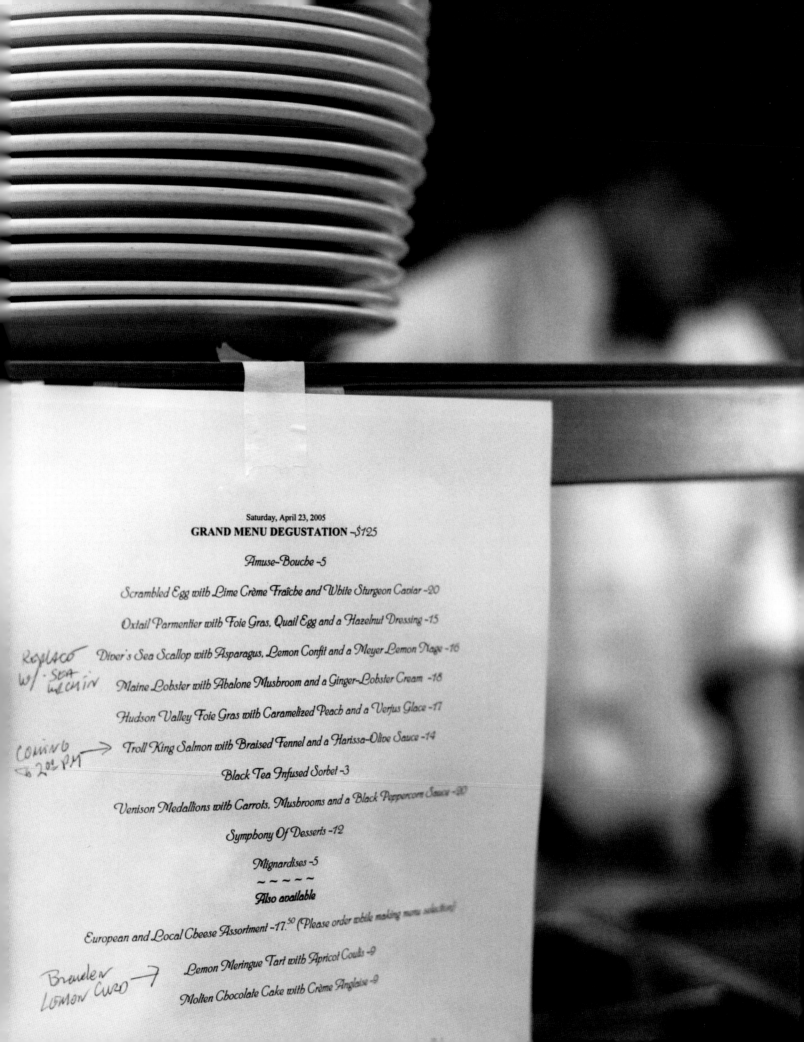

Saturday, April 23, 2005

# GRAND MENU DEGUSTATION –$125

*Amuse-Bouche* –5

*Scrambled Egg with Lime Crème Fraîche and White Sturgeon Caviar* –20

*Oxtail Parmentier with Foie Gras, Quail Egg and a Hazelnut Dressing* –15

*Replace w/ Sea Urchin* *Diver's Sea Scallop with Asparagus, Lemon Confit and a Meyer Lemon Nage* –16

*Maine Lobster with Abalone Mushroom and a Ginger-Lobster Cream* –18

*Hudson Valley Foie Gras with Caramelized Peach and a Verjus Glace* –17

*Coming to 2:05 PM* → *Troll King Salmon with Braised Fennel and a Harissa-Olive Sauce* –14

*Black Tea Infused Sorbet* –3

*Venison Medallions with Carrots, Mushrooms and a Black Peppercorn Sauce* –20

*Symphony Of Desserts* –12

*Mignardises* –5

~ ~ ~ ~ ~
## Also available

*European and Local Cheese Assortment* –17.⁵⁰ *(Please order while making menu selection)*

*Branden Lemon Curd* → *Lemon Meringue Tart with Apricot Coulis* –9

*Molten Chocolate Cake with Crème Anglaise* –9

## INTRODUCTION by Thierry Rautureau

One of the questions that I am most often asked—both by customers and by people I meet when traveling around the country—is "What is Pacific Northwest cuisine?" Every time the subject comes up, my answer is "It's all about the ingredients." We are so blessed in this part of the country to have an astounding supply of local seasonal foods, which come to my kitchen from dozens of different sources.

Among those sources are Veronica Williams, a mushroom forager on Washington's Long Beach Peninsula, and Lora Lea and Rick Misterly, who make Quillisascut goat cheese in Rice, Washington. Klipsun Vineyards is one of the most celebrated suppliers of grapes to the state's winemakers, and they also produce the verjus (sour green grape juice) that I use for sauces and dressings. Ulrika Hilborn, from Whidbey Island, farms a small plot of land that provides me and other local chefs with dozens of products, and she's always willing to try a new crop for me, such as shell beans or baby zucchini with blossoms. Since my first year of business, the Yoshimura family (three generations working side by side), owners of Mutual Fish in Seattle, have been providing me with top-quality local seafood. Don & Joe's Meats in the Pike Place Market is where I can count on getting lambs' tongues and other specialty meats. Thanks to them and the other many suppliers and growers in the area, I never lack for delicious products to cook with. The selection of foods that is available at my doorstep remains a constant source of inspiration.

# "It's all about the ingredients."

One of the highlights of Seattle's food scene is our famous Pike Place Market, which dates back to 1907. I have been to that market countless times over the years, and yet on almost every visit I discover something new, such as dry hibiscus blossoms at World Merchants or tatsoi (a green with a slight mustardy flavor) from an Asian farmer at the day stalls. A key feature of the market are the small farmers who sell specialty produce (often picked that morning). For the first seven or eight years of Rover's, I went to the Pike Place Market three or four times a week, meeting with farmers, going to Don & Joe's Meats for lamb kidneys, and buying fresh yogurt and organic cream at The Pike Place Creamery, as well as making other stops along the way.

These days, the farmers and producers come to our kitchen door, saving me considerable time. Despite the convenience of having the food delivered, nothing beats a "Hi, Thierry" or "Hey, what's up, chef?" when doing the shopping myself. So when I can, I go early in the morning and walk around the market with a cappuccino in hand, checking out the goods and letting ideas flow through my head, all the while planning the menu for that night. That feeling of discovery and following

one's culinary muse has to be the ultimate rush for a chef. The new artichokes are out (I'm thinking, "maybe sautéed with pine nuts and what else?"); the next stall will probably finish that thought with another ingredient, or perhaps take it somewhere very different, maybe to braised with baby leeks instead. Oh, red, black, *and* golden currants are here ("combine them with fish … maybe wild king salmon or perhaps quail instead"). On and on it goes. Two hours later, the trunk is full and it's time to go back to the restaurant and start creating dishes with all that great food. I miss those weekly trips to the Pike Place Market, but I do still get down there as often as I can for a good dose of delicious inspiration.

> "I still maintain that the Northwest is one of the regions, if not the region, of the United States with the best supply of local foods. It is a chef's dream come true …"

Of course, some of the ingredients we use come from outside the Northwest. They include foie gras (from Hudson Valley in upstate New York and Sonoma, California), wild fowl from Scotland during hunting season, and lobster and other seafood from the Atlantic Ocean. But despite my use of these "imported" products, I still maintain that the Northwest is one of the regions, if not the region, of the United States with the best supply of local foods. It is a chef's dream come true, and without these local products, Rover's would not be what it is today—a celebration of the Northwest served up with a French accent.

I was born in a very small farming village of about ten houses in St. Hilaire de Clisson, in the Muscadet region of France, just south of the Loire Valley. Strangely enough, I was born on the kitchen table (the hospital was just too far away). The closest big city to us was Nantes, which happens to be Seattle's sister city, as well as the last city on the Loire River before it spills into the Atlantic Ocean.

Much of my early childhood was spent running in the fields surrounding our house and at my grandparents' farm in nearby St. Hilaire de Loulay, where my family moved when I was seven years old. My grandparents worked the land attached to the Château de la Preuille, an 1810 château with about 40 hectares (roughly 100 acres) of property. Most of it was used for row crops, but there were 10 hectares of Muscadet grapes, which were used by Leon, the wine maker next door. I remember during the *vendanges* (grape harvest) watching the old wooden *pressoir* (grape press) oozing white grape juice into a big vat, which was then pumped into barrels. It's a smell I shall never forget.

My mother's parents rented their land from the *châtelain* (chateau owner). I do not know quite how they paid him, but I know that with ten cows, a few chickens and other fowl, rabbits, pigs, a horse, and some farmland, you can't become rich, especially when raising eleven children during and after the war. The buildings on the farm formed a square around a big central courtyard. To enter, you passed through two giant old wooden doors, crossed a big porch (with living quarters and the big kitchen above and to each side), and came into the dirt courtyard. On the left were the wine-making and storage buildings, in front were the stables and grange, and on the right were the maintenance buildings, the poultry building, the pig building, the old bread oven, and a small passage that led into the vegetable and fruit gardens. I spent many of my weekends and much of the summer in and around this farm while growing up; it is so far from the world I live in today, but it remains a magical place in my memory.

My grandfather's day started with an early rise at—if not before—dawn with a quick cup of coffee, then it was off to milk the cows and feed and tend to the animals. By nine o'clock, he was back inside for a healthful breakfast, which often included the leftover broth from the night before to which a little red wine was sometimes added, a combination that is called *faire chabrol* (a flavor I am still not sure about). He might also have had a piece of sautéed ham, charcuterie, and/or cheese, all washed down with some of that terrible wine he made (sorry, *grandpère!*). By ten o'clock, he was ready to go into the field, riding in a horse-drawn flatbed cart. Some days in summer, he would cut half a field of clover with his sickle and feed it to the cows and the horse, while in winter, he would pick sugar beets to feed the animals. I remember walking with my brother in the muddy field, laboriously picking giant beets to help my grandfather, drinking the sweet rainwater that had accumulated inside big cracks that formed in their tops. That sweet water was nectar, and I would love to have my boys try it some day.

In the kitchen, there was always a fire in the oversized fireplace (with the exception of the hottest days of summer), a big cast-iron cauldron hanging in it most of the time. The other heating and cooking source was a woodstove about four feet long and two feet wide, which included an oven where all the baking was done. The cauldron was used to make all kinds of soups, as well as pot au feu. My grandmother would always finish her pot au feu by holding one or two sugar cubes in a pair of iron tongs just above the fire. As soon as the sugar started to caramelize, she would drop them into the cauldron, and the liquid would instantly get some light brown color. As a kid, I was always amazed by that technique.

The other great piece in the kitchen was a large wooden table in the middle of the room with about a dozen wood-and-straw chairs around it. This table was the center of most of the activity in the house. We, of course, ate our meals there, but meal prep also took place at that table, as well as card playing in the afternoon and leisurely after-dinner conversations. The kitchen floor was made of hard concrete and the walls were white chalk. On the east wall an old seven-foot-tall clock that chimed every fifteen minutes, day and night, and on the north wall was a buffet (plate cupboard) so big that it held all the linens, glassware, plates, and silverware. On the south wall was the fireplace and the woodstove, and on the left side of the fireplace was *la hûche à pain* (bread hutch), where the country sourdough bread was kept.

In the morning, when staying at my grandparents' house, my brother, sister, and I would wake up and go into the kitchen where there was the constant aroma of a wood fire. My grandmother would take some of that morning's milk and bring it to a boil on the woodstove to make the most delicious hot chocolate for us. We would then take a slice of the coarse country bread, poke a fork into it, and hold the bread over the fire, filling the whole kitchen with the wonderful smell of toasted bread. We would then slather the warm toast with salted butter made on the farm, and sometimes some homemade jam. The morning aroma of that kitchen was a most comforting one, and it still lingers in my memory.

In addition to taking care of the chores inside the house, my grandmother also tended to the fowl and the garden. Since there were lots of children, she always had help. Some days I would go into the garden with my grandmother to help pick vegetables, then she would have me catch a chicken on the way back to the farmhouse. After it was killed and feathered, my grandmother would either roast it in the wood oven with sea salt and thyme or boil it slowly in the cauldron with vegetables, bay leaf, and thyme. Still at other times the chicken would be cut into pieces and stewed with vegetables, mushrooms, and bacon. Another significant memory is of the day I watched the annual slaughtering and butchering of one of the pigs with help from the local butcher, while the women were in the kitchen making sausages, pâtés, meat stews, and other preparations to make use of all the parts. It was a big deal because there was no time to waste. Refrigeration was almost nonexistent, which made the processing a bit intense (or at least it seemed that way from a kid's point of view). Life at the farm was always fascinating, whether it was helping to harvest the wheat or to milk a cow, and I am grateful to have been exposed to such experiences during my childhood.

My mother is an excellent cook and a swift and efficient decision maker when it comes to menu planning. In our house, when we were all seated around the dinner table and about to start our meal, the first thing my mom would always ask was "What are we going to eat at the next meal?" and before the meal was over the next meal was planned. My mother would leave me a list of instructions for specific chores to accomplish before she came home from work: clean the

haricot verts, light the fire under the pot au feu, pick the ripe tomatoes from the garden. She'd add, "I will finish the salad when I get home." Those were among my daily tasks as I grew up. When a special holiday came, my mom took over, prepping and cooking just about everything on her own (I'm sure she didn't trust us to do it as well). We kids were given the trustworthy duties of peeling the vegetables and setting the table. My father busied himself with choosing just the right wines to serve with the *entrée* (starter), the *poisson* (fish), and finally the *assiette de résistance* (main course). Such meals most always started off with an *apéritif maison*, such as his homemade aperitif of fresh green walnuts macerated in eau-de-vie. This group-effort approach to meals created warm memories for me that I like to re-create with my wife and sons, Ryan and Adrian.

My father is the most avid gardener I know. When I was growing up, I never once saw my parents buy a vegetable. To this day, they grow about 95 percent of the vegetables and fruits they need for the year, with enough extras to share with friends and neighbors. My parents own a piece of land two miles from our home where my dad spends most of his free time. He is very patient and attentive to detail, so the garden is always immaculate and perfectly organized. There are rows of cabbages, carrots, leeks, potatoes, haricots verts, peas, melons, red and green lettuces, herbs (thyme, laurel, basil, sage, rosemary, and lavender), a few grapevines, and walnut, pine (for pine nuts), chestnut, and hazelnut trees. Any gardener would be in awe of his work! I love being in my father's garden, a place where I can feel the labor and passion that he puts into the tending and the harvest. I am eternally grateful to have been exposed to this connection with the land and what it produces, a sensibility and connection that I still carry with me today.

> "Gardening is very soothing and is such a part of the circle of life; you grow it, you pick it, you cook it, and you eat it—an ingredient never gets any better than that."

Having watched my father work in his garden with such devotion when I was younger, I now really enjoy being in my own garden and working with my wife, Kathy, to build beds, plant, weed, pick something for dinner, or cut herbs and edible flowers for the restaurant garnish tray. Living just a couple of blocks from work can be very convenient (I do not like commuting!) when it comes to sharing some of the harvest with the restaurant. Gardening is very soothing and is such a part of the circle of life; you grow it, you pick it, you cook it, and you eat it—an ingredient never gets any better than that.

I took my first step on the path to a professional cooking career at the age of fourteen, when I started an apprenticeship in Cholet, a town of 50,000 people in the Anjou region, about thirty miles from my hometown. Those early years were rather demoralizing and shaky; let's just say the chef treated the dog better than me, and he was quite disappointed to see me graduate after two years of hardship. Despite that unfortunate early experience, I grew to appreciate the profession through work at Mont Saint Michel in Normandy, in Chamonix in the Alps, and in Hendaye in the Basque region near Spain.

After a one-year stint in the French Air Force (which I spent in the kitchens of the officer's quarters, fixing some very non-soldierly meals), I decided to head for the United States for some discoveries and adventures. It was 1978, and my first stop was Chicago. I worked at La Fontaine restaurant for three years, where I met some wonderful people. The three French owners, including Jean-Claude Poilevey, who today owns Le Bouchon and La Sardine in Chicago, gave me my first opportunity in America and were extremely supportive in my future endeavors.

Another fabulous person I met in Chicago is my friend, manager, and sommelier extraordinaire Cyril Fréchier. He arrived in the United States about six months after I did and was hired as a server at La Fontaine. We immediately clicked and shared the experience of discovering the United States together. During the summer of 1981, Cyril and I decided to take a trip to San Francisco, then drive down the coast to Los Angeles. It was such an incredible trip. For starters, we had to buy a used car because neither of us had a credit card and the rental company would not take cash (go figure). Our trip was so much fun and so full of discovery, it left us with the feeling that the visit was incomplete. Six months later we moved to Los Angeles, driving there with all our belongings in a van that constantly overheated.

In Los Angeles, both Cyril and I worked at The Regency Club for Joachim Splichal. I moved on after about six months to work with Fred Halpert at Mangia, an Italian restaurant in Rancho Park. This is where I met my wife and partner, Kathy; she was a server and I, of course, was in the kitchen. I was then fortunate to meet once again with chef Laurent Quenioux (I had previously worked with him at The Regency Club), who offered me the sous-chef position at the Seventh

"My goal as a restaurant owner was to be able to practice my art and follow my own culinary passions on an intimate scale."

Street Bistro in downtown Los Angeles. It was the opportunity of a lifetime; to this day I think Laurent is one of the most talented chefs around. His creativity is what attracted me most of all. That and the chance to work as his second hand, being in charge of a kitchen with people pulling you from all sides (not much different from my life today!), the chef expecting everything done exactly as he would do it. I still say that the position of sous-chef is one of the hardest jobs in a kitchen.

Sometime during my three and a half years with Laurent, a light came on and I finally understood that there was a place for me somewhere in the cooking profession, where my creative juices and sometimes childish behavior could both fit in. Watching Laurent creating dishes and menus on the spur of the moment, cooking with such great passion, and finishing every plate with a never-before-seen presentation was a daily high for me. This experience paved the way for what I am doing today.

I started to consider opening a restaurant in Santa Monica when I made a trip to Seattle to be the best man at Cyril's wedding. Cyril and Carolyn had moved to Seattle to be nearer her parents, who lived in Issaquah. A review of a small restaurant called Rover's had recently appeared in the *Los Angeles Times*, calling it a new hot spot for dining in Seattle. On that trip, we had a terrific meal at Rover's, and the chef, Kevin McKenzie, mentioned that the restaurant was for sale. I returned to Los Angeles and worked to convince Kathy, along with a business partner, to move to the beautiful Northwest.

We opened our doors on Monday, August 3, 1987, very quietly starting our Rover's life. The name stayed the same and the menu, too, at least for the first few weeks. We even hired most of the previous employees (one server, David Brumer, was with us until 2003). My goal as a restaurant owner was to be able to practice my art and follow my own culinary passions on an intimate scale. The small size of Rover's and its neighborhood setting offered the perfect ambience. From the beginning, I focused on smaller plates in a *dégustation* format (page 20) rather than full-size entrees, which allows for an orchestration of different flavors that complement and contrast over the course of a meal. The service had to be professional and polished but never obtrusive. Ultimately, I wanted to assure guests of a delicious meal but also make them feel relaxed, as if they were dining in a friend's home.

Well, it took a long time to get off the ground and gain a following, but eventually diners found Rover's, most liked what they ate, and the rest is history. Four years after opening, I bought out my partner and the business continued to grow. Four years later, we built an extension onto the dining room that also serves as a private dining space. In 2003, a more significant expansion was undertaken to create a foyer entrance and to double the size of the kitchen, a development I would have never dreamed of fifteen years ago.

So much has happened over the past seventeen years since we purchased Rover's, that little restaurant in a courtyard in Madison Valley, with only thirty-two seats (now fifty) and barely fifty wines on the list (today well over 500). It is amazing to look back on the transformation, working hard to stay in business through it all. Despite the challenges—the great days and not so great days, evenings with lots of customers and some with none—I still relish having this job that doesn't feel like a job at all. I simply love the adrenaline flow I get from having to create a menu for a regular customer who has never seen the menu or wine list because those choices were always left to Cyril and me. I thrive on that. It caps off the cycle that begins with my purveyors bringing me the best products they can, it continues with the chefs working beside me in the kitchen, and it ends with the servers who link us with the customers and ensure their evening runs smoothly and is enjoyable. It is a crazy business, owning a restaurant, but it is also an incredibly fulfilling one. I can't wait to cook for you the next time you walk through my door. I tip my hat to you and to all my customers who allow me the opportunity to live out my passion at Rover's. Bon Appétit!

—Thierry Rautureau, the Chef in the Hat!!!™

Seattle, 2005

## INTRODUCTION by Cynthia Nims

Working on this book with Thierry has been an outstanding experience for many reasons. Certainly not the least of them was the opportunity to taste—both in his kitchen and again in my own—every recipe in this collection. I can vouch for them all, though I personally won't be rushing to make the Manila clam soup with snails and bone marrow again any time soon.

The process has been like a culinary refresher course, as well. Back among the stockpots, peeling fava beans, making *crème pâtissière*, keeping an eye on reducing sauces, and even speaking French—it all took me back to my cooking school days more than a dozen years ago at La Varenne in France. It was nice to be back in a restaurant kitchen, but I sure don't regret my choice to go the writing route instead!

I was a fan of Rover's from my first meal there in the early 1990s. I remember so clearly that perfect August evening. My husband and I had played hooky from work and taken a ferry ride to Bainbridge Island simply to make the most of the summer day. Capped off with dinner on the patio at Rover's, the day became magical. To Thierry, I was just another guest, but his offer to "just cook for us" on our first visit was one we couldn't refuse…and we were hooked. Now having worked so closely with him on the cookbook, my admiration for his skill and creativity has grown exponentially.

As you'll learn from Thierry's discussions elsewhere in the book (if you haven't experienced it already at Rover's), his is a spontaneous style of cooking. The restaurant does have some signature dishes that are made nearly by rote: Scrambled Eggs with Lime Crème Fraîche and Caviar (page 89), Terrine of Sonoma Valley Foie Gras with Sauternes Aspic and Thyme Brioche (page 60), and Pinot Noir Sorbet (page 169) among them. But only the tiniest percent of what is cooked in the Rover's kitchen ever gets written down; much of it is ephemeral, here tonight, changed, adapted, and retooled tomorrow.

Thierry has definitely mastered the art of culinary improvisation. I love jazz and many times I'd watch him riffing on an idea or an ingredient while creating a recipe and think how much his energy and focus reminded me of watching great jazz performers. He even takes it to an audible level, going all percussion with the pots and utensils while waiting for something to reduce on the stovetop, unconsciously driving that jazz analogy home. (Did you know that the fluted edge of a pair of tongs drawn across the top of a heavy pot makes a nice rat-a-tat kind of sound? Yet another dose of kitchen wisdom from the master.)

The trick comes in freeze-framing that creative spirit long enough to record the moment for future reference, for your reference. Here's how we did it:

First Thierry and I brainstormed on paper the many dozens of potential recipes with seasonal diversity and covering a good range of courses, from cold appetizers through dessert. Then came the fun. A couple of days a week, I'd show up at his kitchen door and set up my laptop on the counter in the middle of the kitchen. It took me a few weeks to realize that a sheet of plastic wrap draped over the keyboard was important to avoid splatter disasters and to make it easier to go from taking notes to peeling beets and back again. We'd usually have a plan of attack—

some specific recipes in mind—but I can't say how many times I heard, *"On va pas faire ça, on va faire autre chose"* ("We're not going to do that, we're going to do something else") before we got started.

After a few sips of coffee, he'd start cooking and I'd start writing, capturing every detail I could, firing up the digital camera to photograph special techniques, midway progress, and final presentations. Thierry's humor is infectious, and it made the long days more than bearable. I had to stay on my toes just to keep up. One day we were working on a lobster recipe and he said something about *homard* (lobster) *shreef* (huh?), which I started typing into my computer, realizing a second too late that he was pulling my leg (Omar Sharif, get it?!). Truly never a dull moment.

Back home at my computer, I'd pore over those notes and photos and write up a full draft of each recipe. Then into my own kitchen to give them a run-through in a home environment with pretty much average everything. My friends loved me. Always happy to be guinea pigs for recipe-testing dinners, these Rover's rounds were particularly popular. Taste, comment, reflect, tweak, rework, and retest as needed. Although some recipes certainly are quite elaborate, I do know that they can all be accomplished in a home kitchen. And many are much easier than you might expect. I feel like something of a culinary interpreter, translating Thierry's distinct style into a format for the home cook. It won't exactly replicate the complete dining experience of a meal at Rover's, but you, your friends, and your family will revel in these tastes from Thierry's kitchen.

# FOOD AND WINE PAIRING PRINCIPLES by Cyril Fréchier, Sommelier

For each recipe in this cookbook, Thierry asked me to make wine recommendations that echo the style of wine and food pairings we offer in the restaurant. The rapport between wine and food is particularly dynamic at Rover's, given the spontaneous creativity of Thierry's cooking and the extensive selections of wines in our cellar. For my part, I rely on a few simple rules that you can use at home as well:

- Wine is meant to complement a dish; it should not become the focal point and dominate the pairing. The more complex, powerful wines will be best served with dishes that have deep, rich flavors or bold seasonings. For lighter, more delicate dishes, crisply fresh or fruity wines tend to be a better choice, as they are less likely to overpower the food.

- Experimentation is the best way to gain knowledge about the pros and cons of pairings: It's hard to know for sure whether a food and wine are compatible until you try them together. As a sommelier, I do this experimentation ahead of time so you, the diner, don't have to. I recollect combinations I've had in the past and mine those experiences to help formulate new pairings. If you make notes about wine and food combinations that you really like (or perhaps don't), over time you'll also have a good base from which to make your own pairings with confidence.

- Finally, food and wine pairing cannot be an exact science—indeed, it should not be a science at all, but an art by which the addition of wine adds complexity and enjoyment to a meal. There is no single "best" wine for a dish, since ultimately your own personal taste will dictate which pairings you like. Use my recommendations as a starting point and feel free to amend them.

Beyond judging for quality when tasting a wine for the first time, I try to understand the wine's *raison d'être*—its reason for being. Acid, tannin, alcohol, dryness, fruit concentration levels—I make note of all these characteristics. But what interests me the most is the personality the wine, the harmony and complexity of the whole. I begin to think how its traits may be used to harmonize with a dish, keeping in mind ingredients Thierry uses throughout the seasons and the styles of recipes he prepares.

When Thierry presents me with a new creation, I first conceptualize the dish, and then focus on its component ingredients, depth, intensity, and degree of flavors; at that point, I can hopefully provide several wine options. More often than not, the idea is sound: the wine is a close relative. Sometimes, though, the pairing is off, the flavors clashing, in which case I revisit my train of thought and consider another candidate. A new lesson has been learned.

With a few exceptions, selected wines are of recent vintages. I admire all of these wines for their qualities, their purity of flavors, and the joy they bring me when I drink them. I hope that you will, too. *Santé.*

## SEASONAL MENUS

Since the beginning of time (well, at least the beginning of time at Rover's), we have featured *dégustation* menus, multicourse tasting menus in the French tradition. To *déguster* is to eat in small bites, which allows you to enjoy thoroughly every morsel of the dish in front of you, to savor it, not simply "eat" it. My philosophy with Rover's is to create a place where diners will enjoy a lot of tantalizing bites over the course of an evening, rather than just one big plate of food. Since we have a small restaurant, I've always been able to focus on each customer's individual dining experience, an element I value greatly. The menu offers three options each night—a menu dégustation, a vegetarian menu dégustation (which I've offered since the first day I opened the restaurant), and a grand menu dégustation. Many guests will choose one of these menus, but regulars and others who are adventurous will ask me simply to cook for them. This is what makes me happiest as a chef, being able to create dishes spontaneously for my guests! I'll sometimes create as many as twelve courses, if I know they're ready for a complete adventure. Other guests who aren't interested in a dégustation menu can choose from à la carte options to suite their taste. It should be a culinary experience, not a gluttonous one.

Below you'll see some examples of tasting menus, orchestrated from recipes in this cookbook. The dégustation menu is a progression of dishes that takes into account a variety of elements—temperature, richness, texture, color, sweetness—that will build and crescendo with the "main" course, typically just before dessert. Every dish we create in the kitchen is taken in the context of what other items the customers will be eating throughout the evening. It's always a balance. In an ideal menu of that kind, the customer will be perfectly happy, not too full, not still hungry. For me, the ultimate pleasure I get as a chef is seeing the glowing, happy face of a customer who has just eaten something delicious and can't wait for the next bite.

---

### SPRING

---

House-Cured Salmon with Yakima Asparagus Salad

Spot Prawns with Cèpes and Pedro Ximenez Noble Sour

Alaskan Halibut with Manila Clams, Petite Peas, and Pepper Cress

Red Beet Sorbet

Bainbridge Island Lamb Loin with Chanterelle and Potato Risotto, Fava Beans,
    and Lemon Thyme Sauce

Honey Mousse Charlotte with Rhubarb Purée

## SUMMER

Heirloom Tomatoes with Roasted Shallots, Pine Nuts, and Sherry Vinaigrette

Corn Flan with Lobster

Whole Roasted Striped Sea Bass with Fennel, Moroccan Olives, and Thyme Vinegar

Infused Tea Sorbet with Fireweed Honey

Sonoma Squab in Artichoke Bottoms with Walla Walla Onion Compote and Lovage Sauce

Raspberry and Blueberry Millefeuille

## FALL

Terrine of Root Vegetables with Horseradish Cream

Manila Clam Soup with Snails, Bone Marrow, and Spaghetti Squash

Red Pot au Feu of Maine Lobster and Root Vegetables

Pinot Noir Sorbet

Venison Medallions with Parsnip Ragout, Apricots, and Mustard Sauce

Pear and Apple Frangipane Tartlets with Caramel and Huckleberry Sauces

## WINTER

Dungeness Crab Salad with Garlic, Roasted Shallots, and Pomegranate Vinaigrette

Diver Sea Scallops with Beets, Foie Gras, and Aged Balsamic Vinegar

Columbia River Sturgeon with Rabbit Kidneys, Truffle Mousseline, and Lovage Glaze

Pink Grapefruit and Vermouth Sorbet

Roasted Pheasant with Brussels Sprouts and Roasted Garlic Sauce

Orange Panna Cotta with Pomegranate Sorbet

## VEGETARIAN

Spring Vegetable Salad with Avocado and Lemon Olive Oil Dressing

Carrot and Ginger Soup with Roasted Cauliflower à la Tom Douglas

Beet and Goat Cheese Tartlets with Walla Walla Sweet Onion Purée

Celery and Fennel Sorbet

Stuffed Cabbage with Green Lentils, Pearl Onions, and Cabernet Sauce

Honey Mousse Charlotte with Rhubarb Purée

# Salads

# SPRING VEGETABLE SALAD

## with Avocado and Lemon Olive Oil Dressing

**MAKES 4 SERVINGS /** The fresh, bright flavors of spring vegetables are as appealing to the palate as their vivid colors are to the eye, here presented almost like a bouquet of flowers. When I was sous-chef at the Seventh Street Bistro in Los Angeles, chef Laurent Quenioux made a similar salad; this version of mine is in honor of him. The avocado, thinly sliced to form a ring in which the salad is composed, should be ripe enough to have good flavor but not too soft; it should give very little when gently squeezed in your hand. You may use small regular carrots or beets rather than ones that are baby-size if you are unable to find them. If using small carrots, cut them crosswise in half, then cut the top halves lengthwise into quarters and cut the bottoms lengthwise in half. For beets, halve them stem end to root end, then cut each half into 8 wedges.

Pierre-Yves Tijou 1999 Savennières "Clos des Perrières," Loire Valley

¼ pound baby carrots, unpeeled

¼ pound baby beets, scrubbed

2 ounces green beans, trimmed

2 ounces freshly shelled English peas

2 ounces snow peas, trimmed

2 ounces asparagus spears, trimmed

2 large ripe but firm avocados

Handful mixed tender greens (red oak,
   green leaf, mizuna, spinach), rinsed
   and trimmed, large leaves torn in
   half or quartered

Lemon Dressing

2 tablespoons freshly squeezed lemon
   juice

2 teaspoons Dijon mustard

⅓ cup olive oil

Sea salt and freshly ground white pepper

Bring 2 saucepans of salted water to a boil over high heat. When the water comes to a boil, add the carrots to 1 pan and the beets to the other. Decrease the heat to medium, and cook until tender, about 7 minutes for the carrots and 20 minutes for the beets. Drain well and set aside separately to cool.

Refill one pan with salted water and bring to a boil; prepare a large bowl of ice water. Add the green beans to the boiling water and cook until vivid green and just barely tender, 2 to 3 minutes. Scoop out the beans with a slotted spoon and plunge them into the ice water to cool them. Repeat with the English peas, snow peas, and asparagus, cooking each separately until just tender, 1 to 2 minutes. Cool the vegetable separately in the ice water, then dry well on paper towels.

*For the dressing,* whisk the lemon juice and mustard together in a small bowl until blended. Slowly add the olive oil, whisking constantly until blended and smooth. Season to taste with salt and pepper, whisking until the salt dissolves.

*continued*

**Garnish**

Chervil sprigs

Sweet cicely sprigs

Garlic chive sprigs

Red Bell Pepper Coulis (page 214)

Yellow Bell Pepper Coulis (page 214)

Shortly before serving, halve, pit, and peel the avocados. Set an avocado half, cut-side down, on the cutting board and cut crosswise into $1/8$-inch-thick slices, holding the slices together as you go. Using your fingers, gently separate the slices to form a strip of partially overlapping slices about 12 inches long. Gently draw the 2 ends around to meet and overlap, forming a round "fence" of avocado. Set this in the center of a plate (use a long narrow spatula to help transfer the avocado) and repeat with the remaining avocado halves. Drizzle about 1 teaspoon of lemon dressing over each avocado half.

Cut the snow peas on the diagonal into thirds. Cut the green beans and asparagus into 2-inch lengths. Combine the snow peas, green beans, asparagus, and English peas in a bowl and drizzle with about half of the remaining vinaigrette. Toss gently to mix, then arrange the mixture in the center of the avocado circles, dividing it evenly, with some of the vegetables decoratively perched up against the avocado edge. Set the bowl aside.

Trim the carrots and beets and slip off their skins. Cut the baby carrots and beets lengthwise in quarters, put them in the reserved bowl (leave pre-trimmed larger carrots and beets as is), and drizzle with about half of the remaining dressing. Toss gently to mix, then arrange the carrots and beets alongside the green vegetables. Add a small tuft of lettuce to fill out the avocado circles.

To serve, top each with a sprig or two of chervil, sweet cicely, and garlic chives. Drizzle the remaining dressing over the salads, and add dots of red and yellow bell pepper coulis around the edge.

# QUAIL AND FRISÉE SALAD

## with Duck Prosciutto, Poached Quail Egg, and Red Wine Vinegar

**MAKES 4 SERVINGS** / This dish is reminiscent of the classic *salade Lyonnaise*, in which frisée is tossed with crisp *lardoons* (bacon pieces) in a red wine vinaigrette and served with a poached egg on top. In place of the bacon, I use duck prosciutto, which I make at Rover's. Traditional prosciutto is made from the leg of the pig, so my duck version also uses the leg of the bird, leaving the delectable breast for other recipes (though many commercial producers of duck prosciutto make theirs with breast meat). My uncle Marcel used to smoke and age his own hams, wrapping the pig leg in thyme and bay leaves. He'd first make a fire in the huge stone fireplace in the farmhouse using bundles of old vines from the family's vineyard. Then he'd hang the leg over the embers to smoke slowly, then he'd age it for as long as six months. What a memory! I can still smell the deep aroma of his house-cured ham. That memory lingers in my own prosciutto.

Domaine des Terres Dorées 2002 Beaujolais "Cuvée à l'Ancienne," France

4 whole quail (about ¼ pound each), rinsed and patted dry

Sea salt and freshly ground black pepper

6 to 7 tablespoons olive oil, plus more if needed

2 teaspoons plus a pinch of minced fresh rosemary

2 tablespoons unsalted butter

1 cup plus 2 teaspoons red wine vinegar

2 teaspoons minced shallots

¼ teaspoon minced fresh thyme

1 ounce duck prosciutto, finely shredded

4 quail eggs

1 head frisée, trimmed, rinsed, and dried

**Garnish**

Rosemary blossoms

Trim away the necks from the quail and cut away the first joint of the wings. Season the cavities of the birds with salt and pepper. Truss each quail by tying the legs together with a long piece of kitchen string, making a butcher's knot (see box). Pull the 2 lengths of string down the side of the bird, between the legs and body, then cross the 2 pieces of string underneath the quail. Bring the string back on top of the bird, holding down the wings, and tie a knot.

Combine 2 tablespoons of the olive oil, 2 teaspoons of the rosemary, and a good pinch each of salt and pepper in a large bowl. Add the quail and toss gently to coat evenly. Set aside to marinate for about 30 minutes, or cover and marinate in the refrigerator for up to 2 hours.

Preheat the oven to 350°F.

Heat a heavy ovenproof skillet over medium-high heat. Add the butter and 2 tablespoons of the olive oil to the pan and heat until the butter melts and is foamy white. Add the quail (reserve the marinade) and decrease the heat to medium. Brown the quail well on all sides,

*continued*

1 to 2 minutes, then set the birds on their backs and transfer the skillet to the oven. Bake until the juices run clear when the thigh is pierced or when you lift the quail and let the juices run from the cavity, about 10 minutes. Take the quail from the oven and cover loosely with foil to keep warm.

Meanwhile, combine 1 cup of the vinegar with 1 teaspoon of the shallot, the thyme, and the remaining pinch of rosemary in a saucepan. Bring to a boil over high heat, then decrease the heat to medium-high and reduce the liquid by half, about 10 minutes. Add the reduction to the reserved marinade and stir to blend evenly, then strain the mixture through a fine-mesh sieve into a small skillet, pressing firmly on the solids to remove as much of the flavorful liquid as possible. Add the prosciutto and the remaining teaspoon of shallot to the vinaigrette and cook over medium-high heat just to warm through. Whisk in another 2 tablespoons of the olive oil and taste the vinaigrette for seasoning, adding more olive oil, salt, or pepper to taste. Set aside.

Fill a small skillet with water and add the remaining 2 teaspoons of vinegar with a pinch of salt. Bring the water to a boil over high heat, then decrease the heat to medium and crack the quail eggs into the water. Poach gently until the whites have set but the yolks are still soft, about 1 minute.

To serve, tear the tender inner frisée leaves into bite-size pieces and put in a bowl. Add the prosciutto and about half of the vinaigrette, toss to mix well, and mound the frisée in the center of individual plates. Cut off and discard the string from the quail. Cut the thigh/leg portions from the bodies and lean them against the frisée on each plate. Cut the breasts from the quail and slice each breast on the diagonal into 4 slices. Arrange around one side of the frisée and drizzle the remaining vinaigrette over and around the quail. Set a poached quail egg on top of each salad and season lightly with salt and pepper, adding more pepper around the perimeter of the salad. Sprinkle the plates with rosemary blossoms.

The "butcher's knot" is a tip from the pros that helps make trussing tasks a bit easier. If you first wrap one end of the string around the other twice, rather than just once, when you pull the ends, the slipknot will hold securely, making it easier to continue with the trussing.

# HEIRLOOM TOMATOES

## with Roasted Shallots, Pine Nuts, and Sherry Vinaigrette

**MAKES 4 SERVINGS** / I love homegrown heirloom tomatoes served simply: sliced with some young goat cheese or fresh buffalo mozzarella on the side, a drizzle of olive oil, and a sprinkle of good sea salt and coarsely ground pepper. That's when I know summer is really here in the Northwest! This embellishment on that theme includes sweet roasted shallots and toasted pine nuts with a flavorful sherry vinaigrette.

Domaine Larredya 2001 Jurançon Sec, France

8 large shallots

3 tablespoons hazelnut or olive oil

1 tablespoon unsalted butter

1 teaspoon minced fresh thyme

Sea salt

1/4 cup sherry vinegar

1/4 cup dry sherry

1/4 cup olive oil

12 ounces small heirloom tomatoes, quartered, or 8 each red, orange, and yellow cherry or baby plum tomatoes, halved

1 tablespoon minced fresh basil

1/2 teaspoon minced fresh chives

1/4 teaspoon minced garlic

Freshly ground black pepper

1/3 cup pine nuts, toasted (page 234)

Garnish

Basil sprigs

Basil Oil (page 216)

Red Bell Pepper Coulis (page 214)

Halve the shallots lengthwise, then cut crosswise into 1-inch pieces. Heat the hazelnut oil and butter in a saucepan or heavy skillet over medium-low heat until the butter melts and is foamy white. Add the shallots, thyme, and a good pinch of salt. Cook, stirring occasionally, until the shallots are nicely browned and tender, 10 to 15 minutes. Add the sherry vinegar and reduce by two-thirds, about 3 minutes. Add the sherry and simmer to reduce by half, 2 to 3 minutes longer, then add the olive oil. Strain the shallots from the vinaigrette, setting both aside to cool.

Put the tomatoes in a large bowl and drizzle with the cooled vinaigrette. Add the basil, chives, and garlic and season to taste with salt and pepper. (There should be a good bit of pepper to contrast the sweetness of the shallots.) Toss gently to mix.

To serve, form a circle of shallots in the center of individual plates. Add the pine nuts to the tomato salad and toss to mix with a slotted spoon, then spoon the tomatoes over the shallots. Top the tomatoes with a basil sprig. Drizzle any remaining vinaigrette from the tomato bowl around, then dot the plates with basil oil and red pepper coulis.

# FENNEL AND CUCUMBER SALAD
## with Pear and Rice Vinegar

**MAKES 4 SERVINGS /** This is a refreshing salad; bright, crisp cucumber slices are paired with fresh fennel and sweet, juicy pear. The surprise ingredient here is Pastis, my favorite of the anisette liqueurs, which echoes the subtle anise flavor of the fennel.

Joseph Phelps 2002 Viognier, Napa Valley

1 fennel bulb

Sea salt

$1/3$ cup Pastis or other anisette liqueur

1 ripe but firm Anjou pear

$1/4$ cup seasoned rice vinegar

1 English cucumber

3 tablespoons olive oil

Freshly ground white pepper

1 tablespoon minced fresh chives

Trim the stalks from the fennel bulb and discard (or use for vegetable stock, page 210), reserving some of the tender fennel fronds for garnish. Halve the fennel bulb lengthwise and cut out the tough core. Separate the layers of fennel, trimming away any tough or browned portions. Cut the fennel lengthwise (with the grain) into thin julienne strips. Put the fennel in a bowl with a pinch of salt and the Pastis. Toss to combine and set aside to marinate for a few minutes, then strain through a sieve into a small saucepan, reserving the fennel.

Bring the Pastis to a boil over high heat, being careful to avoid any flames that may rise up from the pan as the alcohol burns off. Boil until reduced to 3 tablespoons, 2 to 3 minutes. Remove from the heat and set aside to cool.

Peel and core the pear and cut it into julienne strips. Put the pear in a small bowl with the rice vinegar and gently toss to mix. Set aside to marinate for a few minutes, then strain through a sieve into a bowl, reserving the vinegar and pear.

Trim the ends from the cucumber and peel away the skin, then halve the cucumber lengthwise and scrape out the seeds with a small spoon. Thinly slice the cucumber crosswise and put in a large bowl. Stir the reserved rice vinegar into the reduced Pastis, then drizzle this over the cucumber, tossing to coat evenly. Add 2 tablespoons of the olive oil with a pinch of salt and a few grindings of pepper, then toss to combine.

*continued*

Garnish

**Red Bell Pepper Coulis (page 214)**

**Yellow Bell Pepper Coulis (page 214)**

Combine the fennel, the pear, the remaining 1 tablespoon of olive oil and the chives in another bowl. Season lightly with salt and pepper and toss gently.

To serve, lay some of the fennel fronds on each chilled plate and set a 4-inch ring mold on top so that the fronds are still visible. Use a slotted spoon to transfer the cucumber into the rings, top with the fennel-pear mixture, then carefully lift up the ring without disturbing the salad. (Alternatively, spoon the salad onto the plates in tidy circles.) Drizzle a bit of the remaining vinaigrette from the cucumber bowl around the salads and add dots of red and yellow pepper coulis around the edge. Top each salad with a small frond of fennel.

**GARNISHING**—Most recipes in the book feature a "Garnish" listing at the end of the ingredients list. Don't be too concerned about following those garnish options to the letter. If, for instance, a dessert recipe calls for a bit of crème anglaise to spoon around the plate before serving, you can instead simply whip some lightly sweetened heavy cream to thicken it and use that instead. Likewise, instead of making up a batch of basil oil to drizzle around a dish, you could finish it with a drizzle of extra virgin olive oil or simply omit that final flourish. At Rover's, we have a lot of garnish options on hand at all times, so these finishing touches are easy for us. But at home, you might not want to go to that extra effort for a small drizzle to accent a plate. Those garnish suggestions reflect the way that I would garnish the plate in my restaurant kitchen. I'd rather have you cook the recipe and enjoy it without garnish, rather than have you panic about shrimp roe and chervil sprigs!

# DUNGENESS CRAB SALAD
## with Roasted Garlic, Shallots, and Pomegranate Vinaigrette

**MAKES 4 SERVINGS /** The sweetness that garlic and shallots acquire after roasting is a wonderful complement to the natural sweetness of Dungeness crab, accented here by the sweet-tart flavor of pomegranate—a favorite ingredient of mine. The roasting method is very easy but it takes at least an hour. You might want to roast an extra head or two of garlic at the same time to have on hand for other dishes. It is delicious puréed into a creamy soup, stirred into mashed potatoes, or added to a pan of simple steamed mussels. The roasted garlic will keep for up to a week in the refrigerator.

Kees-Kieren 2002 Riesling Kabinett "Graacher Domprobst," Mosel

1 head of garlic, unpeeled

2 shallots, unpeeled

3 tablespoons plus 4 teaspoons olive oil

Sea salt and freshly ground white pepper

4 slices Thyme Brioche (page 220) or
    8 slices baguette, 1/4 inch thick

1/4 cup plus 1 teaspoon pomegranate
    juice (page 235)

1/4 cup red wine vinegar

6 ounces Dungeness crabmeat (page 232)

2 teaspoons minced fresh chives

Small handful chervil leaves or baby
    watercress

1 teaspoon Basil Oil (page 216) or extra
    virgin olive oil

Garnish

Yellow Bell Pepper Oil (page 218)

Preheat the oven to 375°F.

Peel away the loose papery skin from the head of garlic and trim just enough of the root end to expose some of the garlic flesh and make it easier to squeeze out after roasting. Trim the root end from the shallots as well. Set the garlic and shallots in the center of a large piece of aluminum foil, drizzle with 2 teaspoons of the olive oil and season with salt and pepper. Wrap the package up securely and roast until the garlic and shallots are tender when pressed between your fingers, 1 to 1 1/4 hours. Unwrap and set aside until cool enough to handle.

Trim the brioche slices into rounds about 4 inches in diameter. Heat a skillet over medium heat, then add 2 teaspoons of the remaining olive oil. Add the brioche and toast well on each side, about 3 minutes total. Set aside on paper towels.

Combine 1/4 cup of the pomegranate juice and the wine vinegar in a small saucepan. Bring to a boil over medium-high heat and boil until reduced to 2 tablespoons, 5 to 7 minutes. Remove the pan from the heat, whisk in the remaining 3 tablespoons of olive oil until blended, and set the vinaigrette aside.

*continued*

Pick over the crabmeat to remove any bits of shell or cartilage and set 4 large claw or leg portions aside for garnish. Put the remaining crabmeat in a bowl. Add the pomegranate vinaigrette and chives and season to taste with salt and pepper. Toss well to combine evenly.

Squeeze the roasted garlic and shallots from their skins and coarsely chop. Toss the garlic and shallots with the remaining 1 teaspoon pomegranate juice and season to taste with salt and pepper.

To serve, spoon the garlic-shallot mixture onto the toasted brioche rounds and set them on individual plates. Form the crab salad into 4 large quenelles (page 235) and set them on top of the brioche (or simply spoon the crab salad on top of the garlic-shallot mixture), topping the crab salad with reserved claw or leg portions. Toss the chervil with the basil oil and a pinch of salt in a small bowl. Place the chervil salad alongside and surround all with a drizzle of yellow pepper oil.

# HOUSE-CURED SALMON

## with Yakima Asparagus Salad

**MAKES 4 SERVINGS** / The Yakima Valley in Eastern Washington is a prolific garden for the state, producing everything from wine grapes to apples to hops for beer making. The asparagus harvest is one of the hallmarks of springtime in the Northwest. Try to choose asparagus spears of similar thickness—not too thin, not too fat—for the best presentation. In place of the house-cured salmon, you could instead use cold-smoked salmon, such as the lox-style salmon from Gerard & Dominique Seafoods (page 228). The traditional Northwest hot-smoked or kippered salmon has a more pronounced flavor but could also be used, if you like.

Highfield Estate 2003 Sauvignon Blanc, New Zealand

6 ounces House-Cured Salmon (page 211) or cold-smoked salmon

3 tablespoons extra virgin olive oil

2 tablespoons minced shallots

1 tablespoon minced fresh chives

Freshly ground white pepper

1 pound asparagus spears

2 tablespoons freshly squeezed lemon juice

1 teaspoon Dijon mustard

Sea salt

Garnish

Basil Oil (page 216)

Chervil sprigs

Toasted baguette slices

Finely chop the salmon and put it in a bowl with 1 tablespoon of the olive oil, 1 tablespoon of the shallots, and the chives. Toss to combine evenly, then season to taste with pepper; set aside.

Trim the tough ends from the asparagus so all the spears are about 5 inches long. Use a vegetable peeler to peel away the tough outer layer of skin from the lower portion of any thicker spears.

Bring a large pot of salted water to a boil and prepare a large bowl of ice water. Add the asparagus to the boiling water and cook just until it is evenly bright green and nearly tender, about 2 minutes. Drain the asparagus and plunge into the ice water to cool quickly and set its color. Once cooled, drain the asparagus and pat dry on paper towels.

Combine the lemon juice and mustard in a large shallow dish, then whisk in the remaining 2 tablespoons olive oil and the remaining 1 tablespoon shallots. Season to taste with salt and pepper.

To serve, lightly toss the asparagus in the dressing and arrange 4 or 5 spears alongside each other on individual plates, resembling a raft. Form the salmon mixture into 8 quenelles (page 235) and set 2 quenelles on top of each bed of asparagus (alternatively, you can simply spoon the salmon mixture into a tidy round on top of the asparagus). Drizzle basil oil around the edge of the salad and scatter chervil sprigs over the oil. Set 2 or 3 baguette slices to one side of the salad.

# LOBSTER AND MANGO SALAD

## with Blood Orange–Argan Dressing

**MAKES 4 SERVINGS** / Argan oil is a golden-orange, nutty-flavored oil that is extracted from the tree's nuts. It is a full-flavored oil, ideal for finishing dishes just before serving, but like most nut oils it also withstands heat well and can be used for cooking.

Domaine Georges Vernay 2002 Condrieu "Les Terrasses de l'Empire," France

2 ripe mangoes

1/4 pound haricots verts or thin regular green beans, trimmed

2 live lobsters (about 1 1/2 pounds each)

1/2 teaspoon minced shallots

1/2 teaspoon minced fresh chives

1/2 head baby Bibb or other tender lettuce, rinsed, dried, and torn into bite-size pieces

Dressing

2 teaspoons Dijon mustard

1/4 cup freshly squeezed blood orange juice or navel orange juice

1 1/2 tablespoons seasoned rice vinegar

2 tablespoons argan or canola oil

Sea salt and freshly ground white pepper

Garnish

Minced fresh chives

Freshly ground black pepper

With a sharp knife, cut down along each side of the mango, cutting as close to the flat, fibrous pit as possible to end up with 2 halves. Peel each half, then cut 2 of the mango halves into thin lengthwise slices and arrange them in a fan pattern just off center on plates. Cut the remaining mango into 1/4-inch dice and put in a large bowl; set aside.

Bring a saucepan of salted water to a boil and prepare a bowl of ice water. Add the haricots verts to the boiling water and cook until bright green and just tender, 1 to 2 minutes (a bit longer for larger beans). Drain well and plunge the beans into the ice water to cool them quickly. When cold, drain the beans and dry them on paper towels. Set aside.

Cook the lobster and pick the meat from the shells (page 234). Cut the lobster tail on the diagonal into slices about 1/4 inch thick. Halve 2 lobster claws horizontally and coarsely chop the remaining claws and lobster meat; set aside.

*For the dressing,* put the mustard in a bowl and gradually whisk in the orange juice and vinegar. Whisk in the oil until blended and season to taste with salt and pepper. Drizzle half of the dressing over the diced mango, add the shallot and chives, and gently toss to coat. Chop about one quarter of the green beans and add them to the mango mixture with the lettuce and toss to combine well.

Lay the remaining green beans in a spoke pattern over the mango slices and lay the lobster tail slices over the beans. Place 1 claw piece on top. Add the remaining lobster to the salad and toss. To serve, spoon the salad alongside the mango and lobster on each plate. Drizzle the remaining dressing over the lobster slices and sprinkle with the chives and a bit of black pepper.

# Soups

# GREEN ASPARAGUS SOUP
## with Meyer Lemon Cream

**MAKES 4 SERVINGS /** I like to use thicker spears of asparagus for this soup. They not only contribute meatier flesh to the purée, but thicker spears—despite impressions to the contrary—are no less tender than thinner ones. If the asparagus you're using is on the thin side, reduce the initial cooking time to about $1^1/2$ minutes. To ensure that the texture of this soup is silky smooth, I always pass the purée through a fine-mesh sieve to remove any lingering solid pieces, though if you promise to purée it thoroughly until very smooth in a blender, you can skip that step.

Weingut Felsner 2002 Grüner Veltliner Alte Reben Rohrendorfer Leithen, Austria

1 pound asparagus spears

4 tablespoons unsalted butter

$^1/2$ onion, chopped

1 teaspoon fresh thyme leaves

$^1/2$ teaspoon minced garlic

3 cups Vegetable Stock (page 210)

Juice of $^1/2$ Meyer lemon or large regular lemon

1 cup crème fraîche, homemade (page 212) or store-bought, or heavy cream

Sea salt and freshly ground white pepper

Remove the tough ends of the asparagus spears by bending each spear near its base until the end snaps off naturally. Cut off about 3 inches from the tips of 12 stalks to use for garnish. Bring a large pot of salted water to a boil and prepare a large bowl of ice water. Add the asparagus spears to the boiling water and cook until bright green and nearly tender, 1 to 2 minutes. Scoop out the spears with a slotted spoon and plunge into the ice water to cool quickly. Return the water to a boil, add the reserved asparagus tips and cook until bright green and nearly tender, about 1 minute. Scoop the tips out with a slotted spoon and cool in the ice water as well. When the asparagus is cold, drain well and place in a single layer on paper towels to dry. Set aside the asparagus tips and cut the spears into 1-inch pieces.

Heat the butter in a saucepan over medium heat until melted and foamy white. Add the onion, thyme, and garlic and cook, stirring occasionally, until the onion begins to soften, 2 to 3 minutes. Stir in the asparagus pieces, then add the vegetable stock and lemon juice. Bring the stock just to a boil over high heat, then decrease the heat to medium-low, stir in the crème fraîche, and simmer until the asparagus is very tender, 15 to 20 minutes.

**Lemon Cream**

1/2 cup crème fraîche, homemade
(page 212) or store-bought, or
heavy cream

Juice of 1/2 Meyer lemon or large regular
lemon

Sea salt and freshly ground white pepper

**Garnish**

Coarsely chopped toasted hazelnuts
(page 234)

Hazelnut oil

Strain the asparagus mixture through a sieve into a bowl, returning the liquid to the saucepan. Bring to a boil over medium-high heat and boil to reduce by one-third. Meanwhile, purée the asparagus mixture in a blender or food processor until very smooth. If the purée is quite thick, add a couple tablespoons of water to lighten it. Pass the purée through a fine-mesh sieve into a bowl, pressing on the solids with the back of a rubber spatula to extract as much purée from the fibrous bits as you can. Stir the asparagus purée into the reduced stock mixture. Taste the soup for seasoning, adding salt and pepper if necessary; keep warm over low heat. Cut the reserved asparagus tips lengthwise in half (unless the tips are already quite thin).

*For the lemon cream,* whip the crème fraîche with the lemon juice in a bowl until medium peaks form. Season to taste with salt and pepper, whisking to blend fully.

To serve, ladle the asparagus soup into warm shallow soup bowls. Form the lemon cream into 4 large quenelles (page 235) and set them in the center of the soup. Lean the reserved asparagus tips up against the lemon cream and scatter the hazelnuts over the cream. Drizzle the top of each soup with hazelnut oil.

# CARROT AND GINGER SOUP

## with Roasted Cauliflower à la Tom Douglas

**MAKES 4 SERVINGS** / I never thought of cauliflower as a good candidate for roasting. But my good friend and Seattle's most popular chef, Tom Douglas, proved otherwise to me one night with a dinner at his house. That's the inspiration for the centerpiece around which this simple—but amazingly flavorful—soup is served. Freshly juiced carrots and ginger will produce the best results here. If you don't have a juicer, you can cheat with store-bought 100% carrot juice. For the ginger juice, you can very finely grate a large piece of fresh, young ginger onto a plate, then transfer the ginger pulp to a fine sieve and press with the back of a spoon to extract the juice. Older ginger has a tough, stringy texture from which it will be harder to extract juice.

René Muré 2001 Pinot Blanc "Côte de Rouffach," France

¼ large head (about ½ pound) cauliflower

2 tablespoons olive oil

2 teaspoons minced fresh thyme

Sea salt and freshly ground white pepper

2 cups fresh carrot juice (from about 2½ pounds carrots)

¼ cup fresh ginger juice (from about ¼ pound fresh ginger)

⅔ cup unsalted butter, cut into pieces and chilled

Preheat the oven to 400°F.

Cut the cauliflower into small florets, trimming away excess stalk. Heat an ovenproof skillet over medium heat. Add the olive oil, then the cauliflower, and toss gently in the oil. Sprinkle the cauliflower with the thyme and a good pinch each of salt and pepper. Toss to coat evenly with the seasonings, then transfer the skillet to the oven and roast, stirring once or twice, until the cauliflower is lightly browned, tender, and aromatic, 18 to 20 minutes.

Meanwhile, combine the carrot and ginger juices in a saucepan and bring to a boil over medium-high heat. Decrease the heat to medium and whisk in the chilled butter, a few pieces at a time, so that it melts creamily into the soup. Season to taste with salt and keep the soup warm over low heat until ready to serve.

To serve, form a mound of the roasted cauliflower in the center of warm shallow soup bowls and ladle the carrot-ginger soup around.

# PEA SOUP

## with Dungeness Crab and Chervil Cream

**MAKES 4 SERVINGS /** This is a very easy recipe, full of color and the fresh, bright flavors of springtime. Young, tender English peas will give the best results, although you can use top-quality frozen peas instead. If purchasing bulk crabmeat rather than cooking and cleaning a whole crab yourself, be sure to ask for at least 4 whole leg portions to use for garnish.

Adelsheim Vineyard 2002 Pinot Blanc, Willamette Valley, Oregon

4 cups Lobster Stock (page 209) or
  Vegetable Stock (page 210)

3 cups freshly shelled English peas
  (from about 3 pounds whole pods)

Sea salt and freshly ground white pepper

6 ounces Dungeness crabmeat (page 232)
  plus 4 nice leg pieces

1 teaspoon minced shallots

1 teaspoon minced fresh chives

1 teaspoon hazelnut or olive oil

¼ teaspoon minced garlic

Chervil Cream

¼ cup heavy cream

2 teaspoons minced fresh chervil

¼ teaspoon hazelnut oil

Sea salt and freshly ground white pepper

Garnish

Carrot Oil (page 219)

Chervil sprigs

Bring the lobster stock to a boil in a saucepan over medium-high heat. Add the peas with a pinch of salt and cook until bright green and tender, 2 to 3 minutes. Strain the peas through a sieve into a bowl, return the stock to the saucepan, and set the pan aside. Purée the peas in a blender or food processor with about 1 cup of the stock until very smooth. Press the mixture through a fine-mesh sieve into a bowl, pressing on the skins to remove as much flavorful purée as possible.

Return the stock to a boil and reduce by one-third, 3 to 5 minutes. Remove the pan from the heat and stir in the pea purée; set aside.

Set aside 4 whole leg pieces of crab to use for garnish. Put the remaining crab into a bowl, using your fingers to break up any large pieces and to remove any bits of shell or cartilage. Add the shallots, chives, hazelnut oil, and garlic and season to taste with salt and pepper. Toss well to combine evenly.

*For the chervil cream,* whip the cream in a small bowl until soft peaks form. Whisk in the chervil and hazelnut oil and season to taste with salt and pepper.

To serve, gently reheat the pea soup over medium heat and taste for seasoning, adding salt or pepper if needed. Form the seasoned crabmeat into 2-inch mounds in the center of warm shallow soup bowls, using a ring mold if you have one. Set the reserved crab leg portions on top, and ladle the warm soup around the crab. Spoon the chervil cream over the crab, add a drizzle of carrot oil, and top the chervil cream with a sprig of chervil.

# BUTTERNUT SQUASH SOUP

## with Apple and Hazelnut Baked in Phyllo

**MAKES 4 SERVINGS /** Although Oregon is the largest producer of hazelnuts in the U.S., I also get hazelnuts from organic producers in the Puget Sound area, such as Penn Cove Organics on Whidbey Island and Holmquist Hazelnut Orchards in Lynden, Washington. Note that some phyllo producers now sell half-size sheets of phyllo rather than the more common full-size 14- by 18-inch sheets. If you purchase the smaller sheets, form 2 triple-layer sheets and halve each lengthwise.

Bressan 2002 Pinot Grigio, Friuli, Italy

1 butternut squash (about 1½ pounds)

10 tablespoons unsalted butter

2 teaspoons hazelnut or olive oil

1 Granny Smith apple

3 tablespoons plus 1 teaspoon minced shallots

¼ teaspoon minced garlic

2 pinches minced fresh thyme

4 cups Vegetable Stock (page 210)

½ cup hazelnuts, toasted (page 234) and coarsely chopped

¼ cup Calvados

2 teaspoons minced fresh chives

Sea salt and freshly ground white pepper

3 sheets phyllo dough

3 tablespoons crème fraîche, homemade (page 212) or store-bought, or heavy cream

2 tablespoons Frangelico

Garnish

Beet Coulis (page 215)

Pumpkin seed or hazelnut oil

Trim the ends from the butternut squash and halve it lengthwise. Use a large spoon to scoop out the seeds and fibrous flesh from the center. (The seeds can be cleaned and tossed with olive oil and salt to roast for a tasty snack.) Cut the squash into large pieces for easier handling. Use a small knife to peel away the skin carefully from the squash and coarsely chop the flesh.

Heat 6 tablespoons of the butter with the hazelnut oil in a large saucepan over medium heat until the butter melts and is foamy white. Add the squash and cook, stirring occasionally, until it begins to soften but not brown, 5 to 7 minutes. Using a paring knife, peel the skin from the apple so that some of the flesh still clings to the skin. Add the apple skin to the squash with 3 tablespoons of the shallots, the garlic, and a pinch of the thyme (reserve the peeled apple). Cook, stirring, until the shallots and garlic are tender and aromatic, about 5 minutes. Stir in the vegetable stock and simmer until the squash is very tender, about 20 minutes longer. Stir in the hazelnuts, then, working in batches, purée the soup in a blender or food processor until very smooth. Strain the soup through a fine-mesh sieve back into the pan and set aside.

Core the reserved apple and cut it into ¼-inch dice. Heat 1 tablespoon of the remaining butter in a small skillet over medium heat until melted and foamy white. Add the apple with the remaining

*continued*

1 teaspoon of shallots and remaining pinch of thyme. Sauté until the apple just begins to soften but still holds its shape, 1 to 2 minutes. Add the Calvados, carefully ignite it with a long match, and flambé until the flames subside. Remove the pan from the heat, stir in the chives, and season to taste with salt and pepper.

Preheat the oven to 450°F.

Melt the remaining 3 tablespoons of butter in a small saucepan, then remove from the heat. Lay 1 of the phyllo sheets on the work surface with the long side facing you and lightly brush with some of the melted butter. Lay another sheet on top and brush it with butter as well. Repeat with the third sheet of phyllo dough. Cut the phyllo vertically into 4 even strips 4$^1$/$_2$ inches wide and 14 inches long. Spoon $^1$/$_4$ of the apple filling onto 1 phyllo strip, about 2 inches up from the end of the strip. Fold the bottom edge of the dough up over the filling to enclose it, then fold in about 1 inch on each of the two long edges. Fold the filled corner over to form a triangular packet, then continue to fold up to the end of the phyllo strip like a flag (or simply fold straight upward several times to make a square packet). Brush the top of the packet with more melted butter and set it on a heavy baking sheet. Repeat with the remaining 3 phyllo strips and apple filling. Bake the apple-hazelnut phyllo packets until crisp and well browned, 10 to 12 minutes.

While the phyllo packets are baking, finish the soup. Stir in the crème fraîche and Frangelico, then use an immersion blender to incorporate fully. Taste the soup for seasoning, adding more salt or pepper if necessary, and gently reheat over medium heat.

To serve, ladle the hot soup into warm shallow soup bowls. Garnish with dots of beet coulis around the edge of the soup, lightly drizzle the soup with pumpkin seed oil, and set a phyllo packet in the center of each bowl.

# MANILA CLAM SOUP

## with Snails, Bone Marrow, and Spaghetti Squash

**MAKES 4 SERVINGS /** I admit this is a rather unusual combination of clams, snails, and rich bone marrow, all surrounding nutty and slightly sweet spaghetti squash. Specialty food shops sometimes carry cooked snails that are ready-to-use, as do online gourmet suppliers such as ChefShop. For the bone marrow, ask your butcher for 4 veal marrow bone pieces that are about 2 inches thick (1 to $1^1/_2$ pounds total). Bring a pan of generously salted water to a boil, then reduce the heat to medium, add the bones, and gently simmer for 1 to 2 minutes. Do not boil or overcook the marrow, or it will begin to fall apart. Lift out the bones with a slotted spoon and let cool, then push the marrow from the bones, using the handle of a wooden spoon or whisk, or with a marrow spoon.

Clemens-Busch 2002 Riesling Spätlese Pündericher Marienburg Trocken, Germany

---

1 spaghetti squash (about $2^1/_2$ pounds)

1 tablespoon plus 2 teaspoons pistachio or hazelnut oil

$^1/_2$ teaspoon fresh thyme leaves plus $^3/_4$ teaspoon minced fresh thyme

2 cloves garlic, halved

Sea salt and freshly ground black pepper

4 cups Lobster Stock (page 209)

$^1/_4$ cup minced shallots

20 Manila clams, scrubbed

$^1/_2$ cup (1 stick) plus 5 tablespoons unsalted butter

$^1/_2$ cup dried bread crumbs (preferably made from Thyme Brioche, page 220)

$^3/_4$ teaspoon minced fresh chives

4 pieces veal bone marrow

20 cooked Burgundy snails

1 teaspoon champagne or white wine vinegar

Preheat the oven to 350°F.

Trim the ends from the squash, halve it lengthwise, and scoop out and discard the seeds and fibrous flesh from the cavities. Set the squash halves, cut-side up, on a large piece of aluminum foil. Drizzle with 1 tablespoon of the pistachio oil, sprinkle with $^1/_4$ teaspoon of the thyme leaves, and put the garlic into the cavities. Season the squash with salt and pepper, wrap securely in the foil, and bake until the squash is tender when pierced with the tip of a knife, about 2 hours. Set the squash aside until it is cool enough to handle. Lift out the garlic and reserve it, then use a fork to scrape the tender flesh from the skin and put it in a skillet. Drizzle with the remaining 2 teaspoons of pistachio oil and toss to mix evenly, separating the thin strands of the squash. Set aside. Decrease the oven temperature to 200°F.

Put the lobster stock in a saucepan with the shallots, the remaining $^1/_4$ teaspoon of thyme leaves, and the reserved garlic. Bring to a boil over medium-high heat. Add the clams, cover the pan, and cook until the clams have opened, 5 to 7 minutes total. Begin checking for opened clams after 1 minute, scooping them out with a slotted spoon and into a bowl; continue to check for cooked clams every 20 to 30 seconds. Discard any clams that haven't opened after about

*continued*

Garnish

Minced fresh chives

8 minutes of cooking. Return any accumulated clam liquid in the bowl back into the pot.

Return the stock to a boil and simmer over medium heat until reduced by one-third, 8 to 10 minutes. Remove from the heat and let cool for a few minutes, then pour the stock into a blender. Cut $1/2$ cup of the butter into pieces, add it to the blender, and process until smooth. (Blending hot liquids creates extra pressure; it's important to firmly hold down the lid. Work in batches if necessary to help avoid overflow.) Strain the soup into a small saucepan and keep warm over low heat.

Combine the bread crumbs, $1/2$ teaspoon of the minced thyme, $1/2$ teaspoon of the chives, and a good pinch each of salt and pepper in a bowl. Toss to mix thoroughly. Add the bone marrow and toss to coat evenly with the crumbs, then set aside on a plate. Remove the clams from their shells and toss them in the crumbs as well.

Heat 2 tablespoons of the remaining butter in a large skillet over medium-high heat until melted and foamy white. Add the snails with the remaining $1/4$ teaspoon of minced thyme and $1/4$ teaspoon of chives, and season with salt and pepper. Toss well and cook until warmed through, 2 to 3 minutes. Drizzle the vinegar over the snails, transfer them to a small rimmed baking sheet, and keep warm in the oven.

Wipe out the skillet and heat 1 tablespoon of the remaining butter over medium-high heat until melted and foamy white. Add the crumb-coated bone marrow and cook just until warmed through and the crumbs are well browned, 1 to 2 minutes. Transfer the marrow to the baking sheet with the snails.

Wipe out the skillet and heat the remaining 2 tablespoons of butter over medium-high heat until melted and foamy white. Add the crumb-coated clams and cook just until warmed through and the crumbs are well browned, 1 to 2 minutes. Add them to the baking sheet. Reheat the squash over medium heat.

To serve, form a circle of spaghetti squash (about $2^1/2$ inches across) in the center of warm shallow soup bowls, using a ring mold if you like. Arrange the clams, bone marrow pieces, and snails around the outer edge of the squash, alternating them, then ladle the hot soup over and sprinkle with chives.

# STEAMED PENN COVE MUSSELS
## and Fennel with Iranian Saffron

**MAKES 4 SERVINGS** / Penn Cove mussels from Whidbey Island are some of the best mussels available and one of the trademark Northwest products. I prefer using saffron from Iran, because I find it to be more flavorful and vividly colored. You can use saffron from Morocco or Spain, but you may want to add an extra pinch. The garnish of lightly sautéed fennel julienne, flambéed with a splash of Pastis, echoes the flavors of the Mediterranean and makes me think of sitting under a shady tree along the seashore in the south of France.

Josmeyer 2001 Gewürztraminer "Les Folastries," France

4 shallots, thinly sliced

3 large cloves garlic, halved, plus a pinch
of minced garlic

3 thyme sprigs

2 curly parsley sprigs

1 bay leaf, preferably fresh, partly torn

10 white or black peppercorns

2 cups dry vermouth

1 cup dry white wine

1 large fennel bulb

2 tablespoons olive oil

Sea salt and freshly ground white pepper

2 tablespoons Pastis or other anisette
liqueur

1 plum tomato, halved

1 teaspoon saffron threads

1 1/2 pounds live Penn Cove mussels,
scrubbed and debearded (page 234)

3 tablespoons crème fraîche, homemade
(page 212) or store-bought

1 tablespoon unsalted butter

Combine the shallots, halved garlic cloves, thyme sprigs, parsley sprigs, bay leaf, and peppercorns in a saucepan. Add the vermouth and wine, bring just to a boil over high heat, then decrease the heat to medium and simmer for 10 minutes.

Meanwhile, trim and discard the stalks from the fennel bulb (or save to use in vegetable stock, page 210), reserving some of the tender fennel fronds for garnish, if not using bronze fennel. Halve the fennel bulb lengthwise and cut out the tough core. Separate the layers of fennel, trimming away any tough or browned portions, and cut the fennel lengthwise (with the grain) into 1/8-inch-thick slices. Heat a skillet over medium heat, then add the olive oil. Add the fennel and cook, stirring, until it begins to soften, 1 to 2 minutes. Add the pinch of minced garlic, season with salt and pepper, and toss to mix. Continue cooking until the fennel is just barely tender, 3 to 5 minutes longer. Add the Pastis, very carefully ignite the alcohol with a long match, and flambé until the flames subside. Set aside until ready to serve.

When the broth has reduced, strain it through a sieve into a large saucepan, pressing well on the solids with the back of a spoon to remove as much flavorful liquid as possible. Add the tomato and saffron to the broth, return to a boil over medium-high heat, and simmer for 2 to 3 minutes. Add the mussels, cover the pan, and

*continued*

**Garnish**

**Finely minced shallots**

**Minced fresh chives**

**Bronze or green fennel fronds**

cook, shaking the pan gently once or twice, until the mussels have opened, 3 to 5 minutes total. Begin checking for opened mussels after 1 minute, scooping them out with a slotted spoon into a bowl; continue to check and remove the cooked mussels every 20 to 30 seconds. Discard any mussels that haven't opened after 5 or 6 minutes of cooking.

Return the saffron broth to a boil, adding any accumulated mussel juices from the bowl to the pan; cover the mussel bowl with aluminum foil to keep warm. Boil the broth until reduced by one-third, 5 to 7 minutes. Slip off the tomato skins and discard.

Whisk the crème fraîche into the saffron broth and set aside to cool slightly. Purée the broth in a blender until smooth, working in batches if necessary. (Blending hot liquids creates extra pressure; it's important to hold down the lid firmly. A chef's trick is to cover the blender lid with a kitchen towel, to catch any drips or splatters.) Add the butter to the blender with the final batch. Strain the broth through a fine-mesh sieve into the same saucepan and keep warm over medium heat. Taste for seasoning, adding more salt or pepper if necessary. Reheat the fennel over medium heat and remove the mussels from their shells.

To serve, spoon the sautéed fennel into the center of warm shallow soup bowls. Take all but 4 of the mussels from their shells and arrange the shelled mussels around the fennel. Discard one half of the shell from the remaining mussels and set the mussels on top of the fennel. Ladle the hot broth around the fennel, scatter shallots and chives over the mussels, and finish with a frond of bronze or green fennel.

# SOFT-SHELL CRAB BISQUE
## with Morels and Duck Egg

**MAKES 4 SERVINGS** / This is a particularly big hit with regulars at Rover's who never fail to swoon when it's on the menu. Soft-shell blue crabs from the East Coast are a springtime favorite even here in the Northwest. They begin appearing mid- to late April and continue through the summer. For the hard-cooked egg garnish, use the small holes on a box grater and finely grate the white and yolk separately onto a small plate or piece of waxed paper for easy handling. I prefer small, bite-size morel mushrooms for this recipe, but if the morels you're using are on the large side, halve them lengthwise before roasting.

René Dauvissat 2000 Chablis 1er Cru "La Fôret," France

4 soft-shell crabs (about 1/2 pound total), trimmed (see box)

2 tablespoons olive oil

3 tablespoons minced shallots

3/4 teaspoon minced fresh thyme

1/2 teaspoon plus a pinch of minced garlic

1 plum tomato, coarsely chopped

1/4 cup brandy or Armagnac

3 cups Lobster Stock (page 209)

4 to 6 ounces small morel mushrooms, cleaned (page 236)

Sea salt and freshly ground white pepper

3 tablespoons plus 2 teaspoons unsalted butter, at room temperature

1 teaspoon hazelnut oil

10 basil leaves

Coarsely chop the crabs. Heat a saucepan over medium heat, then add the olive oil and crab pieces and toss for a few seconds. Add the shallots with 1/2 teaspoon of the thyme and 1/2 teaspoon of the garlic. Sauté until the crab browns lightly and becomes aromatic, 2 to 3 minutes. Add the tomato and brandy. Very carefully light the alcohol with a long match and flambé until the flames subside. Simmer until the liquids have reduced slightly, 2 to 3 minutes.

Add the lobster stock to the pan, bring to a boil over medium-high heat, then decrease the heat to medium-low and simmer gently until it is quite aromatic and the tomato is very tender, about 40 minutes. The liquid should not boil vigorously; reduce the heat if needed so that it remains at a low simmer.

Meanwhile, preheat the oven to 400°F. Cut a large piece of aluminum foil and put the morels in the center. Season with salt and top with bits of the 2 teaspoons of softened butter. Drizzle the hazelnut oil over the mushrooms, and add the remaining 1/4 teaspoon of thyme and pinch of garlic. Wrap the foil up and around the morels, though not too snugly. Set the foil packet directly on an oven rack and roast until the mushrooms are tender and aromatic, about 30 minutes.

**Garnish**

1 hard-cooked duck or chicken egg, yolk and white finely grated separately

Toasted baguette slices, lightly brushed with olive oil

Chopped fresh chives

Let the crab mixture cool slightly, then purée the mixture, in batches, in a blender, adding the remaining 3 tablespoons of softened butter and the basil leaves with the last batch. (Blending hot liquids creates extra pressure; it's important to hold down the lid firmly. A chef's trick is to cover the blender lid with a kitchen towel, to catch any drips or splatters. Work in batches if necessary to help avoid overflow.) Pass the soup through a fine sieve and keep warm over low heat until ready to serve.

To serve, pile the roasted morels in the center of warm shallow soup bowls. Ladle in the soft-shell crab bisque, sprinkle the hard-cooked egg white and yolk on the baguette slices, and set them on top of the morels, just to one side. Scatter the chives over the bisque.

**SOFT-SHELL CRABS**—Soft-shell crabs are a springtime delicacy that come from the Chesapeake Bay and other points on the eastern seaboard where the blue crab is king. Their beautiful blue shells are typically quite hard, but in order to grow, the crabs slip out of their too-small shells and grow new larger ones, which take a few days to form. The crab harvested in this soft-shell state are almost completely edible, the shell thin enough to eat. You just need to use kitchen shears or a large heavy knife to cut off the front "face" of the shell. Lift up one side of the soft top shell (carapace) and use the shears to snip away the feathery gills, then repeat on the other side of the carapace. Turn the crab over and lift up the apron, the flap of shell across the bottom of the crab, and cut it away from the body. The soft-shell crab is now ready to cook.

# Cold Appetizers

# MARTINI OF SPOT PRAWNS

## with Cucumber, Caviar, and Vodka

**MAKES 4 SERVINGS /** This is one of the most elegant martinis you'll ever come across. It contains a little splash of vodka to add some spirited flavor, but in this martini what really stars are delicate, sweet spot prawns. Most come from Alaska, but they are also harvested around the San Juan Islands. Spot prawns sometimes come with their roe attached; if you like, you can dry the roe and use it for garnish (page 81). This recipe would also be delicious with slices of lobster tail or pieces of sweet Dungeness crabmeat in place of the spot prawns when they are not available.

Pol Roger 1993 Champagne Blanc de Blancs de Chardonnay, France

3 tablespoons vodka

4 tablespoons olive oil

2 teaspoons Dijon mustard

Sea salt and freshly ground white pepper

1 large English cucumber, peeled, seeded, and cut into medium dice

12 to 16 large spot prawns, peeled

1 tablespoon minced shallots

1 tablespoon minced fresh chives

1 ounce white sturgeon caviar

Garnish

Whole chives

Fennel fronds

Chervil sprigs

Whisk the vodka, 2 tablespoons of the olive oil, and the mustard together in a bowl and season to taste with salt and pepper (I like a real good pinch of pepper here). Whisk well to blend. Add the cucumber and toss to coat evenly. Set aside to marinate while cooking the shrimp.

Heat a large skillet over medium-high heat, then add the remaining 2 tablespoons of olive oil and swirl gently to coat the skillet. Add the spot prawns and sear well on both sides, about 1 minute total. Add the shallots and sauté until the shallots begin to soften, 1 minute longer. Remove the pan from the heat, add the chives, and season to taste with salt and pepper. Toss to mix well, then transfer the spot prawns to a plate to avoid overcooking.

Using a slotted spoon, scoop the dressed cucumber into 4 martini glasses (about 6-ounce volume) or small dishes. Add the shrimp to the cucumber bowl and toss to coat in the dressing. Top each cucumber salad with 3 or 4 spot prawns, curved side up, in a spoke pattern. Add a generous spoonful of caviar to the center and drizzle some of the remaining vodka dressing around the edge. Garnish with a scattering of chives, fennel fronds, and chervil.

# LAMBS' TONGUES AND SPANISH WHITE ANCHOVIES
## with Yellow Finn Potatoes and Watercress Salad

**MAKES 4 SERVINGS /** Lambs' tongues are a delicacy you should be able to find in (or to order from) a specialty meat market. The anchovies I use are imported from Spain and are known as *boquerones;* they are meatier and less salty than the anchovies commonly found in the United States. They are preserved in a white wine and vinegar marinade and are so delicious they can be served alone.

Didier Dagueneau 2002 Pouilly Fumé "Pur Sang," France

1 pound lambs' tongues (3 to 4 tongues)

1/2 celery stalk, coarsely chopped

1/2 carrot, peeled and coarsely chopped

6 to 8 thyme sprigs

4-inch piece of dark green leek top

1 bay leaf, preferably fresh, partly torn

6 white peppercorns

4 tablespoons freshly squeezed lemon juice

2 teaspoons Dijon mustard

Sea salt and freshly ground white pepper

1/2 cup olive oil

1 pound Yellow Finn potatoes

2 shallots, minced

1 tablespoon minced fresh chives

1 teaspoon minced garlic

8 Spanish white anchovy fillets marinated in white wine, halved lengthwise

1/4 cup loosely packed tender watercress leaves

Garnish

Minced fresh chives

Rinse the lambs' tongues very well under cold running water. Put the tongues in a large saucepan with cold water to cover generously and bring to a boil over high heat. While the water is heating, cut a piece of cheesecloth about 8 inches square. Put the celery, carrot, thyme sprigs, leek green, bay leaf, and peppercorns in the center of the cheesecloth and tie the packet securely with kitchen string.

Use a spoon to skim off the scum that rises to the surface of the water, then decrease the heat to medium, add the seasoning packet, and simmer the lambs' tongues until they are very tender and the skin easily peels away, 2 to 2 1/2 hours. The water should not boil; reduce the heat if needed to maintain a moderate simmer. Add more boiling water if needed so that the tongues are fully covered throughout the cooking.

When the tongues are tender, scoop them out, reserving the cooking liquid but discarding the seasoning packet. When the tongues are cool enough to handle, peel away and discard the skin. Return the tongues to the cooking liquid and refrigerate until fully chilled, at least 2 hours. (The tongues can be prepared to this point one day in advance.)

Whisk the lemon juice and mustard together in a small bowl and season to taste with salt and pepper. Slowly whisk in the olive oil until emulsified. Set aside.

Put the potatoes in a saucepan, add cold salted water to cover, and bring to a boil over high heat. Decrease the heat to medium and simmer until the potatoes are just tender, 15 to 25 minutes, depending on their size. Drain the potatoes, set aside until cool enough to handle, then peel away the skin. Cut the potatoes into $1/4$-inch dice, put them in a bowl, and drizzle about $1/4$ cup of the lemon dressing over. Add the shallots, chives, and garlic and season to taste with salt and pepper. Toss gently to combine evenly, then cover and refrigerate for at least 1 hour and up to 2 hours. Reserve the remaining dressing.

When the lambs' tongues are cold, drain them and thoroughly pat dry with paper towels. Thinly slice the tongues crosswise, put them in a shallow dish, and drizzle with about 3 tablespoons of the reserved dressing. Toss the tongues to coat evenly, then set aside to marinate for about 15 minutes. Meanwhile, set the potato salad out at room temperature to warm it just a bit.

To serve, form a tidy 3-inch circle of the potato salad just off center on each plate, using a small ring mold, if you like. Arrange the lambs' tongue slices on top of the potatoes, overlapping them slightly. Roll up the strips of anchovy into spirals and set them on top of the tongue. Toss the watercress with a couple tablespoons of the dressing and mound it to one side of the potato-lamb salad. Sprinkle chives over all and drizzle the remaining dressing around the edge of the potato salad.

# TERRINE OF SONOMA VALLEY FOIE GRAS

## with Sauternes Aspic and Thyme Brioche

**MAKES ABOUT 20 SERVINGS** / Foie gras terrine gets its silky, elegant texture from very gentle, slow cooking. The raw lobes are first marinated in Sauternes and thyme and then packed into the mold. Because the terrine makes a good number of portions, it's an ideal recipe to prepare for a large celebration dinner or holiday buffet. For luxurious cocktail fare, cut each terrine slice into quarters and set the pieces on small rounds of toasted brioche or on toasted baguette slices. Top the foie gras with a small dollop of the diced aspic and serve. The terrine can be made up to 2 days in advance. Any extras will keep for 3 days, well wrapped and refrigerated.

Château Bastor La Montagne 1997 Sauternes, France

---

2 whole foie gras (about 3 pounds total)

3 cups Sauternes or late harvest riesling

Sea salt

1 teaspoon minced fresh thyme

2 gelatin sheets or 2 teaspoons unflavored gelatin powder

Garnish

Fleur de sel

Toasted Thyme Brioche rounds (page 220)

Set the foie gras on the counter for about 1 hour, which will make it easier to handle.

Meanwhile, make a press for the terrine by cutting a few pieces of heavy cardboard just large enough to fit inside the rim of the terrine mold. Wrap the stacked cardboard pieces in a few layers of plastic wrap to form a secure packet. Set aside.

Separate the 2 lobes of each foie gras to expose some of the veins and nerves. Using the blunt edge of a small knife, lightly cut into the lobes and around the veins and nerves, then scrape the edge along the length of the veins to separate them from the lobes. Save any pieces of the foie gras that break away as you work. Then use the blunt edge of the knife to scrape away any red spots or blemishes from the surface of the foie gras. Make a lengthwise cut, about 3/4 inch deep, into the 2 larger lobes, then gently pull apart the two sides (without fully separating the halves) and look for and remove more veins and nerves. Put all the pieces of foie gras in a shallow dish and evenly drizzle with 2 cups of the Sauternes. Lightly salt the foie gras on all sides and sprinkle with the thyme. Marinate in the refrigerator for 45 minutes, turning the pieces after 20 minutes.

Preheat the oven to 200°F.

Place one of the larger lobe pieces in the bottom of the terrine mold, smoothest-side down. Add the other lobe pieces to fill the terrine, pressing down well to form an even layer. Cut a piece of parchment paper large enough to cover the terrine or use its lid; set the terrine in a baking dish. Add about 1 inch of hot water (about 180°F) to the baking dish and carefully place in the oven. Bake for 40 minutes.

Take the terrine from the oven, lifting it from the water bath. Remove the parchment paper and carefully pour a little of the fat from the terrine into a bowl. Set the prepared cardboard press on the terrine, then, holding it securely against the terrine, pour all the remaining terrine liquid into the bowl; refrigerate the liquid. Set the terrine in a shallow dish, place several heavy cans or foil-wrapped bricks on top of the cardboard, and refrigerate overnight. Make sure the weight is evenly distributed to ensure that the top of the terrine will be even.

For the aspic, if using gelatin sheets, break them into pieces and soften in a bowl of cold water for 5 to 10 minutes, then drain. If using powdered gelatin, sprinkle it over 3 tablespoons of cold water in a small dish and set aside to soften, about 5 minutes. Warm the remaining 1 cup of Sauternes in a small saucepan over medium heat for 1 to 2 minutes. Very carefully light the alcohol with a long match and flambé until the flames subside (the wine won't flame as dramatically as higher-alcohol spirits do); set aside to cool slightly. Add the softened gelatin to the warm wine, stirring until it is thoroughly melted. Pour the Sauternes into a 9-inch square baking dish or other similar dish (the liquid should be about $1/2$ inch thick). Remove any bubbles by popping them with a wooden skewer or a fork. Refrigerate until the aspic has set, at least 1 hour (make sure the dish is sitting flat so the aspic will have an even thickness).

At least 6 hours before serving, take the bowl of cooking liquid from the refrigerator. Press down on the surface of the solidified fat to separate it gently from the liquid below. Lift up the fat and use a small knife to scrape away all the congealed liquid on the underside of the fat. Put the clean fat in a small bowl and set over a small saucepan of warm water to melt it very gently without heating it.

Remove the weights from the terrine. Scrape away the fat from the surface of the terrine and discard or save for another use. Pour the melted clean fat over the surface of the terrine and refrigerate until the fat sets, at least 4 hours. Put a metal tray, baking sheet, or piece of marble in the freezer to chill. Take the aspic from the refrigerator and use a small knife to cut the aspic into a small dice, then use a small spoon to scrape up and separate the pieces. Refrigerate until ready to serve.

To serve, carefully run a thin-bladed knife around the sides of the terrine. Unmold the terrine onto the chilled tray and use the knife blade to scrape away any gelled cooking liquid from the sides of the terrine. Dip the knife blade into warm water and wipe it dry, then cut the terrine into $1/2$-inch-thick slices and set them on chilled plates. Sprinkle the foie gras with a pinch of fleur de sel and spoon a small pile of the aspic alongside. Arrange a few slices of warm toasted thyme brioche alongside (not touching the terrine or aspic directly) or pass the brioche separately.

# TUNA SASHIMI

## with Sea Beans and Wasabi Sesame Dressing

**MAKES 6 SERVINGS /** Sea beans (also known as samphire and salicornia) are a distinctive wild treat that is gathered along the seashore in the Northwest. Availability is unpredictable, but generally these bright green, crisp "beans" with the gentle taste of the sea can be found in the summer and fall. The sea beans I use at Rover's come primarily from Veronica Williams, a forager on Washington's Long Beach Peninsula, though specialty stores such as Uwajimaya (page 230) also carry them. If you are unable to find sea beans, asparagus makes a reasonable substitute. Cut the spears into roughly 2-inch pieces, then halve or quarter them lengthwise. When blanching, salt the water generously to replicate more closely the brisk seaside flavor of sea beans.

Bernard Schoffit 2002 Riesling Grand Cru "Rangen de Thann," France

1 pound sashimi-grade ahi tuna

2 teaspoons minced fresh chives

1 teaspoon minced shallots

1 tablespoon plus 1 teaspoon dark
   sesame oil

1/4 teaspoon grated fresh ginger

1/4 teaspoon minced garlic

Sea salt and freshly ground white pepper

6 to 8 ounces sea beans

2 tablespoons soy sauce

1/2 teaspoon wasabi powder

Garnish

Basil Oil (page 216)

Basil leaves

Cut 6 paper-thin slices of the tuna to use as garnish and set aside. Cut the remaining tuna into 1/4-inch dice and put in a bowl. Add the chives, shallots, 1 teaspoon of the sesame oil, the ginger, and garlic and season to taste with salt and pepper. Toss gently but thoroughly; set aside while preparing the sea beans.

Trim away and discard any tough stems from the sea beans. Bring a large saucepan of water (not salted) to a boil and prepare a bowl of ice water. Add the sea beans to the boiling water and cook until tender and bright green, 1 to 2 minutes. Drain and plunge into the ice water to cool them quickly, then drain well again and spread the sea beans out on paper towels to dry. Combine the soy sauce, the remaining 1 tablespoon of sesame oil, and the wasabi in a bowl and whisk well to blend. Add the blanched sea beans and toss to coat evenly.

To serve, use a slotted spoon to scoop out the sea beans and arrange them in circles in the centers of the plates, reserving the dressing. Lightly oil a 2-inch ring mold and set on top of one of the sea-bean circles. Spoon one-sixth of the diced tuna mixture into the mold, pressing down with the back of a spoon to form an even layer. Lift off the ring and repeat with the remaining tuna. Wrap the reserved slices of tuna around the outside of the tuna sashimi. Drizzle the reserved dressing and some basil oil around the sea beans and top the tuna with a basil leaf.

# SALMON GELÉE

## with Leeks and Smoked Salmon

**MAKES 4 SERVINGS** / Typically, salmon is not used to make fish stock because its flavor is so distinctive and pronounced it could overpower the other ingredients in a recipe. This is one exception, however; richly flavored salmon stock lightly set with gelatin becomes the base for tender sautéed leeks and smoked salmon. Check ahead with your fishmonger about the availability of salmon bones (a salmon head can be included as well), as they may not be on hand at all times. In place of the cold-smoked salmon, you could instead make our House-Cured Salmon (page 211) and use that, cut into paper-thin slices.

Domaine Ravenneau 2002 Chablis Grand Cru "Les Clos," France

2½ pounds salmon bones

½ cup (1 stick) unsalted butter

3 tablespoons Tomato Oil (page 217)
  or olive oil

1 large Walla Walla sweet onion or
  yellow onion, coarsely chopped,
  plus ½ onion, finely chopped

3 celery stalks, chopped

2 plum tomatoes, coarsely chopped

10 to 12 curly parsley sprigs

6 or 7 thyme sprigs

3 cloves garlic, crushed

1 tablespoon tomato paste

3 bay leaves, preferably fresh, partly torn

10 cracked white peppercorns

1½ cups dry vermouth

3 large egg whites

Sea salt

Rinse the salmon bones well under cold running water. Trim away and discard any fins. If the blood line down the backbone of the fish is still present, scrape it away with a small spoon. Cut the bones into 2-inch pieces.

Heat the butter in a large pot over medium heat until melted and foamy white, then stir in the tomato oil. Add the salmon bones, stirring to coat with the butter, then add the coarsely chopped onion, celery, tomatoes, parsley sprigs, thyme sprigs, garlic, tomato paste, bay leaves, and peppercorns. Stir to mix, then add the vermouth. Add enough cold water to cover the bones and vegetables by about 1 inch (6 to 8 cups). Bring just to a boil over medium-high heat. Use a large spoon to skim away the scum that rises to the surface, then decrease the heat to medium and simmer for 30 minutes (do not let the stock boil or it will become bitter and cloudy; decrease the heat to medium-low if needed). Remove the pan from the heat and set aside until cooled slightly, skimming away any fat that collects on the surface.

Line a large fine-mesh sieve with a damp, thin, clean kitchen towel or several thicknesses of cheesecloth. Slowly pour the stock through the sieve into a large bowl. Avoid shaking or stirring the pot, so that as many of the solids remain in the bottom of the pot as possible. Discard

1½ gelatin sheets or 1½ teaspoons
   unflavored gelatin powder

2 tablespoons olive oil

2 large leeks, white and pale green parts
   only, halved lengthwise, rinsed well,
   and sliced

Freshly ground white pepper

2 ounces thinly sliced cold-smoked
   salmon or House-Cured Salmon
   (page 211)

Tarragon Cream

½ cup crème fraîche, homemade
   (page 212) or store-bought

½ teaspoon minced fresh tarragon

Sea salt and freshly ground white pepper

Garnish

Tender tarragon sprig tops

Salmon roe

the vegetables and other solids. Put 6 cups of the stock in a saucepan (the remaining stock can be saved for another use) and bring to a boil over medium-high heat. Boil until reduced by about half, about 20 minutes, then set aside to cool to room temperature.

Put the egg whites in a saucepan and whisk until frothy. Add the finely chopped onion and whisk to mix, then whisk in the cooled stock. Set the pan over medium-high heat and simmer until a "raft" of egg white and onion has formed on top of the stock and the stock comes to a boil. Decrease the heat to medium and simmer for a few minutes longer. Use a ladle to form a hole in the center of the raft. Ladle out the clarified stock through the hole and pour through a fine-mesh sieve into a clean saucepan. Continue ladling until nearly all the stock is removed (it's better to leave some stock behind than to disturb the egg white mixture enough to break it up into the stock). Taste the stock for seasoning and add salt if necessary.

If using gelatin sheets, break them into pieces and soften in a bowl of cold water for 5 to 10 minutes, then drain. If using powdered gelatin, sprinkle it over 3 tablespoons of cold water in a small dish and let soften for about 5 minutes. While the gelatin is softening, warm the clarified salmon stock over medium heat. Add the softened gelatin to the warm stock, stirring until it has thoroughly melted. Ladle the stock into large shallow soup bowls and refrigerate until set, about 1 hour.

Heat a skillet over medium heat, then add the olive oil. Add the leeks with a pinch each of salt and pepper and cook gently until the leeks become very tender but not colored, 15 to 20 minutes, decreasing the heat if necessary. Remove from the heat and let cool.

*For the tarragon cream,* stir the crème fraîche and the tarragon together in a dish until well blended. Season to taste with salt and pepper. Refrigerate until ready to serve.

To serve, place a mound of the leeks in the center of the salmon gelée in each bowl. Arrange slices of salmon around the leeks. Form the tarragon cream into 4 small quenelles (page 235), set them on top of the leeks, and top each with a tender tarragon sprig top. Garnish with a few salmon eggs set on the gelée around the leeks.

# SMOKED SALMON AND CRISPY POTATO TIAN

## with Crème Fraîche

**MAKES 4 SERVINGS** / A tian is a traditional rustic gratin of vegetables, such as zucchini, tomato, and eggplant, and a classic dish from the south of France. This version is decidedly a new interpretation. Just outside Seattle is Gerard & Dominique's, a company that makes delicious cold-smoked salmon that is especially perfect for this recipe. You can also use a good virgin olive oil in place of the walnut oil, if you are unable to find it, though the nutty oil wonderfully echoes the slight nuttiness of the Yukon Gold potatoes.

Pikes 2003 Clare Valley Riesling, Australia

6 ounces thinly sliced cold-smoked salmon

1 tablespoon crème fraîche, homemade (page 212) or store-bought

1 tablespoon argan or olive oil

1 teaspoon minced shallots

1/2 teaspoon minced fresh curly parsley

1/2 teaspoon minced fresh chives

Crispy Potato Tian

2 Yukon Gold potatoes (about 12 ounces total)

1/4 cup clarified unsalted butter (page 231)

1/4 teaspoon minced garlic

Pinch minced fresh thyme

1 tablespoon minced fresh chives

1 tablespoon crème fraîche, homemade (page 212) or store-bought

Sea salt and freshly ground white pepper

Garnish

Basil Oil (page 216)

Red Bell Pepper Coulis (page 214)

Yellow Bell Pepper Coulis (page 214)

From 4 of the salmon slices, cut a strip 3 inches by 7 inches and set these pieces aside for finishing the dish. Cut the trimmings and remaining salmon into julienne strips and put them into a bowl with the crème fraîche, argan oil, shallots, parsley, and chives. Stir gently until evenly mixed. Set aside.

*For the potato tian,* peel the potatoes and cut into a 1/4-inch dice. Heat a large skillet over medium-high heat, then add the clarified butter. Add the potatoes and sauté until just crisp on the outside and tender on the inside, 6 to 8 minutes. Add the garlic and thyme and toss for 30 seconds, then transfer the potatoes to paper towels to drain and cool slightly. Combine the potatoes, chives, and crème fraîche in a small bowl and season to taste with salt and pepper. Stir to mix well.

To serve, set a 3-inch ring mold in the center of a plate and spoon the smoked salmon mixture into the mold, pressing with the back of the spoon to form an even layer. Top with the potato mixture, forming an even layer, and gently pack with the back of the spoon, then carefully lift up the mold. Repeat with the remaining salmon and potato mixtures. (Alternatively, simply form the salmon and potato layers neatly with a small spoon.) Wrap the reserved smoked salmon pieces around the outside of the tians, and drizzle basil oil, red pepper coulis, and yellow pepper coulis around each plate.

# TERRINE OF ROOT VEGETABLES

## with Horseradish Cream

**MAKES 4 SERVINGS /** This is a little adventure of a recipe, an artistic combination of root vegetables in different colors that create a beautiful presentation for serving. I prefer using pink or yellow beets here; they have the same sweet flavor of regular red beets without the pervasive magenta juices, which would tint the whole terrine. If the vegetable stock you're using isn't full-flavored, start with $1^1/2$ cups and reduce it to about 1 cup to concentrate the flavor. You could also make the terrine in one large dish (about a 2-cup capacity) instead of the ramekins, then simply slice it and serve. For a vegetarian rendition, use 1 teaspoon of agar in place of the gelatin.

Verget 2002 Pouilly-Fuissé "La Roche," France

4 small yellow, white, or orange carrots (about 7 ounces total), trimmed but unpeeled

$1/4$ pound pink baby beets or 1 small beet, scrubbed

1 large carrot, peeled and trimmed

1 turnip, peeled and trimmed

1 large leek, white and pale green part only, halved lengthwise and rinsed well

1 to 2 teaspoons olive oil

2 teaspoons minced shallots

1 teaspoon minced fresh thyme

Sea salt and freshly ground white pepper

1 gelatin sheet or 1 teaspoon unflavored powdered gelatin

1 cup Vegetable Stock (page 210)

Bring a saucepan of generously salted water to a boil over high heat. Add the 4 small carrots, decrease the heat to medium, and simmer until the carrots are tender, 5 to 7 minutes. Drain the carrots and set aside to cool. Put the beets in the same saucepan with cold salted water to cover and bring to a boil over high heat. Decrease the heat to medium and simmer until the beets are fully tender, about 20 minutes (longer for small or medium-size beets). Drain the beets and set aside to cool.

Using a mandoline or a sharp knife, cut the large carrot lengthwise into $1/8$-inch-thick slices. Cut the turnip crosswise into $1/8$-inch-thick rounds. Cut the leek halves lengthwise in half and separate the layers.

Bring a large pot of salted water to a boil. Add the carrot strips and cook until very tender, 5 to 7 minutes. Lift out with a slotted spoon and drain on paper towels, taking care to keep the strips intact. Return the water to a boil, add the turnip slices and cook until tender, 2 to 3 minutes. Lift out with a slotted spoon and drain well on paper towels. Return the water to a boil again and add the leek strips, cooking until tender, 3 to 5 minutes. Lift out with a slotted spoon and drain well on paper towels. Set the vegetables aside to cool.

## Horseradish Cream

¹/4 cup crème fraîche, homemade
(page 212) or store-bought, or
heavy cream

1 tablespoon finely grated fresh
horseradish or prepared horseradish

2 teaspoons Vegetable Stock (page 210)

1 teaspoon marine cider vinegar or rice
wine vinegar

Sea salt

## Frisée Salad

2 teaspoons sherry vinegar

1 teaspoon Dijon mustard

2 tablespoons extra virgin olive oil

Sea salt and freshly ground white pepper

2 cups loosely packed frisée

## Garnish

Carrot Coulis (page 215), made with
yellow or orange carrots

Fleur de sel

Lightly coat four ³/4-cup ramekins with olive oil. Use a 1¹/4-inch round cutter to cut circles from the turnip slices (save the trimmings to add to a vegetable soup or to mashed potatoes). Use the turnip rounds to line the bottom of each ramekin, overlapping the rounds slightly in an attractive pattern that will be visible when unmolded. Alternatively, for a simpler presentation, cut 4 rounds from the turnip slices just a bit smaller in diameter than the ramekin bottoms and use one round to line each ramekin.

Lay a strip of leek across the center of the ramekin, pressing it down into the bottom and letting the ends hang evenly over the side of the dish. Repeat with a carrot strip, placing it to one side of the leek so it slightly overlaps the leek. Continue alternating strips of leek and carrot until the ramekin bases are completely and evenly covered.

Using your fingers, peel away the skin from the baby carrots and beets. Cut the beets into ¹/4-inch-thick wedges. Cut 2 of the carrots lengthwise into thin slices, then crosswise in pieces of varying lengths so that they will fit across the surface of the terrine in a single layer. Finely dice the remaining 2 carrots.

Lay the carrot slices in each ramekin and sprinkle with half of the shallots, half of the thyme, and a small pinch each of salt and pepper. Top with a layer of the beet wedges followed by the diced carrots, then season with the remaining shallots, the remaining thyme, and another small pinch each of salt and pepper. Fold the carrot and leek ends over the top of each ramekin to enclose the filling and set aside.

If using a gelatin sheet, break it into 3 or 4 pieces and soften in a bowl of cold water for 5 to 10 minutes, then drain. If using powdered gelatin, sprinkle it over 2 tablespoons of cold water in a small dish and set aside to soften, about 5 minutes. Warm the vegetable stock in a small saucepan over medium heat, seasoning to taste with salt. Add the softened gelatin to the stock, stirring until it thoroughly melts. Slowly ladle the stock over the ramekins, allowing time for it to seep in and around the vegetables. When the stock reaches the top of the vegetables, refrigerate until fully set, at least 1 hour, or up to a day ahead.

*continued*

*For the horseradish cream,* whisk the crème fraîche, horseradish, vegetable stock, and vinegar together until smooth. (If using heavy cream, whip it until soft peaks form, add the remaining ingredients, and continue whisking to medium peaks.) Season to taste with salt and refrigerate until ready to serve.

*For the frisée salad,* whisk the vinegar and mustard together in a small bowl. Whisk in the olive oil until blended, then season to taste with salt and pepper. Add the frisée and toss to coat evenly.

To serve, wrap a warm, damp kitchen towel around the side and bottom of a ramekin to soften the gelatin a bit, then run a thin knife blade around the edge and unmold onto a cutting board. Repeat with the remaining terrines, then cut each crosswise in half. Set a terrine in the center of each plate, separating the halves slightly. Drizzle the horseradish cream around each terrine and top the cream with dots of carrot coulis. Add a tuft of frisée salad alongside, sprinkle the tops of the terrines lightly with fleur de sel, and serve.

# Preserving

When the summer season is in full swing, so is the kitchen at Rover's. At this time of year, the Northwest erupts with local stone fruit: cherries, nectarines, apricots, plums, and peaches. For local chefs and home cooks alike, it's an ideal time to visit Seattle's historic Pike Place Market, where farm stalls overflow with tree-ripened fruit. In addition to stone fruit, we also preserve rhubarb, huckleberries, and pickles (which I use in salads and add diced to sauces that accompany meat and fowl). By preserving some of this summertime bounty, on a whim in the middle of winter, I'm able to grab a jar and bring a little bit of summer to dishes such as Wild Boar and Banana Squash with Huckleberry Pepper Sauce (page 157), Seared Hudson Valley Foie Gras with Nectarine Chutney and Verjus Sauce (page 78), or Honey Mousse Charlotte with Rhubarb Purée (page 178). And we are sure to use all our preserved foods before the new preserving season begins.

Each week during the summer, I'll typically order twice as much fruit as I need, half to be used fresh and half to be preserved. First come the cherries in late June, followed by apricots, then peaches and nectarines, and finally plums (with some overlap, of course). So the kitchen keeps busy during the summer and early fall months preserving the fruit we use during winter and spring. On most summer nights, the last thing still cooking in the kitchen is jars of fruit being processed in large pots, simmering to seal.

Most of the fruit is cooked in a light syrup, which allows us the most flexibility when used because the fresh flavor of the fruit is altered very little this way. It also allows me to use the fruit in both sweet and savory recipes. Some of our other preparations include champagne syrup (for peaches), vanilla syrup (adding whole split beans to cherries and nectarines), and heavy brandied syrup (for cherries).

All this is reminiscent of my childhood and my parent's *cave* (basement wine storage area), half of which would be filled with jars of white asparagus, haricots verts, tomato sauce, salsify, jams, and a great many other items from our garden that my mom would preserve during the growing season to sustain us through the winter.

# Hot Appetizers

# CHANTERELLE FLAN
## with Amontillado Sherry Sauce

**MAKES 6 SERVINGS /** Sherry and mushrooms are a friendly flavor combination that just can't be beat. For cooking, I like to use amontillado sherry, which has a subtle nutty character and a bit more sweetness than dry fino sherry. An optional serving suggestion would be toasted crostini served alongside the flan, perhaps spread with soft cloves of roasted garlic or tangy fresh goat cheese to complement the rich flan.

Conde de Valdemar 1998 Rioja Reserva, Spain

4 tablespoons unsalted butter

1/2 pound chanterelle mushrooms, cleaned (page 236), trimmed, and halved, or quartered if large

1 tablespoon minced shallots

1 teaspoon minced fresh thyme

1/2 teaspoon minced garlic

Sea salt

1/2 cup amontillado sherry

2 large eggs

2 large egg whites

1 cup heavy cream

Pinch freshly grated or ground nutmeg

Freshly ground white pepper

Heat the butter in a saucepan over medium heat until melted and foamy white. Add the chanterelles, shallots, and thyme, and sauté over medium-high heat until the mushrooms begin to release their liquid, 2 to 3 minutes. Add the garlic and a good pinch of salt and continue sautéing until the mushrooms are tender, about 5 minutes longer. Stir in the sherry, cook for 1 to 2 minutes longer, then remove from the heat and let cool slightly. Purée the mixture in a blender or food processor until very smooth. Set aside.

Preheat the oven to 275°F. Lightly butter six 1/2-cup ramekins and set them in a shallow baking dish.

Whisk the eggs and egg whites together in a large bowl until very well blended. Whisk in the cream, nutmeg, and a good pinch each of salt and pepper. Whisk in the warm chanterelle purée. Ladle the chanterelle custard into the prepared ramekins. Add enough hot water to the baking dish to come about halfway up the sides of the ramekins, then cover the baking dish tightly with aluminum foil. Insert the tip of a small knife into the center of the foil and lift up slightly to create a "tent" to prevent condensation from dripping down onto the surface of the flans. Carefully transfer the baking dish to the oven and bake until the custard is set (a knife inserted into the center of the flan will come out clean), 25 to 30 minutes.

**Amontillado Sherry Sauce**

1¹/₂ cups amontillado sherry

2 tablespoons minced shallots

1 cup Vegetable Stock (page 210)

¹/₄ cup heavy cream

2 tablespoons unsalted butter

Sea salt and freshly ground white pepper

**Garnish**

Chervil or sweet cicely leaves

*Meanwhile, make the sauce.* Bring the sherry to a boil in a saucepan over medium heat. Boil to reduce by one-fourth, 2 to 3 minutes, then add the shallots and cook until the liquid has reduced in total by three-fourths, 6 to 8 minutes longer. Add the vegetable stock, return to a boil, and cook until reduced by half, about 5 minutes. Add the cream, return to a boil, and cook until slightly thickened, 3 to 5 minutes. Remove the pan from the heat and whisk in the butter so that it melts creamily into the sauce. Season the sauce to taste with salt and pepper.

To serve, carefully remove the ramekins from the water and wipe them dry. Let sit for 15 minutes. Use your fingers to press gently on the surface of the flans, pulling the edge away from the sides of the ramekin to facilitate unmolding (you can run a thin-bladed knife around the edge if necessary). Invert the chanterelle flans onto warm plates, spoon the sherry sauce around the flans, and top the flans with chervil leaves.

# DIVER SEA SCALLOPS

## with Beets, Foie Gras, and Aged Balsamic Vinegar

**MAKES 4 SERVINGS /** This is an easy recipe with just a few ingredients—be sure to choose the best so the dish really shines. Pull out the best balsamic (aged at least 25 years) for the final drizzle before serving. Both the scallops and the foie gras should be served immediately after being seared. If you have limited space or equipment, sear the foie gras and keep it warm on a plate in a low oven, then pour out the excess fat, wipe out the pan, and sear the scallops.

Allegrini 2001 Palazzo della Torre IGT, Veneto, Italy

---

$3/4$ **pound small red beets, scrubbed**

**2 tablespoons olive oil**

**Sea salt**

$1/2$ **pound large dry-pack sea scallops**

**4 slices foie gras (1$1/2$ to 2 ounces each)**

**Garnish**

**Aged balsamic vinegar**

**Extra virgin olive oil**

**Beet Oil (page 219)**

**Minced fresh chives**

Put the beets in a small saucepan of cold salted water and bring to a boil over high heat. Decrease the heat to medium and simmer until the beets are tender, about $1^1/4$ hours. The beets should be fully covered with water as they cook; if needed, add more hot water. Drain the beets well and set aside until cool enough to handle. Trim the beets and slip off the skins, then cut the beets into $1/4$-inch-thick wedges.

Heat a skillet over medium heat, then add 1 tablespoon of olive oil to the pan. Add the beets and a pinch of salt and cook, tossing gently, until warmed through, 3 to 5 minutes.

Heat both a large and a medium skillet over high heat. Season the scallops with salt. Score the foie gras slices with the tip of a knife in a diamond pattern and season with salt. Add the remaining 1 table-spoon of oil to the large skillet, then add the scallops and sear until nicely browned but still opaque in the center, about 1 minute total. Meanwhile, add the foie gras slices to the hot, dry medium skillet and sear until well browned but still tender in the center, about 30 seconds per side. (See page 232 for notes on cooking foie gras.)

To serve, arrange the beet wedges in a small pile to one side of center on warm plates. Halve each scallop horizontally and arrange over the beets, slightly overlapping them. Top the scallops with the foie gras. Drizzle the balsamic vinegar, extra virgin olive oil, and beet oil around the beets and sprinkle minced chives over the foie gras.

# SEARED HUDSON VALLEY FOIE GRAS

## with Nectarine Chutney and Verjus Sauce

**MAKES 4 SERVINGS /** Verjus, French for "green juice," has been a key ingredient in kitchens as far back as the Middle Ages and is regaining its popularity. It is made from immature grapes culled from vines early in the grape-growing season, usually in the summertime, so the remaining grape clusters can more easily mature. The clear, light, very acidic juice is only lightly fermented, so it contributes a bright flavor to sauces; here, it is the ideal complement to rich foie gras. The verjus I use at Rover's is from the celebrated Klipsun Vineyards on Red Mountain in Eastern Washington.

Château Ste. Michelle 2003 Riesling "Eroica," Washington State

---

½ cup sugar

Juice of ½ lemon

2 nectarines, halved and pitted

1 tablespoon olive oil

2 tablespoons minced shallots

¼ teaspoon minced garlic

¼ teaspoon minced fresh thyme

1 tablespoon verjus

1 tablespoon clover honey

1 teaspoon minced fresh chives

Sea salt and freshly ground white pepper

4 slices foie gras (2 to 3 ounces each)

Bring a saucepan of water to a boil over high heat and prepare a bowl of ice water. Add the sugar and lemon juice to the boiling water, stirring to help the sugar dissolve, then add the nectarine halves. Decrease the heat to medium-low and simmer just long enough to make it easy to peel off the skin, 1 to 2 minutes. Use a slotted spoon to lift out 2 of the nectarine halves from the water and cool them in the ice water, then set aside on paper towels to drain. Simmer the remaining halves until tender when pierced with a knife, 3 to 5 minutes longer. Transfer the nectarine halves to a plate and set aside.

Peel away the skin from the briefly cooked nectarine halves and cut them into a ½-inch dice. Heat a skillet over medium heat, then add the olive oil. Add the shallots, garlic, and thyme and cook until tender and aromatic, 1 to 2 minutes. Add the diced nectarine and cook over medium-high heat for about 2 minutes, then stir in the verjus and honey. Cook until slightly thickened, 2 to 3 minutes longer. Remove the skillet from the heat, stir in the chives, and season to taste with salt and pepper. Peel the reserved nectarine halves and cut into very thin slices. Set aside.

**Verjus Sauce**

³/₄ cup verjus

3 shallots, thinly sliced

1 teaspoon fresh thyme leaves

1 bay leaf, preferably fresh, partly torn

1¹/₂ cups Veal Stock (page 206)

4 tablespoons unsalted butter, cut into
    pieces and chilled

Sea salt and freshly ground white pepper

**Garnish**

Carrot Coulis (page xx)

Minced fresh chives

*For the verjus sauce,* combine the verjus, shallots, thyme, and bay leaf in a saucepan. Bring to a boil over high heat and boil to reduce by about two-thirds, 5 to 7 minutes. Add the veal stock and reduce by half, 8 to 10 minutes longer. Add the butter pieces, swirling the pan so that the butter melts creamily into the sauce. Strain the sauce through a sieve into a smaller saucepan, and season to taste with salt and pepper; keep warm over low heat. Gently reheat the nectarine chutney over low heat.

Score the foie gras slices with the tip of a knife in a diamond pattern and season with salt. Heat a skillet over high heat, add the foie gras, and sear until well browned but still tender in the center, 30 to 45 seconds per side. (See page 232 for notes on cooking foie gras.)

To serve, arrange the nectarine slices in a fan pattern, slightly overlapping them, on warm plates. Spoon the chutney over the nectarine slices, set the foie gras on top, and drizzle the verjus sauce around the nectarine slices. Drizzle some carrot coulis over the sauce and sprinkle the foie gras with minced chives.

# SPOT PRAWNS

## with Cèpes and Pedro Ximenez Noble Sour

**MAKES 4 SERVINGS** / Pedro Ximenez is a grape used in Spain to make sweet wine, from which this "noble sour" is made. It is very slightly sour, hinting at vinegar, but so low in acidity that the deep brown liquid is commonly served as an after-dinner *digestif.* Look for Pedro Ximenez noble sour in specialty food shops, such as ChefShop (page 228). If you're unable to find it, you can combine 6 tablespoons of balsamic vinegar with a pinch of sugar and boil gently until reduced to about 1/4 cup. If your spot prawns have their roe attached, see the box on page 81 for tips on drying it to use as a garnish.

Salon 1990 Blanc de Blancs Champagne, France

1 tablespoon olive oil

1 tablespoon plus 1 teaspoon finely minced shallots

1/4 cup Pedro Ximenez noble sour

2 tablespoons plus 1 teaspoon walnut oil

1 teaspoon sherry vinegar

1/2 pound cèpe mushrooms, cleaned (page 236)

1 tablespoon unsalted butter

1/2 teaspoon minced fresh thyme

1/4 teaspoon minced garlic

Sea salt and freshly ground white pepper

2 teaspoons minced fresh chives

3/4 pound spot prawns, peeled

Garnish

Red Bell Pepper Coulis (page 214)

Fleur de sel

Heat a small skillet over medium heat, then add the olive oil. Add 1 tablespoon of the shallots and cook until just tender, about 30 seconds. Add the Pedro Ximenez, 1 tablespoon of the walnut oil, and the sherry vinegar. Cook until slightly reduced, 2 to 3 minutes. Remove from the heat and set aside.

Preheat the oven to 200°F.

Trim the mushrooms if needed. Cut the caps from the stems. Halve the stems lengthwise (or quarter if quite large) and cut the caps and stems into 1/4-inch-thick slices.

Heat a large skillet over medium-high heat, then add the butter and 1 tablespoon of the walnut oil and heat until the butter is melted and foamy white. Add the mushrooms and sauté until beginning to soften, 1 to 2 minutes. (It's important that the mushrooms not be crowded in the skillet or they will give off lots of liquid and become soggy; cook in 2 batches or in 2 separate skillets if necessary.) Add the remaining 1 teaspoon of shallots, the thyme, and garlic and season to taste with salt and pepper. Cook, stirring often, until the mushrooms are fully tender, 2 to 3 minutes longer. Transfer the mushrooms to a plate and sprinkle the chives over; keep warm in the oven.

SEASON | SPRING        81

Toss the shrimp with the remaining 1 teaspoon of the walnut oil and season with salt and pepper. Heat the clean, large skillet over high heat, add the shrimp and cook, turning once, just until lightly browned on the outside but still tender and partly translucent in the center, about 1 minute total.

To serve, arrange the cèpes in a flat 3-inch circle in the center of warm plates and arrange the shrimp on top in a spiral pattern. Drizzle the Pedro Ximenez sauce over the shrimp, add dots of red bell pepper coulis around the shrimp and mushrooms, and top the shrimp with tiny pinches of fleur de sel.

**DRIED SHRIMP ROE**—The tiny orange eggs (roe) from shrimp can be dried and used as an interesting garnish on dishes such as this, the brightly colored roe offering a nice bit of crunch as well. The roe is ideally added to a dish just before serving, because cooking at high heat will bring out stronger flavors.

Remove the roe from the shrimp when peeling them and set aside in a small bowl. Bring a small saucepan of salted water to a boil, then add the roe and boil for just 5 to 10 seconds. Drain the roe well in a fine-mesh sieve, then put on a rimmed baking sheet and spread in an even layer. Dry the roe in the oven at its lowest setting, preferably no more than 150°F, for 1 to 2 hours. If you have a gas oven with a pilot light, you may not need to turn it on at all; just leave the baking sheet in the oven overnight to dry.

When the roe has dried, set aside to cool to room temperature. Gently rub the roe between your fingers to separate any eggs that are still clinging together. Refrigerate in an airtight container for up to 3 weeks.

# MACKEREL

## with Tomato Confit and Caper Vinaigrette

**MAKES 4 SERVINGS** / Mackerel is a fish that is not commonly found in markets, but I love its robust flavor; it's worth making a special request of your fishmonger. An ideal accompaniment—in keeping with the Provençal flavors of this dish—would be fennel braised with a splash of Pastis. Capers are the pickled buds of a shrub native to Morocco and Turkey. Caper berries—olive-sized and sold with the stem still attached—are the mature fruit of the same shrub, but they have a less intense flavor than regular capers.

Château Simone 2001 Palette Blanc, France

1 pound plum tomatoes, halved
  lengthwise

Sea salt and freshly ground white pepper

6 to 8 thyme sprigs

1/2 cup plus 1 tablespoon olive oil

4 pieces mackerel fillet (about 1/4 pound
  each)

2 teaspoons Turmeric Oil (page 218,
  optional)

Caper Vinaigrette

8 large caper berries

8 large pitted cured black olives,
  quartered

8 large green olives, such as picholine,
  pitted and quartered

1 tablespoon drained nonpareil capers

4 teaspoons marine cider vinegar or white
  wine vinegar

2 teaspoons minced shallots

Preheat the oven to 300°F.

Place the tomato halves in a small roasting pan, cut-side up, and season with salt and pepper. Top the tomatoes with the thyme sprigs, drizzle with 1/2 cup of the olive oil, and bake for 1 1/4 hours, or until the tomatoes are very tender and aromatic, turning the tomatoes after about 45 minutes and basting them with the oil 4 or 5 times. Set the pan of tomato confit on a wire rack and let cool. Increase the oven temperature to 350°F.

*For the caper vinaigrette,* halve the caper berries just to one side of the stem so that the stem is fully attached to one half; set the halves with the stems aside for garnish. Quarter the remaining halves and put into a saucepan with the black and green olives and capers. Add the vinegar, shallots, chives, thyme, and garlic. Measure out 1/4 cup of the tomato confit oil from the pan, add to the caper vinaigrette, and season to taste with salt and pepper. Toss well to mix and set aside to marinate while cooking the mackerel.

1 teaspoon minced fresh chives

¼ teaspoon minced fresh thyme

¼ teaspoon minced garlic

Sea salt and freshly ground white pepper

Garnish

Green fennel sprigs

Minced fresh chives

Heat a large skillet over medium-high heat, then add the remaining 1 tablespoon of olive oil. Season the mackerel with salt and pepper and add to the hot skillet, drizzling the turmeric oil around them, if using. Brown the mackerel well on both sides, 2 to 3 minutes total, then transfer the skillet to the oven and bake until only a bit of translucency remains in the center, 3 to 4 minutes. Remove the skillet from the oven; carefully peel away the skin and remove the dark band of flesh (which is quite strongly flavored) from just under the skin.

To serve, gently warm the caper vinaigrette over medium-low heat, stirring to combine well, 2 to 3 minutes. Peel away and discard the skins from the tomato confit halves and place 3 halves, cut-side down, next to each other in the center of warm plates. Lay the mackerel on top of the tomatoes and spoon the warm caper vinaigrette over, drizzling the liquid over and around the fish. Top the fish with the reserved caper-berry halves, add a few small fennel sprigs around the fish, and sprinkle chives over all.

# CORN FLAN
## with Lobster

**MAKES 8 SERVINGS** / Sweet summer corn and rich lobster play off one another beautifully in this appetizer. I like to use white corn here, though yellow corn can be used as well. You could use about $1/2$ pound of Dungeness crabmeat in place of the lobster, if you like, preferably larger leg and claw pieces, as they will make the most attractive garnish.

McCrea Cellars 2002 Viognier, Washington State

4 ears tender white corn, husks and silks removed

4 cups heavy cream

4 large eggs

2 large egg yolks

Pinch freshly grated or ground nutmeg

Sea salt and freshly ground white pepper

2 live lobsters (about $1^1/2$ pounds each)

1 cup Lobster Stock (page 209)

$1/2$ cup (1 stick) unsalted butter, cut into pieces and chilled

Garnish

Blanched julienned carrot

Shrimp Roe (page 80)

Beet Coulis (page 215)

Chervil sprigs

Preheat the oven to 300°F. Lightly butter eight $1/2$-cup ramekins and set them in a large baking dish.

Cut the kernels from the ears of corn. Using the back of the knife, scrape away the tender flesh that clings to the cobs and set aside. Bring a small saucepan of salted water to a boil, add $1/2$ cup of the corn kernels, and blanch for 1 to 2 minutes. Drain well and set aside for garnish.

Combine the cream, the remaining corn kernels, and the tender corn flesh in a saucepan with $1/2$ teaspoon of salt. Bring just to a boil over medium-high heat, then decrease the heat to medium and simmer until the corn is very tender and the liquid has reduced slightly, 10 to 12 minutes. Strain the corn through a sieve into a bowl, reserving the corn-infused cream. Purée the corn kernels with $1/2$ cup of the corn-infused cream in a blender or food processor until very smooth. Strain the corn through a fine-mesh sieve into a bowl, pressing on the tough skins to extract as much of the flavorful purée as possible.

Whisk the eggs and egg yolks together in a large bowl until well blended, then whisk in the corn purée and enough of the remaining corn-infused cream to equal 4 cups. Season the custard mixture with the nutmeg, a good pinch of salt, and a small pinch of pepper. Ladle the custard mixture into the prepared ramekins. Add enough boiling water to the baking dish to come about halfway up the sides of the ramekins, then cover the pan tightly with aluminum foil. Insert the tip of a small knife into the center of the foil and lift up slightly to create a "tent" to prevent condensation from dripping down onto the surface of the flans. Carefully transfer the baking dish to the oven and bake until the custard is set (a knife inserted into the center of the flan will come out clean), 25 to 30 minutes.

Meanwhile, cook the lobster and pick the meat from the shells (page 234), reserving the tail and claw meat. Set aside.

Bring the lobster stock to a boil in a small saucepan over medium-high heat and boil to reduce by one-third, 3 to 5 minutes. Decrease the heat to low and whisk in the butter, a couple of pieces at a time, swirling the pan gently so the butter melts creamily into the sauce. Remove the pan from the heat and add the lobster pieces and reserved corn kernels to the sauce to warm through.

To serve, carefully remove the ramekins from the water and wipe them dry. Use your fingers to press gently on the surface of the flans, pulling the edge away from the sides of the ramekin to facilitate unmolding (you can run a thin-bladed knife around the edge if necessary). Invert the corn flans into the centers of warm plates. Cut the reserved lobster tails into $1/2$-inch medallions and slice the reserved claws horizontally in half. Arrange the lobster tail medallions around the flan, setting the claw portions on top. Drizzle the sauce over the lobster tail and scatter the reserved corn kernels around the flan. Garnish with julienned carrot and shrimp roe, adding a drizzle of beet coulis around the outer edge of the sauce. Top the flan with a small chervil sprig.

# FROGS' LEGS

## with Fava Bean Purée and Summer Black Truffle

**MAKES 4 SERVINGS** / When I was a kid, I used to go fishing in a pond close to my house and come home with a hundred frogs' legs, having no idea that I'd one day be cooking them in my own restaurant kitchen. In the Northwest, the late springtime treat of plump, green fava beans serves as a base for delicate roasted frogs' legs, the fava purée embellished with summer truffles that come to me from Provence. If you're unable to find truffles, another seasonal option is fresh morel mushrooms. Finely chop about 2 ounces of them and sauté in a couple teaspoons of butter over medium-high heat with a pinch each of thyme and shallot until tender, about 5 minutes.

Domaine Jean-Philippe Fichet 2002 Puligny-Montrachet 1er Cru "Les Referts," France

2 cups peeled fava beans (from about 2 pounds pods, page 232)

1/2 cup Vegetable Stock (page 210) or water, or more if needed

1 tablespoon olive oil

Sea salt

2 teaspoons minced summer black truffle, plus 8 thin slices

6 tablespoons unsalted butter

1 pound frogs' legs (6 to 8 pairs)

1/2 teaspoon minced fresh thyme

Freshly ground white pepper

3 shallots, thinly sliced

1 cup Poultry Stock (page 207)

### Garnish

Microgreens, such as celery sprouts, tatsoi sprouts, or watercress sprouts

Chive Oil (see Basil Oil, page 216) or extra virgin olive oil

Bring a large pot of generously salted water to a boil. Add the fava beans and simmer until just tender but still bright green, 3 to 4 minutes. Drain well and spread out on paper towels to dry. Put the beans in a blender or food processor. Warm the vegetable stock in a small saucepan over medium heat; add to the blender with the olive oil and a good pinch of salt. Purée until smooth, scraping down the sides of the blender as needed and adding a bit more stock if the purée is too thick; it should have the texture of soft mashed potatoes. Transfer the purée to a heatproof bowl, stir in the minced truffle, and set over a saucepan of simmering, not boiling, water to keep warm.

Preheat the oven to 350°F.

Heat 4 tablespoons of the butter in a large skillet over medium-high heat until melted, medium brown, and slightly nutty smelling. Season the frogs' legs with the thyme, salt, and pepper. Add them to the skillet and brown well on both sides, about 5 minutes total. Scatter the shallots over and around the frogs' legs and season the shallots with salt. Transfer the skillet to the oven and roast until the meat is cooked through and the shallots are tender and lightly caramelized, 10 to 12 minutes.

Meanwhile, bring the poultry stock to a boil in a small saucepan over medium-high heat. Boil until reduced by two-thirds, 8 to 10 minutes. Add the remaining 2 tablespoons of butter, swirling the pan gently so that the butter melts creamily into the stock. Season the jus to taste with salt and pepper.

Remove the skillet from the oven and transfer the frogs' legs to a plate. Carefully remove the meat from the legs, keeping it in large pieces as much as possible. Taste the fava bean purée for seasoning, adding more salt or pepper if needed.

To serve, spoon a circle of the fava bean purée just off center on warm plates. Lay the frogs' leg pieces on the purée in a spoke pattern. Cut the truffle slices in half or in quarters and slip them between the frogs' leg pieces so that the slices stand upright. Drizzle the poultry jus over the meat. Spoon the roasted shallots on the opposite side of the plate, arranging them out flat. Toss the microgreens with a drizzle of chive oil and a pinch of salt and arrange the greens on top of the shallots.

# SMOKED DUCK SALAD

## with Duck Prosciutto, Foie Gras, and Plum Confit

**MAKES 4 SERVINGS /** This is a meat-lover's salad in which the plums of late summer and early fall provide a nice tangy contrast to the rich, full flavors of smoked duck breast, duck prosciutto, and foie gras. The added touch of peppery arugula further enhances the balance of the dish.

Duckhorn 2002 Merlot, Napa Valley

2 tablespoons unsalted butter

3 red plums, halved and pitted

5 tablespoons red wine vinegar

1 tablespoon sugar

1 tablespoon minced shallots

1/2 teaspoon minced fresh thyme

1/4 teaspoon minced garlic

3 tablespoons canola oil

1 tablespoon water

Sea salt and freshly ground black pepper

6 ounces smoked duck breast

2 ounces duck prosciutto

1 1/2 cups loosely packed baby arugula, rinsed and dried

4 slices foie gras (1 1/2 to 2 ounces each)

Garnish

Minced fresh chives

Preheat the oven to 400°F. For the plum confit, heat the butter in a large ovenproof skillet over medium heat until melted and foamy white. Add the plum halves, cut-side down, and drizzle with 4 tablespoons of the vinegar. Sprinkle with the sugar and roast in the oven for 10 minutes. Baste the plums with the cooking liquid and roast for another 10 minutes. Baste once again, then add the shallots, thyme, and garlic to the skillet. Continue roasting until the plums are very tender and aromatic, 10 to 15 minutes longer. Lift off and discard the plum skins, then transfer all but 1 of the plum halves to a plate to cool. Reserve the cooking liquid.

Put the reserved plum half and the cooking liquid in a blender and purée until very smooth. Add the oil, the remaining 1 tablespoon of vinegar, and the water and purée until blended. Strain the mixture through a fine-mesh sieve into a bowl and season to taste with salt and pepper.

Cut the smoked duck breast and duck prosciutto into very thin slices. Thinly slice the plum confit halves and arrange in a row to one side of each plate, slightly overlapping them. Lay the smoked duck breast slices alongside, slightly overlapping the plums, then place the prosciutto slices so they are slightly overlapping the smoked duck. Toss the arugula in the plum dressing. Set a pile of arugula to one side of the plate and drizzle the remaining dressing around.

Score the foie gras slices with the tip of a knife in a diamond pattern and season the slices with salt. Heat a skillet over high heat, add the foie gras, and sear until well browned but still tender in the center, about 30 seconds per side. (See page 232 for notes on cooking foie gras.) To serve, set the foie gras on top of the salad and scatter the chives over all.

# SCRAMBLED EGGS
## with Lime Crème Fraîche and White Sturgeon Caviar

**MAKES 4 SERVINGS** / If there is one signature dish at Rover's, this is it. I didn't invent this recipe—it has been prepared many times by many chefs—but this is my rendition of the contemporary classic. Every customer familiar with dining here knows that this is often one of the first exquisite bites of the evening. I serve the delicate scrambled eggs and caviar in an eggshell nestled in a simple, elegant egg cup. You could also serve the eggs in espresso cups. Ideally, the eggs should be removed from their shells a few hours before serving to allow time for the shells to dry fully (refrigerate the eggs until you're ready to cook them). Once dry, the thin membrane coating the inside of the eggshell will be easier to remove before spooning in the tender scrambled eggs.

Bollinger RD 1988 Champagne, France

4 large eggs

1 tablespoon unsalted butter

1$^1$/$_2$ teaspoons minced shallots

$^1$/$_4$ teaspoon minced fresh thyme

2 teaspoons minced fresh flat-leaf
    parsley

Sea salt and freshly ground white pepper

1 ounce white sturgeon caviar

Lime Crème Fraîche

3 tablespoons crème fraîche, homemade
    (page 212) or store-bought

1 teaspoon freshly squeezed lime juice

Sea salt and freshly ground white pepper

Garnish

Chervil leaves

Trim about $^1$/$_2$ inch from the smaller tapered end of each egg (see box on page 91). Pour the egg into a bowl; reserve the shell and discard the top cap. Repeat with the remaining eggs. Bring a saucepan of water to a boil. Add the eggshells and gently use a large spoon to keep them submerged. Boil for 3 minutes, then scoop out the shells with a slotted spoon and set upside down on paper towels to dry thoroughly. (Or use an empty egg carton if you have one.)

*For the lime crème fraîche,* whisk the crème fraîche in a small bowl until light, then add the lime juice and whisk until firm peaks form. Season with a small pinch of salt (keep in mind that the caviar will add saltiness) and pepper. If you like, transfer the lime crème fraîche to a small piping bag fitted with a plain tip (it can also be spooned onto the eggs); refrigerate until needed. When the eggshells are well dried, remove as much as possible of the fine white membrane from inside each shell, being careful not to break the shell.

Beat the eggs, preferably with an immersion blender, until thoroughly blended and smooth, about 30 seconds. Strain them through a medium sieve into a bowl to remove any stray bits of shell. Heat the butter in

*continued*

a small skillet over medium heat until melted and foamy white, then add the shallots and thyme and cook until tender and aromatic, about 2 minutes. Add the eggs and cook, whisk constantly and briskly, for 3 to 4 minutes; the eggs should remain creamy and not cook into big clumps. Be sure to draw the whisk all across the bottom of the pan to avoid sticking, moving the skillet on and off the heat as needed to prevent overcooking. Remove the skillet from the heat before the eggs are fully cooked, because the heat of the pan will continue to cook them for a few minutes longer. Stir in the parsley and season to taste with salt and pepper.

To serve, use a small spoon to fill the prepared eggshells with the warm eggs to within $1/4$ inch of the top. Pipe or spoon the lime crème fraîche over the eggs and top with a generous dollop of caviar. Garnish each with a small chervil leaf and set the eggs in egg cups.

**EGG CUPS**—I use an egg trimmer that has a perfectly calibrated spring action to score a ring gently around the top of an eggshell, which we then further trim away with the tip of a small knife, leaving a clean edge along the top of the egg. A home-style alternative—similar to what I used to do before finding the trimmer tool—is to use the wide edge of a large plain pastry tip or a small round cutter that has a diameter of about $1^1/4$ inches. With the egg sitting securely in its carton, rest the rim of the pastry tip or cutter on top of the egg, and use the back of a spoon to gently tap the tip or cutter so it lightly scores the shell. Don't worry as much about creating a perfectly tidy, unjagged edge, but do avoid using too much force, which will crack the egg.

# VEAL SWEETBREAD AND HUDSON VALLEY FOIE GRAS SAUSAGE

## with Couscous and Port Reduction

**MAKES 4 SERVINGS /** This is my indulgent twist on sausage. I rarely use chicken in my kitchen, but in this case the mild meat serves as a great foundation to which diced sweetbreads, foie gras, mushrooms, and truffle are added. The sausage-stuffing attachment of a stand mixer will greatly facilitate filling the sausage casings, though you can do the work with a pastry bag instead.

DeLille Cellars 2002 D2, Washington State

6 ounces veal sweetbreads

1/2 celery stalk, coarsely chopped

1/2 carrot, peeled and coarsely chopped

6 to 8 thyme sprigs

4-inch piece of dark green leek top

1 bay leaf, preferably fresh, partly torn

6 white peppercorns

3 whole cloves

Sea salt

6 tablespoons unsalted butter

1/4 pound oyster mushrooms, cleaned
    (page 236), trimmed, and finely diced

1/2 teaspoon minced shallots

Pinch of minced garlic

Pinch of minced fresh thyme

Freshly ground white pepper

2 teaspoons minced fresh chives

1/4 pound foie gras, cut into 1/4-inch-
    thick slices

Put the sweetbreads in a saucepan with cold water to cover. Cut a piece of cheesecloth about 8 inches square. Put the celery, carrot, thyme sprigs, leek green, bay leaf, peppercorns, and cloves in the center of the cheesecloth and tie the packet securely with kitchen string. Add the seasoning packet and a generous pinch of salt to the pan. Bring to a boil over medium-high heat and count 1 minute from the time the water reaches a full boil. Drain the sweetbreads and rinse under cold running water, then set aside to cool; discard the seasoning packet. When cool enough to handle, trim away the tough membrane from the sweetbreads and cut into a fine dice; set aside. (The sweetbreads will be rare at this point but will cook more later.)

Heat 3 tablespoons of the butter in a skillet over medium-high heat until melted, medium brown, and slightly nutty smelling. Add the sweetbreads, mushrooms, shallots, garlic, thyme, and a pinch each of salt and pepper. Sauté for 1 minute, then add the chives and toss, cooking for about 1 minute longer. Transfer the mixture to a plate and spread out to cool quickly.

Score the foie gras slices with the tip of a knife in a diamond pattern and season with salt. Heat a skillet over high heat, add the foie gras, and sear until well browned but still tender in the center, about 20 seconds per side. (See page 232 for notes on cooking foie gras.) Set aside to cool, then finely dice the foie gras.

1/2 pound boneless, skinless, free-range
  chicken breast

1 large egg white

1/2 cup heavy cream

2 teaspoons finely diced black truffle

About 3 feet medium pork casings

Couscous

2/3 cup Israeli couscous

2 cups Poultry Stock (page 207)

1 tablespoon olive oil

2 teaspoons minced shallots

1/2 teaspoon minced fresh thyme

1/4 teaspoon minced garlic

Sea salt and freshly ground white pepper

Port Reduction Sauce

1 cup ruby or vintage port

2 shallots, sliced

1/4 cup Veal Stock (page 206)

2 tablespoons unsalted butter

Sea salt and freshly ground white pepper

Garnish

Chopped fresh chives

Carrot Coulis (page 215)

Cut the chicken breast into 1-inch pieces and pulse in a food processor until finely chopped. Add the egg white and pulse until smooth. Transfer the chicken mousse to a bowl and set over a large bowl of ice water. Stir in the cream, a little at a time, until evenly blended and smooth. Gently stir in the truffle, foie gras, and sweetbread-mushroom mixture. Bring a small saucepan of water to a boil, add a teaspoon of the sausage mixture, and simmer until cooked through, about 1 minute. Let cool, then taste the mixture for seasoning, adding more salt or pepper to the sausage mixture if needed.

Put the pork casings in a colander and rinse well under cold running water. Attach the sausage-stuffing attachment to your stand mixer and slide the casing onto the stuffing tube. Tie a knot at the end of the casing. Feed the mousse through the grinder (without the blade or the die) and into the casing. (Alternatively, put the mousse in a large piping bag fitted with a large plain tip and squeeze the mousse into the casing. You may need to cut the casing into 4 individual sections so that the casings will slip over the end of the pastry bag, making individual sausages.) Fill the casing without overstuffing; if filled too tight, it will burst during cooking. Twist the casing a few times every 5 to 6 inches to form 4 sausages.

*For the couscous,* put the couscous in a skillet and add the poultry stock, olive oil, shallots, thyme, and garlic. Bring to a boil over medium-high heat, then decrease the heat to medium-low and simmer gently, stirring occasionally, until the couscous is tender, 18 to 20 minutes. Season to taste with salt and pepper; set aside.

*For the port sauce,* combine the port and shallots in a saucepan and bring to a boil over medium-high heat. Boil to reduce by three-quarters, 8 to 10 minutes. Add the veal stock and boil to reduce by half, 3 to 5 minutes. Add the butter and whisk gently so it melts creamily into the sauce. Season the sauce to taste with salt and pepper, then strain it through a sieve into a small saucepan; set aside.

Preheat the oven to 350°F.

*continued*

*To finish the sausages,* heat the remaining 3 tablespoons of butter in a large ovenproof skillet over medium heat until melted and foamy white. Add the sausages and brown gently on all sides, 2 to 3 minutes, being careful not to cook the sausages over too high a heat or the casings might split. Transfer the skillet to the oven and roast the sausages until cooked through, 5 to 7 minutes. Remove the skillet from the oven and let the sausages sit for a minute or two. Meanwhile, gently reheat the sauce and the couscous over medium-low heat.

To serve, cut the sausage into $^1/_2$-inch-thick slices on the diagonal. Spoon the couscous into the center of warm plates and lean the sausage slices against the couscous, overlapping them slightly. Drizzle the port reduction around the sausages, sprinkle chives over the sausages and couscous, and drizzle carrot coulis around the couscous and sausages.

# BUTTER-POACHED SCALLOPS ON CELERIAC PURÉE

## with Meyer Lemon Nage and Lemon Confit

**MAKES 4 SERVINGS** / Poaching in butter is a technique most often used to cook fish and shellfish gently, resulting in an elegant flavor and a silky texture. That richness is tempered here by the bright citrus flavor of Meyer lemon juice. If you are unable to find Meyer lemons, which are available during winter months, you can use regular lemons. In place of the lemon confit, you could instead use preserved lemon and cut it into thin slices for the garnish. Also known as celery root, celeriac offers a sweet, nutty flavor and a delicate echo of branch celery's distinctive flavor. Be sure to peel the root fully, not only the thin outer skin but also the slightly woody, tough layer just below. Do your best to buy dry-pack scallops from your fishmonger; they have not been treated with additives to keep them extra plump (which alters the flavor and texture of the scallop).

Trimbach 2001 Riesling "Frederic Emile," France

12 large sea scallops, dry-packed

Sea salt and freshly ground white pepper

**Lemon Confit**

1 Meyer lemon or large regular lemon

1 cup water

1/3 cup sugar

1/4 cup rice wine vinegar

**Celeriac Purée**

1 celeriac (about 1 1/4 pounds)

4 tablespoons unsalted butter

2 tablespoons crème fraîche, homemade (page 212) or store-bought, or heavy cream

Sea salt and freshly ground white pepper

*For the lemon confit,* trim the ends from the lemon just to the flesh; reserve the ends for cooking the celeriac and cut the lemon into 1/8-inch-thick slices. Combine the water, sugar, and vinegar in a large sauté pan or skillet. Bring just to a boil over medium-high heat, stirring occasionally to help the sugar dissolve. Add the lemon slices to the pan in an even layer, overlapping the slices as little as possible. Decrease the heat to very low; it's important that the liquid not boil or the lemon will fall apart. If your stove won't hold a very low temperature, transfer the pan to an oven set at 170°F, covering the lemon slices with a piece of parchment paper to avoid drying out. Gently cook the lemon slices until the rind is translucent and very tender, 2 to 3 hours. Remove the pan from the heat and let cool, then transfer the slices to a plate and set aside. (The confit can be made up to 4 days in advance).

*continued*

**Butter Poaching Liquid**

3 Meyer lemons or large regular lemons

1/2 cup Lobster Stock (page 209)

3/4 cup unsalted butter, cut into pieces

Sea salt and freshly ground white pepper

**Garnish**

Minced fresh chives

Shrimp roe (page 80)

*For the celeriac purée,* trim the stalk end from the celeriac and peel it with a paring knife. Cut the celeriac into quarters, then crosswise into 2-inch pieces. Fill a large saucepan with salted water and add the celeriac and lemon trimmings from the lemon confit (this will help keep the celeriac white as it cooks). Fold a damp, clean kitchen towel into quarters and lay it directly over the celeriac so that it remains fully submerged in the liquid during cooking. (Alternatively, you can top the celeriac with a small heatproof plate to weight it down.) Bring the water just to a boil over medium-high heat, then decrease the heat to medium and simmer gently until the celeriac is tender when pierced with the tip of a knife, 40 to 45 minutes. The liquid should not boil; reduce the heat to medium-low if needed.

Carefully remove the towel with tongs or a large wooden spoon and rinse it well under cold running water, twisting it to remove the excess water; set the towel aside. Drain the celeriac in a colander and let it cool. Transfer the celeriac to the center of the towel, draw the edges of the towel up around the celeriac, and twist firmly, pressing it down into the colander to add extra pressure and remove as much excess liquid as possible. Combine the butter and crème fraîche in a small saucepan and bring just to a boil over medium-high heat, then remove the pan from the heat. Put the celeriac in a food processor, pulse a few times, then add the warm butter–crème fraîche mixture and purée until very smooth. Season to taste with salt and pepper and transfer the purée to a small saucepan; set aside.

Meanwhile, preheat the oven to 170°F.

*To prepare the butter poaching liquid,* section 2 of the Meyer lemons (page 235, reserve the trimmings) and squeeze the juice from the third lemon. Put the lobster stock in a sauté pan and bring to a boil over medium-high heat. Boil to reduce the liquid by one-third, then reduce the heat to medium and gradually whisk in the butter so that it melts creamily into the stock. Add 2 teaspoons of the Meyer lemon juice with a pinch of salt and pepper. Reheat the celeriac purée over medium-low heat while cooking the scallops.

Season the scallops lightly with salt and pepper, then add them to the butter poaching liquid. Cook over medium-low heat until the scallops are evenly opaque on the surface but still translucent in the center, with a texture that is firm on the outside but still springy when pressed, about 5 minutes; make sure that the liquid doesn't overheat and boil. If the scallops are not fully submerged in the poaching liquid, turn them once or twice while they cook. With tongs or a slotted spoon, lift out the scallops, put on an ovenproof plate, and keep warm in the oven. Add the Meyer lemon sections and any remaining juice to the poaching liquid and gently warm over medium heat for 2 to 3 minutes. Taste for seasoning, adding more salt or pepper if necessary.

To serve, lay 2 or 3 lemon-confit slices in the center of warm plates, slightly overlapping them. Form the celeriac purée into 4 large quenelles (page 235) and set one atop the lemon confit on each plate. Cut the scallops horizontally in half and arrange them around the celeriac, leaning them up against the purée. Spoon the Meyer lemon butter sauce over the scallops and celeriac, arranging the lemon segments around the outer edge. Sprinkle chives over the celeriac and top the scallops with tiny pinches of shrimp roe.

# KUSSHI OYSTERS

## with Leeks and Caviar Sabayon

**MAKES 4 SERVINGS /** We have many outstanding types of oysters in the Northwest, to enjoy both raw on the half-shell and in a wide range of recipes. A recent favorite of mine is the kusshi oyster from Vancouver Island, though I've also used kumamoto oysters for this recipe. Rock salt is a great tool for helping keep the oysters steady in the baking pan and on the plate. Be sure to use a generous layer so the shells will be able to settle into the salt. You can also use the salt on the serving plates for the same purpose, which also provides a striking visual element. For a more decadent presentation, top each oyster with a small dollop of extra caviar just before serving. No need to break out a primo champagne for this dish; feel free to use a less expensive one or perhaps a bit of champagne left from a bottle you enjoyed a night or two ago, as long as it was properly stored.

Taittinger 1995 Comtes de Champagne Blanc de Blancs, France

Rock salt

12 small kusshi oysters in the shell

1/2 cup heavy cream

3/4 cup champagne

2 small leeks, white part only, halved
   lengthwise, rinsed, and very thinly
   sliced

Sea salt

3 large egg yolks

2 tablespoons unsalted butter, melted

1 ounce white sturgeon caviar

Garnish

Fennel fronds

Preheat the oven to 400°F. Line a rimmed baking sheet with about 1 inch of rock salt.

Shuck the oysters. Discard the top shells and carefully cut the adductor muscle that attaches each oyster to its bottom shell. Pour the nectar from each oyster into a small dish and reserve. Set the oysters, in their shells, on the prepared baking sheet, gently nestling them into the salt so they rest securely.

Combine the cream and oyster nectar in a small skillet over medium-high heat and boil to reduce by half, 2 to 3 minutes. Transfer to a dish and set aside. Clean the skillet. Put 1/2 cup of the champagne, the leeks, and a pinch of salt in the same skillet over medium heat. Cook, stirring occasionally, just until the leeks are tender and the champagne has fully reduced, 8 to 10 minutes.

Whisk the egg yolks and the remaining 1/4 cup of champagne together in the top of a double boiler or in a stainless steel bowl set over a saucepan of simmering, not boiling, water. Whisk the mixture until frothy and doubled in volume, about 2 minutes. Whisk in the

*continued*

reduced cream and melted butter and continue whisking until the mixture is fluffy and thickened and holds a ribbon for a few seconds when the whisk is lifted, 3 to 5 minutes longer. Remove the pan from the heat and gently fold in the caviar.

Bake the oysters just until warmed, but not cooked through, about 2 minutes. Take the oysters from the oven and turn on the broiler. Top the oysters with an even layer of the leeks, then spoon the sabayon evenly over and broil until the sabayon is lightly browned, about 1 minute.

To serve, make a bed of rock salt on plates (you can reuse the salt from the baking sheet but it will be hot, so use a large spoon to transfer it) and arrange 3 oysters on each plate in a spoke pattern. To finish, add a tuft of fennel to the center of each plate.

**MISE EN PLACE**—*Mise en place* (putting things in their place) is a standard practice you should learn to follow in your kitchen. Cooking is all about organization, so when it is time to get started, you don't need to stop to prepare an ingredient or suddenly realize you are out of something. One of the main reasons chefs look so impressive when cooking is that they just reach for an ingredient that is ready to go and put it in the skillet. That is the benefit of having done the *mise en place*. So get ahead of the game and look like a pro by having your *mise en place* ready before you start cooking.

First off, always read a recipe all the way through—both the ingredients and the method—before you start so there won't be any surprises, such as beans that need to soak overnight or a terrine that has to chill a day before unmolding. Make sure that you have all the necessary ingredients and cooking equipment. Have ingredients cleaned, trimmed, chopped, or otherwise prepped as needed. Our *mise en place* is done in large volumes for the night's cooking, but you might want to invest in some small dishes or small plastic containers to have on hand for your prepped items. (I've seen Cynthia's kitchen shelves, one of which is filled with dozens of ramekins in all sizes and tiny gratin dishes that she says got plenty of use for holding minced thyme, shallots, and garlic while testing these recipes.)

Learning the practice of *mise en place* will do wonders for streamlining your cooking. Once everything's ready to go, you can then concentrate on the cooking process and not get distracted by last-minute chopping.

# PORK BELLY WITH GINGER, HONEY, AND SOY

## and a Cannellini Bean Salad

**MAKES 6 SERVINGS** / Pork belly (*poitrine* in French) is the same cut of the pig that—when cured and smoked—becomes bacon. This recipe adds some delicious Asian touches to slow-cooked pork belly, namely the vibrant flavors of ginger and soy. Try to choose a pork belly portion that has a good balance of meat and fat. The cooking liquid that remains after braising makes a great marinade for grilled chicken, with or without the addition of Dijon mustard. This recipe will be all the better if you choose a top-quality soy sauce. I have also used tamari in this preparation, which is made by the same method as the more common shoyu-style soy sauce but uses only soybeans, while traditional shoyu-style soy sauce is made with a combination of soybeans and wheat.

Domaine Robert Arnoux 1996 Vosne-Romanée "Les Chaumes," France

1 pork belly piece (about 1 pound)

2 tablespoons olive oil (optional)

1/4 pound young, tender ginger, finely grated

4 cloves garlic, coarsely chopped

5 bay leaves, preferably fresh, partly torn

Freshly ground black pepper

2 cups honey, preferably wildflower

2 cups top-quality soy sauce (shoyu or tamari)

3 tablespoons unsalted butter, cut into pieces and chilled

### Cannellini Bean Salad

1/2 cup dried cannellini beans

1/4 cup coarsely chopped onion

1/4 cup coarsely chopped carrot

1/4 cup coarsely chopped celery

*For the bean salad,* put the dried beans in a large bowl and add cold water to cover by at least 3 inches. Cover the bowl with plastic wrap and set aside to soak overnight.

If the pork belly still has the skin on, carefully trim it away. Heat a heavy deep skillet (not nonstick) over medium-high heat. Put the pork belly in the skillet, fat-side down, and sear until browned and the fat begins to render, about 5 minutes; turn the pork a few times, but spend more time on the fat side than on the meaty side. Transfer the pork belly to a plate and set aside. Pour off the fat from the skillet (you can keep it for cooking the aromatics if you wish) and set the skillet aside (no need to clean it).

Preheat the oven to 250°F.

Heat 2 tablespoons of the reserved pork fat, if using (or the olive oil), in a saucepan over medium heat. Add the ginger, garlic, and bay leaves and season generously with pepper. Cook, stirring often, until quite aromatic, 2 to 3 minutes. Add the honey and soy sauce and stir to help the honey dissolve. Return the pork belly to the skillet and pour the soy-honey mixture over. Bring the liquid just to a low boil

*continued*

1/4 cup coarsely chopped dark green
    leek top (optional)

2 cloves garlic, crushed

4 thyme sprigs

2 bay leaves, preferably fresh, partly torn

1 whole clove

2 1/2 cups Vegetable Stock (page 210)
    or Poultry Stock (page 207)

1/2 teaspoon sea salt

1 tablespoon red wine vinegar

1 1/2 teaspoons Dijon mustard

2 tablespoons extra virgin olive oil

Freshly ground black pepper

2 teaspoons minced shallots

1/4 teaspoon minced fresh thyme

Garnish

Chopped fresh chives

over medium-high heat, then transfer the skillet to the oven. Bake
the pork belly, basting it occasionally with the pan liquid, until it is
very tender, about 2 1/2 hours, turning the belly over after 1 hour.
The liquid should not boil; decrease the oven temperature to 225°F
if necessary.

*Meanwhile, make the bean salad.* Cut a 12-inch square of cheesecloth.
Put the onion, carrot, celery, leek green (if using), garlic, thyme sprigs,
bay leaves, and clove in the center of the cheesecloth and tie the
packet securely with kitchen string. Drain the soaked beans and put
them in a saucepan with the stock, salt, and seasoning packet. Set the
pan over medium-high heat and bring the stock just to a boil, skimming away any scum that rises to the surface, then decrease the heat
to medium-low and simmer gently until the beans are tender, about
45 minutes. Remove the pan from the heat and set aside until the
beans and liquid are cool. Drain the beans and discard the seasoning
packet. Whisk the vinegar and mustard together in a bowl until well
blended, then gradually add the olive oil, whisking constantly until
emulsified. Season to taste with salt and pepper. Add the beans, shallots, and thyme and toss well to combine and coat with the dressing.
Set aside at room temperature for up to 2 hours, or cover and refrigerate for up to 6 hours. If refrigerated, bring the bean salad to room
temperature before serving.

When the pork belly is tender, take the skillet from the oven and transfer the pork belly to a cutting board; cover with foil to keep warm.
Strain the cooking liquid into a bowl, measure out 1 cup, and put in
a small saucepan. Bring to a boil over medium heat (save the remaining cooking liquid for another use, if you like). Decrease the heat to
medium-low and simmer until reduced by one-third, 5 to 7 minutes.
(Taste the liquid as it reduces, because less reduction time may be
needed, given the robust flavors of the ingredients. Over reducing
can create flavors that are too strong.) Add the butter and whisk so it
melts creamily into the sauce; keep warm over very low heat.

To serve, spoon the bean salad into the center of each plate. Cut the
pork belly on the diagonal into slices about 1/4 inch thick. Lay the
slices against one side of the bean salad. Spoon the sauce around the
salad and sprinkle chives over the pork belly; serve right away.

# Vegetarian

# QUILLISASCUT GOAT CHEESE IN PHYLLO

## with Ratatouille and Goat Cheese Sauce

**MAKES 4 SERVINGS** / Phyllo is a beautiful thing: paper-thin sheets of dough that cook up crisp and light, a versatile product perfect for various recipes. It's important to cook the vegetables for the ratatouille in a large enough skillet so that they can spread out evenly, cook quickly, and not give off liquid. To cut the skin away from raw bell pepper, first core and seed it, then cut it into strips about 2 inches wide. Lay the strips, skin-side down, on a cutting board and carefully slide the knife blade between the skin and the flesh. You can also use a vegetable peeler, but try to avoid peeling away too much flesh with the skin. At Rover's, we use the pepper trimmings to make our Bell Pepper Oil (page 218).

Chateau Ste. Michelle 2002 Sauvignon Blanc "Horse Heaven," Washington State

---

6 teaspoons olive oil, plus more if needed

1/2 red onion, finely diced

3/4 teaspoon plus a pinch of minced garlic

3/4 teaspoon plus a pinch of minced fresh thyme

1 red bell pepper, cored, seeded, peeled, and finely diced

1 yellow bell pepper, cored, seeded, peeled, and finely diced

3 teaspoons extra virgin olive oil

1 teaspoon minced fresh chives

1 shallot, minced

1 zucchini, halved lengthwise, seeded, and finely diced

Sea salt and freshly ground white pepper

---

Line a rimmed baking sheet with paper towels.

Heat a large skillet over medium heat, then add 2 teaspoons of the (regular) olive oil. Add the red onion, 1/4 teaspoon of the garlic, and 1/4 teaspoon of the thyme. Sauté until aromatic, about 1 minute, then add the red and yellow bell peppers. Increase the heat to medium-high and sauté until tender, stirring often, 1 to 2 minutes longer. Stir in 1 teaspoon of the extra virgin olive oil and 1/2 teaspoon of the chives. Transfer the onion-pepper mixture to the prepared baking sheet, spreading it out so it cools; set aside.

Heat the same skillet over medium heat and add 2 teaspoons of the remaining (regular) olive oil. Add the shallot, another 1/4 teaspoon of the garlic, and another 1/4 teaspoon of the thyme. Sauté until aromatic, about 1 minute. Add the zucchini and sauté until tender, stirring often, 2 to 3 minutes longer. Stir in 1 teaspoon of the remaining extra virgin olive oil, season lightly with salt and pepper, and add the zucchini mixture to the onion-pepper mixture, spreading it out evenly to cool.

*continued*

$^1/_2$ eggplant, peeled, seeded, and finely diced

6 basil leaves, julienned

$^1/_2$ cup (1 stick) plus 2 tablespoons unsalted butter

1 large egg yolk

1 teaspoon water

6 sheets phyllo dough

2 small goat cheese crottins (about 3 ounces each), crumbled

$^3/_4$ cup peeled fava beans (from about $^3/_4$ pound pods, page 232, optional)

Goat Cheese Sauce

1 cup Sancerre or other sauvignon blanc

2 shallots, thinly sliced

$^1/_2$ teaspoon minced garlic

$^3/_4$ cup Vegetable Stock (page 210)

$^1/_2$ cup heavy cream

5 ounces caillé or other fresh goat cheese

$^1/_4$ teaspoon minced fresh thyme

Sea salt

Heat the remaining 2 teaspoons of (regular) olive oil in the same skillet over medium-high heat. Add the eggplant with $^1/_4$ teaspoon of the remaining garlic and $^1/_4$ teaspoon of the remaining thyme. Sauté until tender, 2 to 3 minutes; if the pan is quite dry, drizzle with another teaspoon or so of olive oil (eggplant absorbs oil quickly). Stir in the remaining teaspoon of the extra virgin olive oil, the remaining $^1/_2$ teaspoon of chives, and season lightly with salt and pepper. Add the eggplant to the vegetable mixture on the baking sheet, spreading it out evenly. Scatter the basil over and stir gently to mix the ratatouille mixture.

*For the goat cheese sauce,* combine the wine, shallots, and garlic in a saucepan and bring to a boil over medium-high heat. Simmer until the wine has reduced by half, 5 to 7 minutes. Add the vegetable stock and boil to reduce by half again, about 5 minutes. Add the cream and boil to reduce by one-third, 3 to 4 minutes. Transfer the mixture to a blender and add the goat cheese and thyme. Blend until smooth, then strain the sauce through a fine-mesh sieve into a small saucepan. Taste the sauce for seasoning, adding salt as needed. Set aside.

Preheat the oven to 375°F. Line a baking sheet with parchment paper. Melt $^1/_2$ cup of the butter and set aside. Combine the egg yolk, water, and a pinch of salt in a small bowl. Beat with a fork until smooth.

Lay 1 phyllo sheet on the work surface with the long side facing you, and lightly brush it with some of the melted butter. Lay another phyllo sheet on top and brush it with butter as well. Repeat with a third sheet of phyllo dough. Cut the phyllo vertically into 4 even strips, $4^1/_2$ inches wide and 14 inches long. Repeat with the remaining 3 phyllo sheets.

Garnish

**Basil Oil (page 216)**

**Basil leaves**

**Red Bell Pepper Coulis (page 214)**

**Yellow Bell Pepper Coulis (page 214)**

Spoon about 1 tablespoon of the ratatouille on 1 phyllo strip, about 2 inches up from the end of the strip, and top the ratatouille with a generous tablespoon of the crumbled goat cheese. Fold the bottom edge of the dough up over the filling to enclose it, then fold in about 1 inch on each of the two long edges. Fold the filled corner over to form a triangular packet, then continue to fold up to the end of the phyllo strip like you would fold a flag (or simply fold straight upward several times to make a square packet). Brush the top of the packet with more melted butter and set it on a heavy baking sheet. Repeat with the remaining phyllo strips (all of the goat cheese will be used, but there will be extra ratatouille for serving alongside). Bake the phyllo packets for 10 to 12 minutes, or until crisp and well browned.

Meanwhile, melt the remaining 2 tablespoons of butter in a small skillet over medium heat. Add the fava beans and cook, stirring often, until tender but not browned, 3 to 5 minutes (larger beans may require more cooking time). Add the remaining pinch of garlic and the remaining pinch of thyme and season to taste with salt and pepper. Toss gently to mix and keep warm over low heat.

To serve, spoon a flat circle of the warm ratatouille to one side of each warm plate and top with 2 of the phyllo packets. Spoon the goat cheese sauce around and spoon a small pile of fava beans alongside the phyllo packets. Drizzle some basil oil on top of and around the phyllo packets, then tuck a basil leaf alongside. Add dots of red and yellow bell pepper coulis around the plate.

# WILD MUSHROOM SALAD

## with Potato Galette, Roasted Shallots, and Pecans

**MAKES 4 SERVINGS** / This salad really shows off the Northwest's bounty of wild mushrooms in style. When sautéing mushrooms, it is important to do so over high heat and not crowd the pan, which helps keep the mushrooms from becoming soggy. For the potato galette that serves as the base for this salad, we often make individual galettes in small blini pans, which you can do if you have four skillets that are 3¹/₂ inches in diameter. For this preparation, I prefer to peel the potatoes with a small knife rather than a vegetable peeler, forming the potatoes into a relatively even shape, which makes even rounds when sliced. Choose potatoes of similar size and shape for the best results.

Château Rouget 1998 Pomerol, France

4 whole shallots plus 2 teaspoons minced shallots

3 tablespoons plus 2 teaspoons olive oil

2 teaspoons fresh thyme leaves plus ¹/₄ teaspoon minced thyme

Sea salt and freshly ground black pepper

2 Yukon Gold potatoes (about ¹/₂ pound each)

3 tablespoons clarified unsalted butter (page 231)

3 tablespoons unsalted butter, plus more if needed

8 to 10 ounces mixed wild mushrooms (such as chanterelle, hedgehog, lobster, honey, and/or cauliflower), cleaned (page 236), trimmed, and thinly sliced

Pinch of minced garlic

Preheat the oven to 375°F.

Trim the root ends from the whole shallots. Set the shallots in the center of a large piece of aluminum foil, drizzle with 2 teaspoons of olive oil, sprinkle with 1 teaspoon of thyme leaves, and season with salt and pepper. Wrap the package up securely and roast until tender when pierced with a knife, 1 to 1¹/₄ hours. Set the packet aside to cool.

Meanwhile, peel the potatoes and cut into ¹/₁₆-inch-thick slices with a mandoline or knife. Put 2 tablespoons of the clarified butter in a large bowl and add the remaining 1 teaspoon of thyme leaves with a good pinch each of salt and pepper. Add the potato slices and toss well with your hands, separating the potato slices so they are evenly coated with the butter and seasonings.

Heat the remaining 1 tablespoon of clarified butter in an ovenproof skillet, preferably nonstick, over medium heat just until warm. Remove the skillet from the heat, and arrange the potato slices in an overlapping spiral pattern, beginning around the edge of the pan and working to the center of the pan with the smaller slices, making one even layer with all the potato slices. Cook the potatoes over medium heat until lightly browned, 5 to 7 minutes. Drain off the excess fat

1/4 cup cherry vinegar or red wine vinegar

2 teaspoons minced fresh chives

1/2 cup pecans, chopped and toasted
(page 234)

from the skillet into a small dish. Invert the potato cake onto a flat plate or rimless baking sheet, then carefully slide it back into the skillet to cook until the bottom is browned and the potato is tender, about 5 minutes longer. Remove from the heat and set aside.

Heat the butter in a large skillet over medium-high heat until melted, medium brown, and slightly nutty smelling. Cook each variety of mushroom separately, seasoning each batch with a pinch of salt and pepper and transferring them as they are done to a large bowl, adding more butter to the skillet if needed. Firmer mushrooms may take 5 to 7 minutes, more tender mushrooms just 2 or 3 minutes. When all the mushrooms have been cooked, return them to the skillet and add the minced shallots, minced thyme, and garlic and cook until well combined and aromatic, 1 to 2 minutes. Transfer the mushrooms to the same bowl; set the skillet aside.

Add the vinegar to the skillet and bring to a boil over medium-high heat. Boil until reduced by half, 2 to 3 minutes. Whisk in the remaining 3 tablespoons of olive oil, then remove the pan from the heat and strain the dressing through a sieve over the mushrooms. Add the chives and toss to mix evenly. Peel away and discard the skins from the roasted shallots, then cut them into quarters.

To serve, cut the potato galette into 4 wedges and set a wedge in the center of each warm plate. Scatter the quartered shallots and toasted pecans around the galettes. Using a slotted spoon, spoon the mushrooms onto the potato wedges, flattening them into an even layer, then drizzle the vinaigrette remaining in the bowl around the salad.

# STUFFED CABBAGE

## with Green Lentils, Pearl Onions, and Cabernet Sauce

**MAKES 4 SERVINGS /** This surprisingly elegant stuffed cabbage features wonderfully nutty green lentils, known in France as *lentilles du Puy* (for the region in France where they're grown), which are now available from Northwest growers as well. In my experience, in addition to their distinctive flavor, green lentils also hold up better than other lentils when cooked. The cabernet reduction sauce with its lightly glazed pearl onions is a sophisticated finish.

Andrew Will 2002 Cabernet Sauvignon "Klipsun," Washington State

2 to 3 lovage or celery leaf sprigs

4 thyme sprigs

1 tablespoon chopped shallots plus
  ¹/₂ teaspoon minced shallots

1 clove garlic, chopped

2 cups Vegetable Stock (page 210)

³/₄ cup green lentils

1 small head Savoy cabbage

1 tablespoon olive oil

¹/₂ teaspoon minced fresh chives

Sea salt and freshly ground black pepper

Cut a piece of cheesecloth about 8 inches square and put the lovage sprigs, thyme sprigs, 1 tablespoon of chopped shallots, and garlic in the center. Tie the packet securely with kitchen string. Combine the vegetable stock and lentils in a saucepan, add the seasoning packet, and bring the stock to a boil over medium-high heat. Immediately decrease the heat to medium-low and simmer gently until the lentils are tender but not soft, 35 to 40 minutes.

*Meanwhile, prepare the onions for the cabernet sauce.* Bring a large saucepan of water to a boil. Add the pearl onions and boil for about 30 seconds. Drain well and when cool enough to handle, peel away the skins. Refill the pan with salted water and bring to a boil; prepare a large bowl of ice water. While the water is heating, cut out the core from the cabbage and peel away and discard the tough outer leaves. Peel away 4 large whole leaves (reserve the rest of the cabbage for another use). Add the cabbage leaves to the boiling water and cook just until pliable and still bright green, 2 to 3 minutes. Plunge the cabbage leaves into the ice water to cool quickly, then drain well and pat dry with paper towels.

Drain the lentils well, put them in a bowl, and discard the seasoning packet. Add the olive oil, the ¹/₂ teaspoon of minced shallot, and the chives and season to taste with salt and pepper. Toss the lentils gently to mix.

## Cabernet Sauce

3/4 pound pearl onions, trimmed

4 tablespoons unsalted butter

Sea salt

2 cups Cabernet Sauvignon

1/4 teaspoon minced fresh thyme

1/8 teaspoon minced garlic

1/2 cup Vegetable Stock (page 210)

1 tablespoon crème fraîche,
    homemade (page 212) or store-
    bought, or heavy cream

Freshly ground white pepper

## Garnish

Blanched finely diced carrot

Minced fresh chives

Lovage or celery leaves

Extra virgin olive oil

Cut a piece of plastic wrap about 12 inches long and set it on the counter. Trim away the tough rib from one of the cabbage leaves and set the leaf in the center of the plastic with the outer, more prominently ribbed side downward, partly overlapping the sides of the slit where the rib was removed. Season the cabbage leaf lightly with salt, then top with 1/3 cup of the lentils. Fold the cabbage around the lentils to make a bundle, and draw the plastic wrap up around the cabbage, twisting the plastic to form a well-rounded and snug package. Repeat with the remaining cabbage leaves, making 4 packages in all (the remaining lentils will be used for serving, set them aside).

*For the cabernet sauce,* heat 2 tablespoons of the butter in a large skillet over medium-high heat until melted and foamy white. Add the boiled and peeled pearl onions and a good pinch of salt. Cook, tossing the onions gently, until they are tender and slightly caramelized, 8 to 10 minutes. Add the cabernet to the skillet with the thyme and garlic. Simmer until the wine has reduced by half, 8 to 10 minutes. Add the vegetable stock and reduce by half again, about 10 minutes. Cut the remaining 2 tablespoons of butter into pieces. Decrease the heat to low and add the butter, swirling the skillet gently so the butter melts creamily into the sauce. Stir in the crème fraîche, season to taste with salt and pepper, and keep warm over very low heat.

Prepare a steamer and set the cabbage bundles on a rack above the boiling water. Steam the cabbage until it is heated through, 5 to 7 minutes.

To serve, spoon some of the reserved lentils in a circle in the center of warm plates. Carefully remove the plastic wrap from the cabbage bundles, letting the excess liquid drain off, and set the cabbage bundles on top of the lentils. Spoon the pearl onions and cabernet sauce around the cabbage. Scatter some diced carrot and chives over the sauce, garnish each plate with lovage leaves, and drizzle a bit of olive oil over the sauce.

# BEET AND GOAT CHEESE TARTLETS

## with Walla Walla Sweet Onion Purée

**MAKES 8 SERVINGS /** There are many quality fresh goat cheeses made across the country, any of which is a good candidate for this recipe. The cheese I prefer for these tartlets, however, is the goat cheese caillé from Quillisascut Farms in Eastern Washington (page 230). For the most uniform slices of beet to top the tartlets, I first trim the cooked beets into a neat cylinder shape, then cut across into rounds. You can omit this step if you like, using larger rounds on the outer edge and smaller rounds toward the center. You can also make one large tart rather than individual ones.

Domaine Servin 2002 Chablis 1er Cru "Vaillons," France

4 small beets (about 1 pound), scrubbed (red and/or yellow)

1/2 pound fresh goat cheese, preferably caillé

1/2 recipe Pâte Brisée (page 223)

1 tablespoon minced shallots

1 teaspoon minced fresh chives

1/2 teaspoon minced garlic

1/4 cup heavy cream

Sea salt and freshly ground white pepper

Walla Walla Onion Purée

6 tablespoons unsalted butter

1 small Walla Walla sweet onion, cut into 1/4-inch-thick slices

Sea salt and freshly ground white pepper

3/4 cup Vegetable Stock (page 210)

1/4 teaspoon minced fresh thyme

Put the beets in a large saucepan of cold salted water and bring to a boil over high heat. (If using both red and yellow beets, cook them in separate pans.) Reduce the heat to medium and simmer until the beets are fully tender, about 1 1/4 hours. The beets should be fully covered with water as they cook; if needed, add more hot water to the saucepan. When cooked, drain the beets well and let cool until easy to handle. Peel away the skins and trim the beets into cylinders about 1 1/2 inches in diameter (I use a heavy pastry cutter to do this), then cut crosswise into 1/4-inch-thick slices. (The beet trimmings can be used to make Beet Oil [page 219] or Beet Coulis [page 215].)

Crumble the goat cheese into a small bowl and set aside at room temperature to soften.

*For the onion purée,* heat the butter in a skillet over medium-low heat until melted and foamy white. Add the onion with a good pinch of salt and pepper and cook, stirring occasionally, until very tender and just lightly caramelized, about 30 minutes. Add the vegetable stock and thyme and bring just to a boil over high heat, then decrease the heat to medium-low and simmer until the liquid has reduced by one-third, 8 to 10 minutes. Transfer to a blender or food processor and purée until very smooth. Taste the purée for seasoning, adding more salt or pepper if needed; set aside in a small saucepan.

*continued*

**Garnish**

**Olive oil**

**Minced fresh chives**

**Sea salt and freshly ground white pepper**

**Beet Coulis (page 215)**

Preheat the oven to 350°F.

Roll out the pâte brisée on a lightly floured surface to a thickness of about $1/16$ inch and cut out 8 circles measuring 4 inches across. Line eight 3-inch tartlet pans with the dough, pressing it down well into the edges of the pans. Prick the bottoms of the tart shells well with the tines of a fork. Blind bake the tartlet shells (see box). Remove the pans from the oven and set on a wire rack to cool completely. Decrease the oven temperature to 300°F.

Add the shallots, chives, and garlic to the softened goat cheese and stir to blend evenly. Add the cream and stir until smooth. Season to taste with salt and pepper.

Carefully remove the pastry shells from the pans. Spoon the goat cheese mixture into the pastry shells, pressing gently with the back of a spoon to form an even layer. Arrange the beet slices on top in slightly overlapping circles. Use a large spatula to place the tartlets carefully on a baking sheet and lay a piece of parchment paper over the tartlets to prevent them from drying out. Warm in the oven just until the cheese begins to soften, 8 to 10 minutes. Reheat the onion purée over medium-low heat.

To serve, spoon the onion purée into the center of warm plates, forming a circle about 1 inch larger than the tartlets. Use the large spatula to set the warm tartlets on top of the sauce. Drizzle olive oil over the beet slices, top with a pinch of chives, and sprinkle lightly with salt and pepper. Add dots of beet coulis around the tartlets.

**BLIND BAKING**—The technique I use for blind baking pastry is to line the tartlet pan with a very thin dough and nestle another same-sized pan on top of the dough, so the pastry is evenly sandwiched between the two pans. I then set the pans upside down on a heavy baking sheet, taking advantage of gravity to help ensure that the edges of the tart shells don't collapse. We set another heavy baking sheet on top, to weight down the pans, and bake the whole thing together. It is important that the dough be rolled out quite thinly and evenly, so that the pastry shell will cook uniformly.

Not all tart pans will allow you to use this technique. If their shape does not allow you to fit a second pan inside the first, you can use a more traditional technique for blind baking. After lining the pans with pastry, line the pastry with parchment paper and fill with pie weights or dry beans, then bake until the edges are set. Remove the foil and weights, then continue baking as needed, until fully cooked or until the bottom of the tart shell is no longer translucent.

# HAZELNUT-STUFFED BABY ZUCCHINI BLOSSOMS

## with Heirloom Tomato Salad

**MAKES 4 SERVINGS /** This is a vegetarian dish that we've been serving at Rover's for more than a dozen years in a variety of different presentations; this simple heirloom tomato salad version is one of my favorites. Served here as a main course, the dish could also be a first course, with one or two stuffed zucchini blossoms per serving. I prefer to use zucchini blossoms that have tiny zucchinis already forming—about as big as your thumb—because I like the flavor and texture contrast of the two together. When only blossoms are available, you can certainly use them instead, perhaps with a little sautéed zucchini alongside to make a more substantial dish, if you like.

Zenato 2003 Lugana San Benedetto, Veneto, Italy

12 baby zucchini with blossoms attached

**Hazelnut Stuffing**

2 tablespoons olive oil

1 tablespoon Basil Oil (page 216, optional)

3 small zucchini (about $3/4$ pound total), trimmed, quartered lengthwise, and coarsely chopped

$1/4$ teaspoon minced fresh thyme

$1/4$ cup finely julienned green or purple basil

2 teaspoons minced shallots

$1/2$ teaspoon minced garlic

$2/3$ cup finely ground toasted hazelnuts (page 234)

Sea salt

*For the hazelnut stuffing,* heat a saucepan over medium heat, then add the olive oil and basil oil. Add the zucchini and thyme and cook, stirring occasionally, until the zucchini begins to soften, about 5 minutes. Add the basil, shallots, and garlic and continue cooking, stirring often, until the zucchini is tender, 3 to 5 minutes longer. The zucchini should not brown; reduce the heat to medium-low if needed. Add the ground hazelnuts and stir until evenly blended, then set aside to cool slightly. Transfer the mixture to a food processor and pulse until it is smooth but still has some texture, about 1 minute. Season to taste with salt. Transfer to a bowl and refrigerate, covered, until well chilled, at least 1 hour.

*For the tomato salad,* combine the tomatoes, basil oil, balsamic vinegar, shallots, and chives in a small bowl. Season to taste with salt and pepper and stir to combine evenly. Set aside to marinate for about 1 hour.

Preheat the oven to 350°F. Lightly oil a large rimmed baking sheet.

Bring a large saucepan of salted water to a boil and prepare a large bowl of ice water. Trim the stem end of each baby zucchini at a slight

*continued*

### Heirloom Tomato Salad

3/4 pound heirloom plum or cherry
tomatoes, halved, seeded, and cut
into a large dice

2 tablespoons Basil Oil (page 216) or
olive oil

1 tablespoon balsamic vinegar

2 teaspoons minced shallots

1 teaspoon minced fresh chives

Sea salt and freshly ground white pepper

1 teaspoon finely julienned green or
purple basil

### Garnish

Small green or purple basil sprigs

Nasturtium blossoms

Red Bell Pepper Coulis (page 214)

angle so it tapers to a point. Add the zucchini to the boiling water, pressing down gently with a slotted spoon to make sure they are fully submerged. Simmer until the zucchini is partially tender (they will be cooked further in the oven), 1 to 3 minutes, depending on their size (about 30 seconds if using just flowers). Using a slotted spoon or tongs, lift out the zucchini and immediately plunge into the ice water to cool quickly and set their color.

Put the hazelnut stuffing in a pastry bag fitted with a medium plain tip. Lift out one of the blossoms from the ice water, inserting your finger into the center of the blossom while it's still in the water because the petals are harder to separate once out of the water. Let the blossom drain above the bowl for a few moments, then place the zucchini on a triple layer of paper towels, still holding the petals open with your fingers. Insert the pastry tip into the center of the flower and gently pipe in enough stuffing so that it comes up to the part of the flower where the petal points begin forming. Draw the petal ends up over the filling and gently twist them to enclose the stuffing fully. Using a small sharp knife, make lengthwise cuts in the zucchini about 1/4 inch apart, leaving the zucchini attached at the flower end. Press gently on the zucchini to fan out the slices and set aside on paper towels to drain while stuffing the remaining blossoms. Turn the stuffed zucchini over after a few minutes to drain on the other side.

Arrange the stuffed zucchini on the prepared baking sheet so that the blossoms are not touching. Bake until the stuffing is heated through, about 7 minutes.

To serve, add the julienned basil to the tomato salad and toss to mix. Using a slotted spoon, place the tomato salad in a pile in the center of each plate, leaving the dressing in the bowl. Arrange 3 zucchini blossoms on each plate, leaning them up against the tomato salad. Drizzle some of the reserved dressing over the blossoms. Top each tomato salad with a basil sprig and nasturtium blossom and add dots of red bell pepper coulis around the edges of the plates.

# The Rover's Garnish Tray

Every night before service begins at Rover's, before we open the doors for the first guest, one of the last things prepared in the kitchen is our garnish tray. The large tray (which is layered over another tray of ice), is topped with a dozen or more small dishes that are filled with a range of items that will be used throughout the evening.

Although the selection varies with the seasons, some standards on the garnish tray include minced chives, thyme, shallots, and parsley; sprigs of herbs including chervil, tarragon, flat-leaf parsley, basil (green and opal), sweet cicely, fennel fronds (green and bronze), and lovage, to name a few; and edible flowers, such as nasturtiums, pansies, chive blossoms, calendulas, blue cornflowers, roses, and tulips. Almost all of our flowers and some of the herbs are grown in my home garden and in the garden at the restaurant. Garnishes also include finely diced or julienned red and yellow bell pepper, diced or julienned blanched carrot, truffle, dried shrimp or lobster roe, salmon roe, and microgreens. We also have a good selection of flavored oils (page 216) and coulis (page 214) on hand.

The garnish tray allows us to finish a plate just before it leaves the kitchen with a specific decoration that embellishes and complements the flavors, colors, and textures of the dish. It's important that these garnish elements be prepared in advance, because there isn't the time to stop and mince herbs or julienne carrots just before serving.

# ROASTED OYSTER MUSHROOMS
## and Onions with Sage

**MAKES 4 SERVINGS** / For this recipe I use spring onions, which look like a cross between a full-size regular onion and a green onion: The bulb is more slender than round, and bright green stalks are still attached at the top. If you're unable to find spring onions, you can use quartered regular onions, peeled pearl onions, or even cipollini onions, the small, flat onions popular in Italy. This recipe makes a delicious vegetarian entrée, but it also can be served as a side dish for roasted chicken or pork. If your oven isn't large enough to hold both the onion and the mushroom skillets side by side at the same time, they can be roasted separately. The onions should be roasted first, then reheated just before serving.

Ducato 2002 Lambrusco Montovano, Lombardia, Italy

---

6 young red onions, or 1 large red onion, cut into eighths

6 young white onions, or 1 large white onion, cut into eighths

5 tablespoons unsalted butter

2 teaspoons minced fresh thyme

Pinch of minced garlic

Sea salt

1 cup loosely packed sage leaves (about ³/4 ounce)

2 tablespoons olive oil

2 tablespoons walnut or olive oil

2 tablespoons plus 1 teaspoon minced shallots

³/4 pound large oyster mushrooms, cleaned (page 236) and trimmed

Freshly ground black pepper

1 teaspoon minced fresh chives

1 teaspoon balsamic vinegar

Preheat the oven to 350°F.

Trim the root ends from the onions and trim the green tops to about 3 inches, then halve the onions lengthwise. Heat 3 tablespoons of the butter in a large ovenproof skillet over medium heat until melted and foamy white. Add 1 teaspoon of the thyme and the garlic and sauté until aromatic, 15 to 30 seconds. Arrange the onion halves in the skillet, cut-side down (if using regular onions, simply place all the wedges in the skillet), and season with salt. Scatter the sage leaves over the onions, drizzle with the olive oil, and lightly salt the sage. Transfer the skillet to the oven and roast the onions until they are lightly browned and tender, 40 to 50 minutes, basting the onions with the oil a few times while they roast.

Meanwhile, heat another large ovenproof skillet over medium heat, then add the remaining 2 tablespoons of butter and 1 tablespoon of the walnut oil and heat until the butter is melted and foamy white. Add 2 tablespoons of the shallots and the remaining 1 teaspoon of thyme and cook for a few seconds, then place the mushrooms in the skillet, gill-side down. Drizzle the remaining 1 tablespoon of walnut oil over the mushrooms and season lightly with salt and pepper. Transfer the skillet to the oven and roast until the mushrooms are tender, about 20 minutes, turning the mushrooms halfway through cooking.

**Garnish**

**Pepper cress or young watercress**

Transfer the crispy sage leaves to a cutting board and finely mince them. Put the sage in a small bowl with the remaining 1 teaspoon of shallots, the chives, the vinegar, and about 2 teaspoons of oil from the onion skillet. Season with salt.

To serve, arrange the onion halves, cut-side down, in a fan pattern on warm plates, removing and discarding the top layer of onion, which will be tough. Place the roasted oyster mushrooms on the green tops of the onions. Spoon about half of the minced sage mixture over the onions and mushrooms. Toss the pepper cress with the remaining sage mixture and arrange the salad alongside the mushrooms.

# RED BELL PEPPER FLAN

## with Green Lentils and Rosemary Beurre Blanc

**MAKES 4 SERVINGS** / This colorful dish is richly flavored with silky roasted pepper custard and an ethereal beurre blanc sauce that has been infused with the essence of fresh rosemary. Earthy green lentils served alongside offer a tempting contrast in color, flavor, and texture.

Woodward Canyon 2000 Chardonnay "Celilo," Columbia Valley, Washington State

2 tablespoons olive oil

1 shallot, minced

1 teaspoon minced fresh rosemary

1 clove garlic, minced

1/2 cup green lentils

1 1/2 cups Vegetable Stock (page 210)

Sea salt and freshly ground white pepper

Red Pepper Flan

3 red bell peppers, roasted, peeled,
   and seeded (page 231)

2 large eggs

1/3 cup heavy cream

1/2 teaspoon sea salt

Freshly ground white pepper

Preheat the oven to 300°F. Butter four 1/2-cup ramekins and set them in a baking dish.

Heat a saucepan over medium heat, then add 1 tablespoon of the olive oil. Add the shallot, rosemary, and garlic and cook, stirring occasionally, until aromatic and tender, about 2 minutes. Stir in the lentils until well combined, then add the vegetable stock. Bring to a boil over medium-high heat, then decrease the heat to medium-low and gently simmer, uncovered, until the lentils are tender, about 25 minutes. Drain the lentils, season to taste with salt and pepper, and set aside.

*For the flan,* purée the roasted peppers in a blender or food processor until very smooth. Transfer 1 cup of the purée to a bowl and whisk in the eggs, then the cream, until thoroughly blended. (Depending on the size of the peppers, you may have extra purée, which can be saved for garnish or for another use.) Season with the salt and a pinch of pepper. Ladle the mixture into the prepared ramekins and add enough hot water to the baking dish to come about halfway up the sides of the ramekins. Cover the dish securely with aluminum foil. Insert the tip of a small knife into the center of the foil and lift up slightly to "tent" the center of the foil to prevent the condensation from dripping down onto the flans. Carefully transfer the dish to the oven and bake until the custard sets (a knife inserted into the center of the flan will come out clean), 35 to 40 minutes.

**Rosemary Beurre Blanc**

3/4 cup plus 1 tablespoon unsalted butter

4 shallots, sliced

3 tablespoons chopped fresh rosemary

1 cup sauvignon blanc or other dry
   white wine

1 tablespoon heavy cream

Sea salt and freshly ground white pepper

**Garnish**

Red Bell Pepper Coulis (page 214)

Chervil sprigs

*Meanwhile, prepare the beurre blanc.* Cut the 3/4 cup of butter into about 12 pieces and refrigerate until needed. Heat the remaining 1 tablespoon of butter in a saucepan over medium heat until melted and foamy white. Add the shallots and rosemary and cook, stirring occasionally, until tender and aromatic, 2 to 3 minutes. Add the wine, bring to a boil, then boil until reduced to about 1/4 cup, 10 to 12 minutes.

Meanwhile, heat a small skillet over medium heat, then add the remaining 1 tablespoon of olive oil. Add the lentils and gently reheat them. When the wine has reduced, add the cream to the pan and continue boiling for 2 to 3 minutes longer. Decrease the heat to medium-low and begin to incorporate the chilled butter, 1 piece at a time, whisking until each is thoroughly incorporated before adding the next piece. The butter should melt creamily without becoming oily; remove the pan from the heat as needed to help prevent over-heating. When all the butter has been incorporated, strain the sauce through a sieve into a bowl, discard the solids, and season the sauce to taste with salt and pepper.

To serve, spoon a circle of lentils to one side of each warm plate. Run a small knife around the edges of the flans to loosen them; unmold a flan alongside the lentils on each plate. Spoon the rosemary beurre blanc around the flans, top the sauce with a drizzle and dots of the red bell pepper coulis (and any remaining pepper purée, if you like), and garnish the flans with chervil sprigs.

# Seafood

# WHOLE ROASTED STRIPED SEA BASS

## with Fennel, Moroccan Olives, and Thyme Vinegar

**MAKES 4 SERVINGS** / *Loup de mer* (sea bass) is one of the most beloved fish in France, typically cooked rather simply to show off its distinctive delicate flavor and texture. Striped sea bass from the mid-Atlantic is another of my favorite fish for similar reasons, and it makes a good replacement for French sea bass, which can be hard to find in U.S. markets. Recalling its Mediterranean roots, the *loup de mer* in this recipe is accented with the rich flavors of fresh fennel, briny black olives, fresh thyme, and a splash of Pastis. Plan time to allow the fish to marinate for at least 4 hours before cooking.

Château de Beaucastel 2001 Châteauneuf du Pape Blanc, France

2 small whole striped sea bass (about 1 pound each)

3/4 cup olive oil

10 cloves garlic, finely crushed

2 tablespoons fresh thyme leaves

Sea salt and freshly ground white pepper

2 fennel bulbs

1 cup Moroccan olives, pitted

1/3 cup Pastis or other anisette liqueur

1 tablespoon thyme vinegar or red wine vinegar

Rinse the sea bass well, especially the belly cavities, under cold running water and pat dry with paper towels. Put the bass in a shallow dish and drizzle with 1/4 cup of the olive oil. Scatter the garlic cloves and 1 tablespoon of the thyme over the fish and inside the cavities, and season each with a pinch of salt and pepper, turning the fish over to coat evenly. Cover with plastic wrap and refrigerate for at least 4 hours or preferably overnight.

Shortly before serving, preheat the oven to 350°F.

Trim the stalks from the fennel bulbs and discard (or save to use in Vegetable Stock, page 210), reserving some of the tender fennel fronds for garnish. Halve the fennel bulbs lengthwise and cut out the tough core. Separate the layers of fennel, trimming away any tough or browned portions. Cut the fennel, with the grain, into 1/4-inch-thick slices.

Garnish

Fennel fronds

Chopped fresh chives and/or chervil

Blanched finely diced yellow bell pepper

Blanched finely julienned red bell pepper

Basil Oil (page 216)

Transfer the fish to a large ovenproof skillet and put $1/4$ cup of olives into the cavity of each fish. Add the garlic (from the marinade) to the skillet and drizzle the remaining $1/2$ cup of olive oil over the fish. Sprinkle with the remaining 1 tablespoon of thyme, season with salt and pepper, then scatter the sliced fennel on top of and around the fish. Roast until the fish is just cooked through (the flesh should look opaque rather than translucent) at the thickest part, 25 to 30 minutes, spooning the cooking liquid over the fennel and fish a few times to keep it moist.

Transfer the olives from the bellies of the fish into the skillet. Using 1 or 2 spatulas, carefully lift the fish onto a large plate or platter and cover to keep warm. Add the remaining $1/2$ cup of olives to the skillet as well. Cook over medium-high heat until the fennel is tender and aromatic, 3 to 5 minutes. Add the Pastis, very carefully light the alcohol with a long match, and flambé until the flames subside. Stir in the thyme vinegar and season to taste with salt and pepper.

Peel away the skin from the fish and remove each fillet from the backbone in one piece. Cut the fillets crosswise in half at a slight angle. Form a circle of the fennel-olive mixture in the center of each warm plate and lean 2 fillet pieces against the fennel, one to each side. Drizzle the cooking liquid from the skillet over the fish and garnish to one side with fennel fronds. Sprinkle the fish with chives and diced and julienned bell pepper, then add a drizzle of basil oil all around the plate.

# TOURNEDOS OF COPPER RIVER SALMON
## with Caramelized Turnips and Sea Urchin Sauce

**MAKES 4 SERVINGS** / Copper River is a celebrated run of wild salmon from Alaska, particularly because it comes early in the season—mid-May—before the bulk of summer's salmon comes into the region. To make tournedos, it is best to start with a center-cut piece of salmon fillet that's broader and of uniform thickness. The dish can also be made without forming the fish into tournedos, if you prefer to skip that step. Sea urchin roe is a special treat that I get from Takaharu Hyono, a Japanese supplier of sea urchin and geoduck in Seattle who also supplies the best sushi restaurants in town. The roe's rich, slightly mineral flavor adds a distinctive essence of the sea to the sauce. Whole sea urchin is tricky to clean, but top-quality seafood markets and Asian markets often sell the roe pre-cleaned and ready to use.

Maison Bouchard Père et Fils 1999 Meursault "Perrières," France

1/2 pound baby turnips or small regular
   turnips, trimmed and peeled

4 tablespoons unsalted butter

Sea salt and freshly ground white pepper

2 teaspoons sugar

1 pound salmon fillet, skin and pin
   bones removed

If using bite-size baby turnips they can be left whole, but halve or quarter larger turnips so they are uniformly sized. Heat 2 tablespoons of the butter in a skillet over medium heat until melted and foamy white. Add the turnips with a good pinch each of salt and pepper and toss well. Cook for about 2 minutes, then sprinkle the sugar over and continue cooking, stirring occasionally, until the turnips are tender and nicely caramelized, 3 to 5 minutes longer. Remove from the heat and set aside, then reheat before serving.

Using a thin, sharp knife, cut away the dark flesh from the skinned side of the salmon fillet, then butterfly the salmon: With the knife horizontal to the work surface, start near the thinner belly side of the fillet and cut toward the opposite, thicker side of the fillet—cutting to about 1/2 inch from the far edge (not all the way through). Fold the top half of the fillet open (like a book) to create a flat piece of fish with a fairly even thickness. Turn the entire fillet piece over so that the cut surface is now face down. Roll the fillet up snugly, beginning at the thinner belly side. Set the cylinder on the work surface, seam-side down, and securely tie the fish cylinder at four evenly

*continued*

## Sea Urchin Sauce

1/2 cup dry vermouth

1 teaspoon minced shallots

Pinch of minced fresh thyme

1/2 cup Veal Stock (page 206)

3 tablespoons unsalted butter, cut into
    pieces and chilled

2 lobes sea urchin roe

Sea salt and freshly ground white pepper

## Garnish

Beet Oil (page 219)

Minced fresh chives

Flat-leaf parsley leaves

spaced intervals with kitchen string. Trim the ends of the cylinder, if necessary, so they are very even. Cut between the strings to make 4 tournedos of even size; the string should be in the center of each tournedos. Season the salmon on both sides with salt and pepper.

Preheat the oven to 350°F.

*For the sauce,* combine the vermouth, shallots, and thyme in a saucepan. Bring to a boil over medium-high heat and boil until reduced by half, 2 to 3 minutes. Add the veal stock and boil until reduced again by half, 1 to 2 minutes. Decrease the heat to medium-low and whisk in the butter so that it melts creamily into the sauce. Whisk in the sea urchin roe and season the sauce to taste with salt and pepper. (The sauce may be strained and/or puréed if you prefer.) Keep warm over low heat.

Heat the remaining 2 tablespoons of butter in a large ovenproof skillet over medium-high heat until it is melted, medium brown in color, and slightly nutty smelling. Add the salmon and cook until nicely browned, about 1 minute on each side. Transfer the skillet to the oven and bake until the salmon is medium-rare (still translucent in the center), 2 to 4 minutes. Transfer the salmon to a warm plate, remove the strings from each tournedos, and keep the fish warm. Warm the caramelized turnips over medium heat.

To serve, arrange the caramelized turnips to one side of warm plates. Carefully transfer the salmon tournedos next to the turnips and spoon the sea urchin sauce around. Garnish the plate with dots of beet oil, sprinkle minced chives over the salmon, and add a small sprig of flat-leaf parsley.

# BAKED ALASKAN HALIBUT
## with Morels, Ramps, and Smoked Bacon Butter Sauce

**MAKES 4 SERVINGS /** I always look forward to spring morels, which have a flavor and an aroma distinct from all the other wild mushrooms. Forager Veronica Williams will typically send us the first morels of the season from Long Beach Peninsula around early May, and I can also count on a few months' worth from the Puget Sound area and farther north in British Columbia. When fresh morels aren't available, you can use $1/4$ ounce dried morels reconstituted in warm water for about an hour before draining. Ramps (wild leeks) are a delicious change of pace from the other onions we commonly use in the kitchen. Look for them at specialty markets or farmers' markets in late spring, though small regular leeks can be used in their place. Just add a pinch of garlic to match the slight garlicy flavor of ramps.

Belle Pente 2000 Reserve Pinot Noir Murto Vineyards, Oregon

5 ounces sliced applewood-smoked or other bacon, cut into $1/4$-inch pieces

8 to 10 ounces ramps or small leeks

8 tablespoons (1 stick) unsalted butter

$1/4$ pound morel mushrooms, cleaned (page 236) and halved or quartered if large

2 teaspoons minced shallots

$1/2$ teaspoon minced garlic (or 1 teaspoon if using leeks)

$3/4$ teaspoon minced fresh thyme

$13/4$ cups Fish Stock (page 208)

1 pound skinless halibut fillet, cut into 4 portions

Sea salt and freshly ground white pepper

2 teaspoons minced fresh chives

Garnish

Beet Oil (page 219)

Cook the bacon in a skillet over medium-high heat, stirring occasionally, until crisp and brown, 5 to 7 minutes. Spoon the bacon into a small sieve set over a bowl to drain; reserve the bacon fat for another use, if you like.

Trim the root ends from the ramps and cut each ramp in half to separate the white bulbs from the green tops. Cut the bulbs into $1/4$-inch pieces and leave the green tops whole. (If using leeks, cut off the dark green portions and discard; halve the leeks crosswise, rinse them well, then cut lengthwise into $1/4$-inch-wide strips.)

Preheat the oven to 350°F.

Heat 2 tablespoons of the butter (or use some of the reserved bacon fat, if you like) in a skillet over medium-high heat until melted and slightly nutty smelling. Add the morels and sauté for 30 seconds. Add the white portion of the ramps (or all of the leek strips) with the shallots, garlic, and $1/2$ teaspoon of the thyme. Sauté until the ramps begin to soften, 2 to 3 minutes. Add three-quarters of the bacon, the ramp greens, and $11/4$ cups of the fish stock. Bring just to a boil, then

*continued*

simmer to reduce by three-quarters, 8 to 10 minutes. Add 4 tablespoons of the remaining butter, swirling the pan so it melts creamily into the sauce; keep warm over very low heat.

Put the remaining $1/2$ cup of fish stock in a large ovenproof skillet and warm over medium heat. Whisk in the remaining 2 tablespoons of butter, then add the remaining bacon and $1/4$ teaspoon of thyme.

Season the halibut with salt and pepper and place it in the skillet. Spoon some of the cooking liquid over the fish and bake until almost opaque in the center, 5 to 10 minutes (the timing will depend on the thickness of the fish), basting with the cooking liquid once or twice.

Pour the halibut cooking liquid into the sauce and bring just to a low boil. Stir in the chives and season to taste with salt and pepper.

To serve, spoon some of the ramps, bacon, mushrooms, and sauce onto warm plates. Top with the halibut, spoon the remaining sauce on top, and drizzle beet oil around.

**TRIMMING FISH**—When I prepare most fish before cooking it, I not only remove the skin and pin bones but also trim away the dark flesh that lies just under the skin. This flesh not only detracts from the natural color of the fish's flesh, but it is also strong-flavored and can overpower the other flavors in a dish. I like to use a thin-bladed sharp knife to cut the dark flesh away from the rest of the flesh. But this is an optional step and can be omitted if you prefer.

When cooking whole smaller fish, such as mackerel or young *loup de mer*, with its skin on (which helps keep it moist), I remove the dark flesh after the fish is cooked. I first slip the skin off, then gently scrape away the dark flesh, which easily separates from the cooked flesh.

# COLUMBIA RIVER STURGEON

## with Rabbit Kidneys, Truffle Mousseline, and Lovage Glaze

**MAKES 6 SERVINGS /** I play off the surf-and-turf theme frequently; here, chicken breast and rabbit kidneys serve as the "turf" element, while the sturgeon serves as the "surf" element. The mousseline-topped sturgeon fillet is wrapped in *crépine* (also known as caul fat) and baked whole, then sliced into portions for serving, which helps keep the flesh as juicy as possible. Here I particularly like to use winter Périgord truffle, which holds up best to baking. If you don't have a juicer to make the celery juice garnish, you can simply chop 2 large stalks of celery and process them in a food processor until very finely chopped and beginning to turn watery. Strain the minced celery in a fine sieve set over a bowl, pressing on the solids with the back of a spoon to extract as much of the juice as possible.

Bonneau du Martray 2000 Corton-Charlemagne, France

1 piece sturgeon fillet (about
   1¹/₂ pounds), skin removed

1 teaspoon minced fresh thyme

Sea salt and freshly ground white pepper

6 tablespoons unsalted butter

¹/₂ pound boneless, skinless, free-range
   chicken breast

1 large egg white

¹/₃ cup heavy cream

1 tablespoon minced black truffle

About 3 ounces crépine (caul fat,
   page 232)

8 large oyster mushrooms, cleaned
   (page 236) and trimmed

12 rabbit kidneys

2 teaspoons minced shallots

2 teaspoons minced fresh flat-leaf
   parsley

Season the sturgeon fillet with ¹/₂ teaspoon of the thyme, and salt and pepper. Heat 2 tablespoons of the butter in a skillet over medium-high heat until it is melted, medium brown in color, and slightly nutty smelling. Add the sturgeon and brown well on both sides, 2 to 3 minutes total. Set the fish aside on a plate (it will be cooked more later) and let cool completely, then chill in the refrigerator for 10 to 15 minutes.

Preheat the oven to 350°F.

While the sturgeon is chilling, cut the chicken breast into 1-inch pieces, put it in a food processor, and pulse until finely chopped. Add the egg white and process until the mixture is thoroughly blended and smooth, scraping down the side of the bowl as needed. Transfer the mixture to a bowl and prepare a large bowl of ice with a bit of water in it. Set the bowl on the ice, stirring the chicken mixture while gradually adding in the cream. Season with ¹/₂ teaspoon of salt and a couple pinches of white pepper, stirring to blend evenly; fold in the truffle.

*continued*

**Lovage Glaze**

2 cups Fish Stock (page 208)

3 celery stalks, trimmed

5 tablespoons unsalted butter

Sea salt

2 tablespoons julienned lovage or celery
   leaves

**Garnish**

Celery juice

Trim the *crépine* to a piece about 10 inches square. Spoon the chicken mousseline on top of the chilled sturgeon fillet, using dampened fingers to press it out evenly and smooth the surface. Set the sturgeon on the *crépine*, a few inches from the bottom edge, and fold the nearest edge lengthwise over the fish. Fold the opposite edge over as well, tucking the long edge underneath. Finally, loosely fold the 2 end pieces underneath the fish, not too tightly or the *crépine* might burst while cooking. Trim away any excess *crépine* if necessary.

Heat 2 tablespoons of the remaining butter in a ovenproof skillet over medium-high heat until it is melted, medium brown in color, and slightly nutty smelling. Add the wrapped sturgeon, mousseline-side up, and cook for a few minutes to help seal the *crépinette* ends, 1 to 2 minutes. Decrease the heat to medium and carefully turn the fish over to brown the top, 2 to 3 minutes (if the heat is too high the *crépinette* may split). Turn the fish over so the mousseline is once again facing up. Transfer the skillet to the oven and roast until the mousseline is cooked through, about 20 minutes (cut into the mousseline to check, or use an instant-read thermometer, which should read 140°F). Take the skillet from the oven and let rest for about 10 minutes before serving.

*Meanwhile, prepare the lovage glaze.* Put the fish stock in a small saucepan, bring to a boil over medium-high heat, and boil to reduce by half, 8 to 10 minutes. Trim the celery stalks and peel away the tough strings, then cut the stalks into 2-inch lengths; halve the broader pieces lengthwise so all the pieces are roughly the same size.

When the stock has reduced, remove it from the heat. Heat 3 tablespoons of the butter in a skillet over medium heat. Add the celery with a pinch of salt and cook gently until beginning to soften but not brown, 2 to 3 minutes. Add the reduced stock to the skillet and continue simmering until the celery is tender and the stock has reduced by half again and is thick enough to coat the back of a spoon, about 5 minutes. Add the remaining 2 tablespoons of butter and the lovage and swirl the pan gently so the butter melts creamily into the glaze. Keep warm over very low heat.

Heat 1 tablespoon of the remaining butter in a skillet over medium-high heat until it is melted, medium brown in color, and slightly nutty smelling. Add the oyster mushrooms and cook, turning once or twice, until tender and lightly browned, 3 to 5 minutes. Season the mushrooms lightly with salt and keep warm over low heat.

Heat the remaining 1 tablespoon of butter in a small skillet and season the rabbit kidneys with salt and pepper. Add the kidneys to the hot skillet with the shallots, parsley, and remaining $1/2$ teaspoon of thyme. Cook, stirring often, until the kidneys are evenly browned on all sides, 2 to 3 minutes. Reheat the glaze and celery pieces over low heat.

To serve, arrange the celery pieces alongside one another in the center of warm plates and set the oyster mushrooms to one side of the celery. Cut the sturgeon into 1-inch-thick slices and arrange them, slightly overlapping, on top of the celery and mushrooms. Cut the rabbit kidneys in half at a slight angle and set them on top of the sturgeon. Drizzle the lovage glaze over all and spoon some celery juice around.

# RED POT AU FEU OF MAINE LOBSTER
## and Root Vegetables with Foie Gras and Truffle

**MAKES 4 SERVINGS /** Beef is the classic main ingredient for this simple country recipe, and it's still one of the things I ask my mom to make when I go back home. For this Rover's version, I like to include Thumbelina carrots, baby turnips, baby beets in a rainbow of colors (red beets contributing the namesake color to this recipe), and tiny new potatoes. The recipe can be made without the foie gras and truffle, two luxurious ingredients that aren't absolutely necessary here.

---

Domaine Jacques Prieur 2002 Puligny-Montrachet 1er Cru "Les Combettes," France

---

2 live lobsters (about 1¹/₂ pounds each)

³/₄ pound mixed baby root vegetables, trimmed and halved or quartered

2 tablespoons unsalted butter

1 tablespoon minced shallots

¹/₂ teaspoon minced fresh thyme

3 bay leaves, preferably fresh, partly torn

2¹/₂ cups Lobster Stock (page 209)

1 small black truffle, scrubbed

Sea salt

4 slices foie gras (1¹/₂ to 2 ounces each)

Garnish

Minced fresh flat-leaf parsley

Fleur de sel

Cook the lobsters and pick the meat from the shells (page 234). Cut the tails and claws lengthwise in half and set aside.

Bring a saucepan of salted water to a boil. Add the root vegetables to the boiling water, one type at a time, decreasing the heat to a simmer and cooking them until nearly tender, 3 to 5 minutes (depending on the size and density of the vegetables). Drain well and set aside.

Heat the butter in a large sauté pan or skillet over medium heat until melted and foamy white. Add the shallots, thyme, and bay leaves, then scatter the root vegetables evenly on top. Arrange the lobster pieces in an even layer on top of the vegetables and pour in the lobster stock. Thinly slice the truffle and scatter it over the lobster, then add a good pinch of salt. Cover the pan with a round of parchment paper and bring the liquid just to a simmer over medium-high heat. Decrease the heat to medium-low and simmer gently for about 5 minutes.

Meanwhile, score the foie gras slices with the tip of a knife in a diamond pattern and season with salt. Heat a skillet over high heat, add the foie gras, and sear until browned but still tender in the center, about 30 seconds per side. (See page 232 for notes on cooking foie gras.)

To serve, arrange the vegetables and truffle slices in warm shallow soup bowls, then place the lobster pieces on top and add a slice of foie gras just to one side. Spoon the cooking liquid over the lobster (discard the bay leaves), sprinkle a good pinch of parsley over all, and finish with a pinch of fleur de sel.

# PACIFIC YELLOW EYE SNAPPER

## with Artichokes, Fava Beans, and Bacon

**MAKES 4 SERVINGS** / The lovely white flesh of yellow eye snapper has a mild flavor that is wonderfully versatile, taking particularly well to the bold flavors of the bacon, rosemary, and artichokes that accompany the fish here. Yellow eye is really rockfish, but everyone knows it as snapper; you can use other snapper or rockfish for this recipe, preferably larger, thicker fillets that will hold together well. Halibut fillet would also be good in this preparation. Small fava beans cook quickly, so there is no need to blanch them first. If the beans you're using are large, blanch them first in salted water for 2 to 3 minutes.

Marqués de Riscal 2003 Rueda, Spain

2 large artichokes

1/2 pound slab bacon, cut into 1/2-inch
    pieces

1/2 teaspoon minced fresh rosemary, plus
    the tender tops of 3 to 4 rosemary
    sprigs

1 pound yellow eye snapper fillet, skin
    and pin bones removed, cut into
    4 portions

2 teaspoons argan or extra virgin olive oil

Sea salt and freshly ground white pepper

1 teaspoon fresh thyme leaves, plus a
    pinch of minced fresh thyme

3 tablespoons olive oil

2 shallots, thinly sliced

3 plum tomatoes, peeled, seeded, and
    cut into eighths

2/3 cup peeled fava beans (from about
    2/3 pound pods, page 232)

Pinch of minced garlic

Preheat the oven to 375°F.

Trim the base and leaves from each artichoke so only the bottoms remain (page 231), then use a small spoon to scoop out the chokes. Cut each artichoke bottom in half, then across into 1/4-inch-thick slices.

Cook the bacon in an ovenproof skillet over medium-high heat, stirring often, until about half-cooked, 3 to 5 minutes. Add the artichoke pieces and toss to mix, then put the skillet in the oven and roast for 5 minutes. Stir in the minced rosemary and continue roasting until the artichoke pieces are tender, 5 to 7 minutes longer.

Meanwhile, rub the snapper with the argan oil and season with salt and pepper. Set the fish on a plate and scatter the thyme leaves and rosemary tops over; set aside to marinate for 5 to 10 minutes.

Heat a skillet over medium heat, then add 1 tablespoon of the (regular) olive oil. Add the shallots and tomatoes with a pinch of salt and sauté for 1 minute. Add the fava beans, garlic, and the pinch of minced thyme and sauté until the tomatoes and shallots are tender, 1 to 2 minutes longer.

**Garnish**

Chive blossoms

Calendula petals

Red Bell Pepper Coulis (page 214)

Minced fresh chives

Remove the skillet from the oven (leave the oven set at 375°F) and carefully drain away any excess fat. Add the artichoke-bacon mixture to the shallot-tomato mixture and toss to mix evenly; set aside.

Wipe out the skillet that was used to cook the bacon-artichoke mixture and heat the skillet over medium-high heat. Add the remaining 2 tablespoons of (regular) olive oil, then add the snapper pieces and brown well on both sides, about 2 minutes total. Set the snapper on top of the vegetable mixture, cover the skillet with its lid or with a piece of aluminum foil, and roast in the oven until the fish is just barely opaque in the center, 5 to 7 minutes.

To serve, spoon the vegetable mixture into the center of warm plates and top with the snapper. Drizzle any cooking liquid remaining in the skillet around the vegetables and scatter chive blossoms and calendula petals over all. Add dots of red pepper coulis around the fish and sprinkle it with chives.

# ALASKAN HALIBUT

## with Manila Clams, Petite Peas, and Pepper Cress

**MAKES 4 SERVINGS /** Spring is a delicious time in the Northwest, though the growing season here can be a little slow to get underway. Come the latter part of spring, we've got asparagus, rhubarb, and morels to work with, but one highlight of early spring is the first catch of Pacific halibut that comes into our kitchen, often around mid-March. *Petit, c'est mieux* ("small is better"); I know this, because I'm not all that tall. It's true with green peas, too, so choose petite peas if you can. Larger peas tend to be starchier and less sweet. The peppery bite of cress is a great contrast to the delicate halibut, sweet peas, and briny, rich clams.

Grosset 2003 Riesling "Polish Hill," Clare Valley, Australia

1 cup freshly shelled or frozen petite
  peas, thawed

1 cup dry white wine

2 teaspoons minced shallots

1/2 teaspoon minced fresh thyme

24 Manila clams, scrubbed

4 tablespoons unsalted butter,
  cut into pieces

1/2 pound halibut fillet, skinned

Sea salt and freshly ground white pepper

3 to 4 tablespoons olive oil

1 to 2 ounces pepper cress, tender
  watercress, or baby arugula, rinsed,
  dried, and trimmed, large leaves
  torn in pieces

1 tablespoon Beet Oil (page 219) or extra
  virgin olive oil

**Garnish**

Minced fresh chives

Beet Oil (page 219)

Bring a small saucepan of salted water to a boil and prepare a bowl of ice water. Add the peas to the boiling water and cook just until tender but still bright green, 1 to 2 minutes. Drain well and immediately plunge into the ice water to cool quickly. Drain again and pat dry on paper towels.

Combine the wine, shallots, and thyme in a large saucepan, bring to a boil over medium-high heat, and boil for 2 minutes. Add the clams, cover the pan, and cook until the clams have opened, shaking the pan gently once or twice, 5 to 7 minutes total. Begin checking for opened cooked clams after the first minute, scooping them out with a slotted spoon and into a bowl; continue to check for cooked clams every 20 to 30 seconds. Discard any clams that haven't opened after 8 to 10 minutes.

Add any accumulated clam liquid in the bowl back into the saucepan, then boil to reduce by one-fourth. Strain the liquid through a sieve into a small saucepan and swirl in the butter so that it melts creamily into the clam liquid. Add the peas to the sauce and keep warm over low heat. Cover the bowl of clams with aluminum foil to keep warm.

*continued*

Cut the halibut fillet crosswise into $^1/_2$-inch-thick slices. Season with salt and drizzle with 1 table-spoon of the olive oil, rubbing it evenly over the fish. Heat a large skillet over medium-high heat, then add another tablespoon of the olive oil. Add the halibut and cook until medium (until barely translucent in the center), about 30 seconds per side.

To serve, using a slotted spoon, remove the peas from the sauce and form a small mound of peas in the center of warm plates. Remove the clams from the shells and arrange them in a circle around the peas. Set the halibut slices, slightly overlapping them, on top of the peas. Spoon the sauce over the halibut and sprinkle with chives. Toss the cress with a drizzle of beet oil and a pinch of salt and pepper. Mound the salad on top of the halibut and add a drizzle of beet oil around the clams.

# SEARED AHI TUNA

## with Caramelized Turnip, Foie Gras, and Pomegranate Glaze

**MAKES 4 SERVINGS /** For a stylish presentation, I cut the tuna and foie gras into rounds before cooking. If you prefer to avoid trimmings, you can cut the tuna and foie gras into squarish pieces of similar size for stacking.

Hiedler 2001 Grüner Veltliner "Maximum," Austria

6 tablespoons unsalted butter

1 turnip, peeled, trimmed, and cut into
   1/4-inch dice

2 teaspoons sugar

Sea salt

2 cups pomegranate juice (page 235)

2 tablespoons Fish Stock (page 208) or
   dry white wine

Freshly ground white pepper

1 pound sashimi-grade ahi tuna, about
   1 inch thick

4 slices foie gras (1½ to 2 ounces each)

Garnish

Minced fresh chives

Heat 1 tablespoon of the butter in a skillet over medium-low heat until melted and foamy white. Add the turnip, sugar, and a pinch of salt, tossing to mix. Sauté until the turnip is tender and evenly caramelized, 10 to 12 minutes. Remove from the heat and set aside.

Meanwhile, bring the pomegranate juice to a boil in a saucepan over medium-high heat. Boil until reduced by half, 4 to 5 minutes. Spoon out and reserve about 2 tablespoons of the reduction for garnish and add the fish stock to the pan. Boil to reduce by one-third, 2 to 3 minutes, then remove the pan from the heat. Cut the remaining 5 tablespoons of butter into pieces and add to the pan, swirling gently so that it melts creamily into the sauce. Season the pomegranate glaze to taste with salt and pepper and keep warm over very low heat.

Cut the tuna and foie gras each into 4 rounds about 2½ inches across (or cut the tuna into 4 pieces of roughly similar shape and size and leave the foie gras slices as is). Cut the tuna rounds horizontally in half and season the tuna and foie gras with salt. Heat a large heavy skillet over high heat. Add the foie gras and sear for about 30 seconds on each side. (See page 232 for notes on cooking foie gras.) Transfer the foie gras to a plate and add the tuna to the same skillet. Sear it until browned but leave very rare, 10 to 15 seconds per side.

To serve, spoon the warm caramelized turnip into the center of each plate, spreading it out evenly. Place a round of tuna on the turnip, set a round of foie gras on top, and finish with a round of tuna. Drizzle the pomegranate glaze around, sprinkle chives over the tuna, and top the glaze with a drizzle of the reserved pomegranate reduction.

# Meat

# BAINBRIDGE ISLAND LAMB LOIN
## with Chanterelle and Potato Risotto, Fava Beans, and Lemon Thyme Sauce

**MAKES 4 SERVINGS /** This recipe combines a few delicious late spring and early summer ingredients: lamb, the first chanterelles of the season, flavorful fava beans, and young garlic, which have green stalks attached so they resemble green onions. If you are unable to find young garlic, you can use regular garlic cloves. Ask the butcher for lamb trimmings and/or lamb fat for the sauce. Lemon thyme adds an interesting citrusy flavor to this recipe; you can use regular thyme instead, but double the quantity of whole leaves.

Betz Family Winery 2002 Syrah "La Serenne," Washington State

1 pound lamb trimmings and/or fat

2 tablespoons fresh lemon thyme leaves, plus 1/4 teaspoon minced fresh lemon thyme

1 tablespoon unsalted butter (use 5 tablespoons if not using lamb fat)

1/4 pound chanterelle mushrooms, cleaned (page 236), trimmed, and cut into a 1/4-inch dice

Sea salt

3/4 pound Yellow Finn potatoes, peeled and cut into a 1/4-inch dice

3/4 cup Vegetable Stock (page 210)

3/4 cup heavy cream

1 tablespoon minced shallots

1/2 teaspoon minced garlic, plus 1 clove garlic, crushed

Freshly ground white or black pepper

1 pound boneless lamb loin

If using lamb trimmings or fat, put it in a skillet with a pinch of the lemon thyme leaves and cook over medium heat to render the fat, 10 to 15 minutes; reserve the remaining solids in the skillet.

Heat 2 tablespoons of the rendered lamb fat (or 2 tablespoons of butter) in a saucepan over medium-high heat. Add the chanterelles and cook, stirring, until tender, 3 to 5 minutes. Season with salt, cook 1 minute longer, then stir in the potatoes. Add the vegetable stock, cream, shallots, minced garlic, and minced thyme. Cook over medium heat, stirring often, until the potatoes are tender and the mixture is creamy, about 25 minutes. Season to taste with salt and pepper; set aside, covered, to keep warm.

Preheat the oven to 375°F.

Heat another 2 tablespoons of lamb fat (or 2 tablespoons of butter) in a large ovenproof skillet over medium-high heat. Season the lamb loin with salt and pepper and sear it well on all sides, 1 to 2 minutes total. Set the loin aside on a plate. Add the onion to the skillet with any lamb trimmings and brown well over medium-high heat, 2 to 3 minutes. Add the remaining lemon thyme leaves with the crushed garlic and stir to combine. Set the lamb loin on top and roast in the oven for 8 to 10 minutes, until rare.

*continued*

$^1/_2$ onion, coarsely chopped

2 cups dry white wine

1$^1/_2$ cups Veal Stock (page 206)

8 young garlic shoots, trimmed and
    halved lengthwise, or $^1/_2$ teaspoon
    minced garlic

1 cup peeled fava beans (from about
    1 pound whole pods, page 232)

2 tablespoons extra virgin olive oil

Garnish

Carrot Oil (page 219)

Thyme blossoms

Put the lamb on a plate and set aside, covered with foil, to keep warm. Spoon out all but about 1 tablespoon of the fat from the skillet and add the white wine. Bring to a boil and boil until reduced by three-fourths, 5 to 7 minutes. Add the veal stock and reduce again by three-fourths, about 5 minutes longer.

Meanwhile, heat the 1 tablespoon of butter in a small skillet over medium heat until melted and foamy white. Add the garlic shoots and cook until beginning to turn tender, 3 to 4 minutes. Add the fava beans and continue cooking until both the garlic and the fava beans are tender, 3 to 4 minutes longer. Season to taste with salt.

To serve, spoon the potato risotto into the center of warm plates. Slice the lamb loin into $^1/_2$-inch-thick slices and arrange in a fan pattern, leaning them against the risotto. Spoon the garlic shoot–fava mixture over the potatoes. Strain the sauce through a sieve into a small saucepan and whisk in the olive oil until blended. Spoon the sauce over the lamb, drizzle carrot oil over the sauce, and scatter thyme blossoms over all.

# DUCK WITH FLAGEOLET BEANS
Confit, Foie Gras, and Ducks' Tongues in Marsala Sauce

**MAKES 4 SERVINGS /** Flageolet are small white to pale green beans with a delicate, slightly nutty flavor. They are rarely available fresh, but the dried beans are quite delicious and versatile and can be found in specialty food markets or well-stocked supermarkets. Note that the beans need to soak overnight before cooking, so plan ahead. If you're up for a little duck carving work, you could start with 2 whole ducks (about 5 pounds each) and cut away the breasts needed here, using the legs for confit (page 213) and the bones for Poultry Stock (page 207). The ducks' tongues are optional, so they can be omitted, if you prefer.

Catena Alta 2002 Malbec, Argentina

4 duck breasts (about ½ pound each)

1 teaspoon minced fresh thyme

Sea salt and freshly ground black pepper

1 tablespoon unsalted butter

1 tablespoon minced shallots

½ teaspoon minced garlic

¼ pound Duck Confit (page 213), chopped

2 teaspoons minced fresh parsley

4 slices foie gras (1½ to 2 ounces each)

Flageolet Beans

1 cup dried flageolet beans

¼ onion, coarsely chopped

½ carrot, peeled and coarsely chopped

½ stalk celery, coarsely chopped

2 pieces dark green leek leaf, rinsed and coarsely chopped

2 cloves garlic, crushed

*To prepare the flageolet beans,* put the dried beans in a large bowl and add enough cold water to cover by at least 3 inches. Cover with plastic wrap and set aside to soak overnight.

The next day, cook the flageolet beans. Cut a 12-inch piece of cheesecloth. Put the onion, carrot, celery, leek green, garlic, thyme sprigs, bay leaves, and clove in the center of the cheesecloth and tie the packet securely with kitchen string. Drain the soaked beans and put them in a large saucepan with the poultry stock, salt, and seasoning packet. Set the pan over medium-high heat and bring the stock just to a boil, then decrease the heat to medium-low and simmer gently until the beans are tender, about 45 minutes. Remove the pan from the heat and set aside to cool. Drain the beans; reserve the cooking liquid and discard the seasoning packet. (The beans can be prepared up to 2 days in advance; store in their cooking liquid, covered with plastic wrap, in the refrigerator.)

*For the tongues,* half-fill a large saucepan with cold water. Cut a 12-inch piece of cheesecloth. Put the onion, carrot, garlic, thyme sprigs, bay leaves, and peppercorns in the center of the cheesecloth and tie the packet securely with kitchen string. Add the seasoning packet, ducks' tongues, and salt to the water. Bring the water to a boil over medium-high heat, using a spoon to skim away the scum that will rise to the

*continued*

4 thyme sprigs

2 bay leaves, preferably fresh, partly torn

1 clove

3 cups Poultry Stock (page 207)

1 teaspoon sea salt

Ducks' Tongues

1/4 onion, coarsely chopped

1/2 carrot, peeled and coarsely chopped

2 cloves garlic, crushed

4 thyme sprigs

2 fresh bay leaves, partly torn

1 teaspoon black peppercorns

8 ounces ducks' tongues

2 tablespoons sea salt

surface. Decrease the heat to medium-low and simmer gently until the tongues are tender and the meat pulls easily away from the cartilage, about 1 hour. Let the tongues cool in the cooking liquid, then drain; discard the seasoning bundle. Pull the tongue meat from the cartilage and set aside until ready to serve.

Preheat the oven to 350°F.

Trim away the excess fat from the edges of each duck breast. Score the skin in a diamond pattern, being sure not to cut into the flesh. Sprinkle both sides of the breasts with the thyme, then season with salt and pepper. Heat a heavy ovenproof skillet over medium-high heat. Add the duck breasts, skin-side down, and cook until the skin is medium brown and a good portion of the fat has been rendered, 3 to 5 minutes. Turn the breasts over and brown on the flesh side, about 1 minute, then turn the breasts, skin-side down, again. Transfer the skillet to the oven and roast the duck breasts until the skin side is nicely browned and the meat is still pink, about 5 minutes. Remove the skillet from the oven and set aside until ready to serve, covered with foil to keep warm. Decrease the oven temperature to 200°F.

Heat the butter in a skillet over medium heat until melted and foamy white. Add the shallots and garlic and cook, stirring, until tender and aromatic, 1 to 2 minutes. Add the drained beans, tongue meat, confit, and parsley and cook to warm the beans through, adding 1 to 2 tablespoons of the bean cooking liquid (or water) if the beans seem dry. Season to taste with salt and pepper and keep warm over low heat.

**Marsala Sauce**

³/₄ cup dry Marsala wine

¹/₂ cup Veal Stock (page 206) or Poultry
   Stock (page 207)

1 tablespoon minced shallots

¹/₄ teaspoon minced fresh thyme

2 tablespoons unsalted butter

Sea salt and freshly ground black pepper

**Garnish**

Minced fresh chives

Beet Coulis (page 215)

*For the sauce,* put the Marsala in a small saucepan and bring to a boil over high heat. Boil until reduced by half, 3 to 5 minutes, then add the veal stock, shallots, and thyme and reduce again by half, 2 to 3 minutes longer. Remove the skillet from the heat, add the butter, and swirl the skillet gently so that the butter melts creamily into the sauce. Season to taste with salt and pepper and keep the sauce warm over very low heat.

Spoon the warm bean mixture into the center of warm plates. Cut the duck breasts across, on the diagonal, into slices about ¹/₂ inch thick and lean the slices against one side of the beans, slightly overlapping them. Put the plates in the low oven to keep warm while cooking the foie gras.

Score the foie gras slices with the tip of a knife in a diamond pattern and season with salt. Heat a skillet over high heat, add the foie gras, and sear until well browned but still tender in the center, about 30 seconds per side. (See page 232 for notes on cooking foie gras.)

To serve, cut each slice of foie gras in half and lean the slices against the beans on the opposite side of the duck. Drizzle the sauce over and around the duck slices, scatter minced chives over the duck and foie gras, and add a drizzle of beet coulis around all.

# SONOMA SQUAB IN ARTICHOKE BOTTOMS
## with Walla Walla Onion Compote and Lovage Sauce

**MAKES 4 SERVINGS /** This recipe is in honor of Jean-Louis Palladin, an outstanding chef for whom I had a great deal of admiration. He was also a very funny man...my kind of guy! This is one of his recipes that I remember with delicious fondness. Choose large artichokes so that their trimmed bottoms will be large enough to hold the mousse and squab breast. The filling has a pronounced gamey flavor, so it's not for the faint of heart. If you are unable to find squab liver or gizzard, you can use chicken liver and/or gizzard. For a milder taste, substitute chicken breast for the liver and other offal. A full-service butcher should be able to bone the birds for you; you will need the boneless breasts and the leg/thigh portions for this recipe, but the bones and trimmings can be used to make a wonderful stock to use in place of the veal stock here. Simply follow the instructions for Poultry Stock on page 207.

Delas Frères 2000 Hermitage "Les Bressards," Rhône Valley, France

4 large artichokes

1/2 lemon

Boneless breasts and leg/thigh portions from 4 whole squab (each weighing about 1 pound)

1/4 pound squab liver, gizzard, and/or kidney

1 large egg white

Sea salt and freshly ground white pepper

1 teaspoon minced fresh thyme

About 3 ounces crépine (caul fat, page 232)

2 cups Veal Stock (page 206)

Small handful of lovage or celery leaves

3 tablespoons unsalted butter, cut into pieces and chilled

Preheat the oven to 350°F.

*For the onion compote,* heat the butter and oil in a large skillet over medium heat until the butter is melted and foamy white. Add the onion and toss to coat well. Add the thyme and season generously with salt, tossing to mix. Decrease the heat to medium-low and cook until the onion is just beginning to soften, 4 to 5 minutes. Transfer the skillet to the oven and roast the onions, stirring once or twice, until they are very tender and lightly browned, 20 to 25 minutes. Remove the skillet from the oven, stir in the vinegar and season to taste with pepper; set aside.

Trim each artichoke so only the bottoms remain (page 231), then use a small spoon to scoop out the chokes. Squeeze the lemon half into a large saucepan of cold salted water and add the lemon half as well. Add the artichoke bottoms to the pan and bring just to a low boil over medium-high heat. Decrease the heat to medium, lay a clean dish towel over the surface to help keep the artichoke bottoms submerged, and simmer until about half-cooked, 5 to 7 minutes. Drain well and set aside to cool, then refrigerate until chilled.

**Walla Walla Onion Compote**

3 tablespoons unsalted butter

1 tablespoon argan or olive oil

1 Walla Walla sweet onion, thinly sliced

1 teaspoon fresh thyme leaves

Sea salt

2 teaspoons red wine vinegar

Freshly ground black pepper

Garnish

Lovage leaves

Basil Oil (page 216)

Using the tip of a small, sharp knife, remove the meat from the leg/thigh portions of the squab, avoiding the very tendony meat near the leg end. You should have about 1 ounce of meat in all. Put the meat in a food processor with the squab liver and pulse a few times to chop finely and blend the meats. Add the egg white and process until the mixture is very smooth, 1 to 2 minutes. Season the mixture with $1/4$ teaspoon of salt and a good pinch of pepper, then pulse a few times to mix.

Increase the oven temperature to 400°F.

Remove the skin from the squab breasts. Trim the base of each cold artichoke bottom so they sit level, if needed, then season the bottoms lightly with salt and pepper. Spoon the squab mousse into the artichoke bottoms, smoothing the tops. Sprinkle the squab breasts with the thyme and season with salt and pepper. Place the squab breasts over the stuffing. Cut the *crépine* into 4 pieces about 6 inches square. Gently but snugly wrap each stuffed artichoke in a piece of *crépine* to enclose the filling, neatly tucking the ends underneath so the packets sit upright securely. Trim away excess *crépine* if needed.

Set the artichoke packets, right-side up, in a large ovenproof skillet. Pour in the veal stock, scatter the lovage leaves over and around the packets, and transfer the skillet to the oven. Roast, basting the packets with the stock every 10 minutes or so, until the filling is cooked through and the artichoke bottoms are fully tender, about 30 minutes. Shortly before the squab is done, gently reheat the onion compote over medium heat.

Transfer the artichoke packets to a plate and cover with aluminum foil to keep warm. Set the skillet over medium-high heat and boil to reduce the cooking liquid by half, 4 to 5 minutes. Whisk in the butter so that it melts creamily into the sauce and season to taste with salt and pepper.

To serve, cut each artichoke packet crosswise in half and set 2 halves just off center on each warm plate. Spoon the onion compote between the artichoke halves and spoon the lovage sauce around (leaving the leaves behind in the skillet). Garnish each plate with a lovage leaf and add dots of basil oil around the outer edge of the sauce.

# PARMENTIER OF OXTAIL

## with Foie Gras and Quail Egg

**MAKES 4 SERVINGS /** Monsieur Parmentier is famous in French culinary history for having worked hard to break Europeans of their belief that the potato, a member of the nightshade family, was deadly. His effort is memorialized in the classic recipe *boeuf parmentier,* in which a ground beef mixture is layered with mashed potatoes; this is my upscale twist. You may need to special order oxtail from your butcher, but the rich, delicate meat is definitely worth the extra effort. We use a ring mold in which to layer the parmentier, then lift it off for a neat presentation. If you don't have ring molds on hand, you can simply form the layers freehand, making them as tidy as you can.

Calera 1996 Pinot Noir "Jensen," California

2$^{1}$/$_{2}$ to 3 pounds oxtails, cut into 1$^{1}$/$_{2}$-inch pieces

Sea salt and freshly ground black pepper

8 tablespoons (1 stick) plus 1 tablespoon unsalted butter

1 large carrot, peeled and coarsely chopped

$^{1}$/$_{2}$ onion, coarsely chopped

1 celery stalk, coarsely chopped

6 cups Veal Stock (page 206)

5 thyme sprigs, plus a pinch of minced fresh thyme

2 bay leaves, preferably fresh, partly torn

$^{3}$/$_{4}$ pound Yellow Finn potatoes

1 tablespoon minced shallots

$^{1}$/$_{2}$ teaspoon minced fresh parsley

Pinch of minced garlic

4 slices foie gras (1$^{1}$/$_{2}$ to 2 ounces each)

Preheat the oven to 325°F.

Rinse the oxtails under cold running water and pat dry with paper towels. Trim away any large pieces of excess fat, then season the oxtails generously with salt and pepper. Heat 4 tablespoons of the butter in a large pot over medium-high heat until melted, medium brown in color, and slightly nutty smelling. Add the oxtails and brown well on all sides, 3 to 5 minutes. Add the carrot, onion, and celery and sauté until lightly browned, about 5 minutes. Add the veal stock and bring just to a boil, skimming away any fat that collects on the surface. (The oxtails should be just covered with liquid; add more stock or water if needed.) Add the thyme sprigs and bay leaves, then transfer the pan to the oven and braise, uncovered, until the oxtails are very tender and the meat is falling off the bones, 2$^{1}$/$_{2}$ to 3 hours. The oxtails should be just barely covered with liquid throughout cooking; add hot water to the pan if necessary.

Using a slotted spoon, scoop out the oxtails and put into a large bowl; let cool until easy to handle. Strain the cooking liquid through a sieve into a saucepan, discarding the vegetables and herbs. Skim away and discard the fat that collects on the surface. Bring the liquid to a low boil over medium heat and simmer until reduced by half, about 25 minutes.

*continued*

## Walnut Vinaigrette

2 tablespoons walnut or champagne
    vinegar

2 teaspoons minced fresh chives

$1/4$ teaspoon minced shallots

Pinch of minced fresh thyme

Sea salt and freshly ground white pepper

## Garnish

4 quail eggs

Flat-leaf parsley leaves

Peel and quarter the potatoes (smaller potatoes can simply be halved, so pieces are of relatively even size) and put them in a saucepan of cold salted water. Bring the water just to a boil over high heat, then decrease the heat to medium and simmer until the potatoes are tender when pierced with the tip of a knife, 20 to 25 minutes. Drain well, then spread the potatoes on a baking sheet and let dry in the oven for a few minutes. Press the potatoes through a ricer into the same saucepan or mash them in the pan with a potato masher until smooth. Cut the remaining 4 tablespoons of butter into pieces, add to the potatoes, and stir until the mashed potatoes are blended and smooth, then season to taste with salt and pepper. Set aside over low heat to keep warm.

Remove the oxtail meat from the bones and cartilage, then chop the meat and put it in a small saucepan with the shallots, parsley, garlic, and minced thyme. Add 2 tablespoons of the reduced cooking liquid to moisten it, stirring to mix evenly, then reheat the oxtail mixture over low heat.

*For the vinaigrette,* put the walnut vinegar in a small bowl and slowly whisk in 3 tablespoons of the reduced cooking liquid. Whisk in the chives, shallots, and thyme and season to taste with salt and pepper.

Score the foie gras slices with the tip of a knife in a diamond pattern and season with salt. Heat a skillet over medium-high heat, add the foie gras, and sear until well browned but still tender in the center, about 30 seconds per side. (See page 232 for notes on cooking foie gras.) Drizzle a teaspoon or two of the foie gras fat into the oxtail mixture if you like. Heat the remaining 1 tablespoon of butter in a small skillet over medium heat until melted and foamy white. Crack the quail eggs into the skillet and cook just until the whites are set, 1 to 2 minutes. Trim the white portion with a small plain cutter to form a tidy circle if you like.

To serve, lightly oil four 3-inch ring molds and set them in the center of warm plates. Spoon the oxtail mixture into the molds and top with the mashed potatoes, smoothing the surface evenly with a spatula or knife. Lift off the rings. Set the foie gras slices on top of the parmentier, then top them with the quail eggs. Spoon the walnut vinaigrette around and garnish the potatoes with parsley leaves.

# WILD BOAR AND BANANA SQUASH

## with Huckleberry Peppercorn Sauce

**MAKES 4 SERVINGS** / Wild boar offers the richness of pork with an added gamey element that I love. If your butcher is able to order rack of wild boar, ask him to trim out the loin, saving you the bones and trimmings, which will add delicious flavor to the sauce. You may, however, find it easier to buy a pre-trimmed boar loin; in that case, beef or veal bones and trimmings can be used for the sauce. If you simply can't hunt down wild boar, use beef or pork tender-loin, but check out page 228 for source options. Fresh or frozen blueberries or red currants could be used in place of the huckleberries if you're unable to find them.

Marcarini 1999 Barolo Brunate, Piedmont, Italy

3 tablespoons peanut or canola oil

1 pound boneless wild boar loin

2 teaspoons minced fresh thyme

Sea salt and freshly ground black pepper

1 parsnip, peeled

1 pound banana, butternut, or acorn
  squash, peeled

1 onion, quartered

4 tablespoons unsalted butter

Huckleberry Peppercorn Sauce

9 tablespoons unsalted butter

1¹/₂ pounds boar, beef, or veal trimmings
  and bones (optional)

1 carrot, peeled and chopped

1 celery stalk, chopped

¹/₂ cup huckleberries

2 teaspoons cracked black peppercorns

3 tablespoons red wine vinegar

Rub 1 tablespoon of the oil all over the boar loin, sprinkle with 1 teaspoon of the thyme, and season generously with salt and pepper. Put on a plate, cover with plastic wrap, and marinate at room temperature for up to 1 hour or refrigerate for up to 4 hours, removing the loin from the refrigerator about 20 minutes before cooking it.

Halve the parsnip crosswise, then cut the thinner bottom portion in half lengthwise and the larger top portion lengthwise into quarters. Trim away the tough core from the center of the parsnip pieces; set aside. Using a sturdy, sharp knife, cut away the tough skin from the squash and scoop out and discard the seeds. Cut the squash into 1-inch wedges; set aside. Separate the layers of half the onion and coarsely chop the remaining onion half and reserve to use in the sauce.

*For the huckleberry sauce,* heat 5 tablespoons of the butter in a large saucepan over medium-high heat until melted and foamy white. Add the meat trimmings and bones, if using, and brown well, stirring often, for about 5 minutes. Add the reserved chopped onion, carrot, and celery and cook, stirring often, until well colored, 3 to 5 minutes, scraping up the browned bits from the bottom of the pan so they don't burn. Add ¹/₄ cup of the huckleberries and the peppercorns and cook, stirring, for 2 to 3 minutes longer. Add the vinegar and boil until reduced by half, 1 to 2 minutes. Add the red wine and stir to

*continued*

3 cups (1 bottle/750 ml) dry red wine

4 to 5 thyme sprigs

3 to 4 parsley sprigs

2 bay leaves, preferably fresh, partly torn

3 cups Veal Stock (page 206)

Garnish

Minced fresh chives

Flat-leaf parsley leaves

deglaze any cooked bits in the bottom of the pan, then add the thyme sprigs, parsley sprigs, and bay leaves. Bring to a boil and reduce by two-thirds, about 20 minutes. Add the veal stock and reduce by half, about 20 minutes longer. Lift out and discard the larger bone pieces. Strain the sauce through a sieve lined with cheesecloth into a small saucepan, pressing well on the solids to extract as much flavor as possible. Set aside while preparing the boar.

Preheat the oven to 350°F.

Heat a large ovenproof sauté pan or deep skillet over medium-high heat, then add the remaining 2 tablespoons of oil. Place the boar loin, top (rounded side) down in the pan. Add 2 tablespoons of the butter and brown the loin well on all sides, 2 to 3 minutes total. Transfer the loin to a plate and set aside. Add the remaining 2 tablespoons of butter to the pan and melt over medium heat. Add the squash, parsnip, and onion leaves, turning to coat them in the butter, then sprinkle with the remaining 1 teaspoon of thyme and season with salt and pepper.

Transfer the pan to the oven and bake until the vegetables are about half-tender, 20 minutes. Turn the vegetables over, place the seared boar loin on top, and cover the pan. Continue roasting until the vegetables are tender and the boar is medium (an instant-read ther-mometer should reach about 135°F), 20 to 25 minutes longer. (Note: If using smaller tenderloin, it will need about half the cooking time of a larger loin, so add it to the vegetables about 10 minutes later than for the loin.) Transfer the boar to a cutting board and let rest, covered with foil, to keep warm.

Bring the sauce to a boil over medium-high heat and boil to reduce by three-fourths, 15 to 20 minutes. Whisk in the remaining 4 tablespoons of butter so it melts creamily into the sauce, then add the remaining 1/4 cup of huckleberries. Season the sauce to taste with salt.

To serve, arrange the roasted squash, parsnips, and onion to one side of each warm plate. Cut the boar loin across into 1/2-inch-thick slices and lean the slices against the vegetables, slightly overlapping them. Spoon the huckleberry sauce over the boar, sprinkle minced chives over the meat and vegetables, and garnish the plate with parsley leaves.

# SCOTTISH WOOD PIGEON

## with Braised Cabbage and Rosemary Sauce

**MAKES 4 SERVINGS /** Scottish wood pigeon is a treat that comes to me from Scotland during the winter hunting season, available off and on from late October to mid-February. These small birds have a slight gamey character that makes for a nice change of pace from other fowl I serve. Squab would be a good substitute when you are unable to find wood pigeon, which is available from d'Artagnan (page 228).

Château Angélus 1998 St. Emilion, Bordeaux, France

1/2 head of Savoy or green cabbage

11 tablespoons unsalted butter

1 small onion, halved and thinly sliced

Sea salt

1 teaspoon minced fresh thyme, plus
   1 teaspoon fresh thyme leaves

1/2 teaspoon minced garlic

1 1/2 cups Poultry Stock (page 207)

4 Scottish wood pigeons (about 1/2 pound
   each)

1 tablespoon fresh rosemary leaves

1 1/2 cups water

1 tablespoon dry white wine (optional)

Freshly ground white pepper

Garnish

Minced fresh chives

Rosemary blossoms

Discard the core from the cabbage and carefully cut the cabbage into 4 wedges, keeping them intact. Heat 4 tablespoons of the butter in a large, deep skillet over medium heat until melted and foamy white. Scatter the onion in the skillet and season with salt. Lay the wedges of cabbage on top and salt the cabbage lightly, then sprinkle the minced thyme and garlic over all. Cover the pan and cook over medium heat for 5 minutes. Carefully turn the cabbage wedges over and cook, covered, for 5 minutes longer. Add the poultry stock to the skillet, cover, and continue cooking until the cabbage is tender when pierced with the tip of a knife, about 15 minutes longer.

Meanwhile, rinse the pigeons well under cold running water and pat dry with paper towels. Cut the breast portions away from the bone, then bend back and remove the thigh/leg portion from each bird. Coarsely chop the bones and reserve for the sauce. Salt the meat portions. Heat 2 tablespoons of the remaining butter in a large skillet over medium-high heat until it is melted, medium brown in color, and slightly nutty smelling. Add the pigeon pieces, skin-side down, and cook for 1 minute. Turn the pieces over, sprinkle with the thyme leaves, and cook until just a bit rosy in the center, about 2 to 3 minutes longer.

Preheat the oven to 200°F.

*continued*

Heat 2 tablespoons of the remaining butter in a small skillet over medium-high heat until melted and foamy white. Add the reserved pigeon bones and brown well, stirring occasionally, for 5 to 7 minutes. Add the rosemary and cook until aromatic, 1 to 2 minutes longer. Add the water and simmer until reduced by half, 5 to 7 minutes; remove from the heat.

When the cabbage is tender, carefully transfer the cabbage and onion to a plate and keep warm in the low oven. Add the cooking liquid to the bones in the skillet. Bring to a boil and boil to reduce by half, 5 to 7 minutes. Strain the sauce through a sieve into a small saucepan and whisk in the remaining 3 tablespoons of butter so it melts creamily into the sauce. Add the wine and season to taste with salt and pepper. Keep warm over low heat.

To serve, spoon the onion in the center of warm plates and top with a cabbage wedge. Cut the pigeon breast portions into thin slices, fan them out slightly, and lean the breasts against the cabbage. Set the leg portions alongside and spoon the rosemary sauce over the meat and cabbage. Sprinkle chives over the breast meat and rosemary blossoms around the plate.

# VENISON MEDALLIONS

## with Parsnip Ragout, Apricots, and Mustard Sauce

**MAKES 4 SERVINGS /** During the summer we do a lot of preserving (page 71) at Rover's, so that we have flavorful, bright-colored apricots on hand throughout the year to use in a variety of recipes. They make a great addition to this recipe, as the fruit's moderately tart flavor is a great complement to the rich game, while echoing the sweetness of the parsnips. If you are unable to find venison medallions, you can use beef tenderloin or filet mignon steaks; simply adjust the cooking time as needed because they are larger than their venison counterpart.

Beaux Frères 2002 Pinot Noir, Willamette Valley, Oregon

2 large parsnips (about ³/₄ pound total), peeled and trimmed

6 tablespoons unsalted butter

³/₄ cup Poultry Stock (page 207)

1¹/₂ teaspoons plus a pinch of minced fresh thyme

Sea salt

2 tablespoons crème fraîche, homemade (page 212) or store-bought

¹/₄ cup champagne vinegar or white wine vinegar

2 teaspoons minced shallots

4 top-quality canned or preserved apricots, halved

1 teaspoon fireweed honey

Freshly ground black pepper

2 venison tenderloins (about 1 pound total)

3 tablespoons clarified unsalted butter (page 231)

2 cups Veal Stock (page 206)

¹/₄ cup Dijon mustard

Preheat the oven to 200°F.

Halve the parsnips lengthwise, then across in half or in thirds. Cut out and discard the tough core from the center and cut the parsnips into julienne strips. Heat 4 tablespoons of the butter in a skillet over medium-high heat until melted and foamy white. Add the parsnips with the poultry stock, the pinch of minced thyme, and a pinch of salt. Cook until the parsnip is just tender and the stock has evaporated, 5 to 7 minutes, reducing the heat if necessary to avoid browning. Stir in the crème fraîche, then remove the skillet from the heat and set aside until ready to serve.

Combine the vinegar, shallots, ¹/₂ teaspoon of the minced thyme, and the remaining 2 tablespoons of butter in a small saucepan. Bring to a boil over medium-high heat and boil to reduce by half, 2 to 3 minutes. Cut each apricot half into 4 pieces and add them to the pan with the honey. Toss over medium heat just until the apricots are evenly coated and warmed through, 1 to 2 minutes. Season to taste with salt and pepper and keep warm over low heat.

Sprinkle the venison with the remaining teaspoon of minced thyme and season with salt and pepper. Slice the tenderloin across to make medallions about 1 inch thick. Heat the clarified butter in a large skillet over high heat. Add the medallions and brown well, about

*continued*

Garnish

**Beet Coulis (page 215)**

**Minced fresh chives**

**Flat-leaf parsley leaves**

1 minute on each side. Transfer the medallions to a heatproof plate and keep warm in the low oven (they will gently continue to cook to medium). Gently reheat the parsnips.

Add the veal stock to the skillet and bring to a boil, scraping up any flavorful browned bits stuck to the bottom of the pan. Boil to reduce by two-thirds, 5 to 7 minutes. Remove the skillet from the heat and whisk in the mustard, then season to taste with salt and pepper.

To serve, spoon a mound of the parsnip ragout just off center on each warm plate. Cut each venison medallion into slices on the diagonal and arrange in a fan pattern, leaning them up against the bottom edge of one side of the parsnip ragout. Spoon the apricot pieces along the other side of the parsnip and drizzle the mustard sauce over and around the meat. Top the sauce with dots of beet coulis, scatter chives over the meat and apricots, and add a leaf of parsley to finish.

# ROASTED PHEASANT

## with Brussels Sprouts and Roasted Garlic Sauce

**MAKES 4 SERVINGS** / Tiny baby Brussels sprouts, extra tender and sweet, are a special treat I get now and then during the winter. Choose the smallest Brussels sprouts you can find, cutting larger Brussels sprouts in half or in quarters. Tapenade is a Mediterranean paste of black olives, garlic, olive oil, and herbs. Here, a dollop of it is spread over the potatoes just before serving. We make our own tapenade at Rover's and use it for a variety of dishes, but you can also purchase good-quality tapenade if you prefer; my favorite is from Mustapha Gourmet Imports (page 229).

Solena 2001 Syrah "Del Rio," Oregon

2 pheasants (about 2 pounds each)

2 whole heads of garlic, plus 5 or 6 cloves

5 tablespoons olive oil

1 teaspoon fresh thyme leaves, plus
    1 teaspoon minced fresh thyme

Sea salt and freshly ground black pepper

11 tablespoons unsalted butter, plus
    more if needed

1/2 onion, sliced

2 Yukon Gold potatoes (about 1 pound)

2 to 3 tablespoons clarified unsalted
    butter (page 231)

2 cups Poultry Stock (page 207)

8 to 10 ounces baby or small Brussels
    sprouts, trimmed

1/4 cup black olive tapenade

Garnish

Minced fresh chives

Carrot Coulis (page 215)

Cut off the neck and first wing joints from the pheasants; reserve along with any giblets for the sauce (discard the liver or save for another use). Trim away any excess fat from the pheasants and put in a small skillet. Warm over medium heat to render the fat, which will be used later (this step is optional).

Thinly slice the individual garlic cloves (if the cloves are large, first cut them in half and remove the green germ). Make a dozen incisions into the skin of each pheasant with the tip of a small, sharp knife and insert a garlic slice into each slit. Rub the birds all over with 2 tablespoons of the olive oil and sprinkle inside and out with the minced thyme and season with salt and pepper. To truss the pheasants, tie the legs of 1 bird together with a long piece of kitchen string, making a butcher's knot (page 29). Pull the 2 lengths of string down the side of the bird, between the legs and body, then cross the 2 pieces of string underneath the pheasant. Bring the string back on top of the bird, holding down the wings, and tie a knot. Repeat with the second pheasant.

Preheat the oven to 375°F.

Peel away the loose papery skins from the whole heads of garlic and trim off a bit of the root end to expose some of the garlic flesh and

*continued*

make it easier to squeeze out after roasting. Set the heads of garlic in the center of a square of foil, drizzle with 1 tablespoon of the olive oil, and season with salt and pepper. Wrap the package up securely and roast until the garlic is soft when pressed between your fingers, 1 to 1¼ hours. Set aside until cool enough to handle.

Meanwhile, heat a large skillet over medium heat, then add the remaining 2 tablespoons of olive oil and 1 tablespoon of the butter and heat until the butter is melted and foamy white. Place the pheasants in the skillet, on their sides, and brown well for 1 to 2 minutes. Using tongs, turn the birds onto their other sides and brown well, then turn onto their breasts to brown for 1 to 2 minutes longer. Avoid too-high a heat or the skin might burst. (If you don't have a skillet large enough to accommodate both pheasants at once, brown one bird at a time and proceed with roasting the pheasants in a roasting pan.) Add the sliced onion to the skillet with the wings and neck trimmings. Place the birds, breast-side up, on top of the onions. Transfer the skillet to the oven and roast until the cavity juices run clear (insert a long wooden spoon or carving fork into the cavity, lift up slightly, and tip juices out into the skillet to check), 40 to 45 minutes.

Meanwhile, peel the potatoes and cut into ¹/₁₆-inch-thick slices with a mandoline or knife. Put 2 tablespoons of the clarified butter in a large bowl and add the thyme leaves with a good pinch each of salt and pepper. Add the potato slices and toss well with your hands, separating the potato slices so they are evenly coated with the butter and seasoning.

Heat 1 tablespoon of the pheasant fat (or 1 tablespoon of the clarified butter) in a ovenproof skillet, preferably nonstick, over medium heat just until warm. Remove the skillet from the heat and arrange the potato slices in an overlapping spiral pattern, beginning around the edge of the pan and working to the center of the pan with the smaller slices, making one even layer of potatoes. Cook the potatoes until lightly browned, 5 to 7 minutes. Drain off the excess fat from the skillet into a small dish. Invert the galette onto a flat plate or unrimmed baking sheet, then carefully slide it back into the skillet and cook until the bottom is browned and the potato is tender, about 5 minutes longer. Remove from the heat and keep warm.

Heat ½ cup of the poultry stock in a saucepan over medium heat. Cut 6 tablespoons of the butter into pieces and add to the warm stock, whisking so that the butter melts creamily. Add the Brussels sprouts with a pinch of salt and decrease the heat to medium-low. Cook gently, stirring occasionally, until the Brussels sprouts are tender, 8 to 12 minutes (depending on their size).

When the birds are done, transfer them to a carving board. Add the remaining 1½ cups of poultry stock to the same skillet and bring to a boil over high heat. Boil until the liquid is reduced by half, 8 to 10 minutes. Strain the liquid through a sieve into a saucepan. Squeeze the roasted garlic cloves from their skins, add them to the saucepan, and cook for 1 to 2 minutes, pressing on the

*continued*

cloves to break them up. Purée the sauce with an immersion blender or transfer to a blender to purée, then return to the pan. Cut the remaining 4 tablespoons of the butter into pieces and whisk so that it melts creamily into the sauce. Season to taste with salt and pepper and keep warm over low heat. Put the potatoes in the oven to reheat gently.

Trim away the legs from the pheasants and separate the thigh portions from the legs. Trim away the thigh bones, running the tip of a small knife down the length of the bones on both sides. Cut the breast meat away from the body and cut it on the diagonal into slices about $1/2$ inch thick, trimming away any excess fat. Slice the thigh meat as well.

To serve, invert the potato cake onto a cutting board and spread with the tapenade. Cut the potato cake into 4 wedges and set a wedge in the center of each warm plate. Lay the breast slices on the tapenade, slightly overlapping them, and set a leg alongside with thigh meat slices around the edge. Pour the roasted garlic sauce over and around the pheasant. Spoon the Brussels sprouts around the pheasant and sprinkle chives over the pheasant. Garnish with dots of carrot coulis around the outer edge.

# Sorbets

## PINOT NOIR SORBET

**MAKES ABOUT 1 QUART /** This Rover's signature recipe has been a regular on our multicourse menus since 1988. When grating ginger, use a very fine grater (I use a Microplane grater) to extract the maximum essence of ginger. For the citrus zest, use a standard vegetable peeler to peel away the zest in lengthwise strips, leaving behind as much of the bitter white pith that is underneath as possible.

4 cups pinot noir or other spicy red wine

*3/4 C. Sugar. FN*

Zest from 2 oranges

Zest from 2 lemons

1½ teaspoons finely grated peeled young ginger

5 thyme sprigs

4 bay leaves, preferably fresh, partly torn

1 small (3-inch) cinnamon stick

20 black peppercorns

5 cloves

Combine the wine, sugar, orange and lemon zests, ginger, thyme sprigs, bay leaves, cinnamon, peppercorns, and cloves in a saucepan. Bring the wine to a boil over medium-high heat, stirring to help the sugar dissolve, then remove the pan from the heat and set aside to steep for about 45 minutes.

Strain the wine mixture through a sieve into a bowl and set over a larger bowl of ice water until fully chilled, stirring occasionally. Pour the mixture into an ice cream maker and freeze according to the manufacturer's instructions. Transfer the sorbet to an airtight container and freeze until set, at least 2 hours.

To serve, scoop the sorbet into small chilled dishes.

## INFUSED TEA SORBET
### with Fireweed Honey

**MAKES ABOUT 3 CUPS /** I am a big fan of the Mighty Leaf Tea Company, whose teas I recommend here. The blend of different teas makes for a compelling combination of flavors, but you could use any flavorful dark teas you have on hand.

3 cups water

²/₃ cup fireweed honey

¼ cup sugar

4 teaspoons freshly squeezed lemon juice

1 bag orchid oolong tea

1 bag ginger twist tea

1 bag jasmine mist tea

1 bag orange jasmine tea

Combine the water, honey, sugar, and lemon juice in a saucepan and bring to a boil over medium-high heat, stirring to help the honey and sugar dissolve. Remove the pan from the heat, add the tea bags, and set aside to infuse for 10 minutes.

Remove the tea bags from the pan, squeezing as much liquid as possible from the bags, then discard them. Transfer the sorbet base to a bowl and set over a larger bowl of ice water until fully chilled, stirring occasionally. Pour the mixture into an ice cream maker and freeze according to the manufacturer's instructions. Transfer the sorbet to an airtight container and freeze until set, at least 2 hours.

To serve, let the sorbet sit on the counter for 15 to 20 minutes (or in the refrigerator for about 1 hour) before scooping it into small chilled dishes.

# PINK GRAPEFRUIT AND VERMOUTH SORBET

**MAKES ABOUT 2 CUPS /** This refreshing sorbet also can be served as a cocktail. Scoop a small ball of the sorbet into chilled martini glasses, add vodka, and serve. I prefer Noilly Prat brand vermouth, because its flavor is the most distinctive of those I've tasted.

2 large pink grapefruits

$1/4$ cup dry vermouth

2 tablespoons sugar

Peel and section 1 of the grapefruits (page 235), reserving the juice and segments separately. Juice the remaining grapefruit and combine with the reserved juice. You should have about 1 cup total. Whisk the grapefruit juice, vermouth, and sugar together in bowl until the sugar dissolves. Pour the mixture into an ice cream maker and freeze according to the manufacturer's instructions. Transfer the sorbet to an airtight container and freeze until set, at least 2 hours.

To serve, let the sorbet sit on the counter for 15 to 20 minutes (or in the refrigerator for about 1 hour) before scooping into small chilled dishes. Arrange the grapefruit segments around the sorbet and serve

**SORBET AT ROVER'S**—We make a lot of sorbet at Rover's. With the multicourse set menu format that most of our customers prefer, I offer a sorbet course as a palate cleanser, typically between the fish and the meat courses. It's for that reason that many of the sorbets we make have savory elements in them, though sugar is always included. Of course, sorbets are among our dessert offerings as well, as an element on the "Symphony of Desserts" plate. You can also simply serve the sorbets alone, perhaps with butter cookies (page 226) alongside, or as an accent to a wide variety of recipes.

I use invert sugar to make sorbet because it gives sorbet a smoother texture (thanks to smaller sugar crystals) so it doesn't freeze as hard as it would otherwise. Invert sugar is regular sucrose that has been treated with acid and heat and is available in cake decorating shops and through specialty pastry suppliers. Another option when making sorbet is to add a bit of egg white—about $1/4$ per recipe, whipped almost to soft peaks—to the sorbet mixture shortly before it has finished churning in the ice cream maker. The whipped egg white lightens the texture of the frozen mixture, making it easier to scoop.

Sorbet made without egg white or invert sugar should be allowed to sit at room temperature for 15 to 20 minutes (or in the refrigerator for about an hour) before serving. (Smaller batches of sorbet will need less sitting time.) Sorbet that contains a little alcohol also does not freeze as solid, needing less sitting time at room temperature or sometimes none at all.

## HIBISCUS SORBET

**MAKES ABOUT 2 CUPS** / Dried hibiscus flowers, which have a subtle citrus flavor, give this sorbet a beautiful deep crimson color. The dried flowers are available in spice shops and specialty food stores.

2 cups water

$2/3$ cup sugar

$1/2$ cup freshly squeezed orange juice

$1^{1}/2$ ounces dried hibiscus flowers

Combine the water, sugar, orange juice, and hibiscus flowers in a saucepan and bring to a boil over medium-high heat, stirring to help the sugar dissolve. Remove the pan from the heat and set aside for about 15 minutes. Strain the mixture through a sieve into a bowl and set over a larger bowl of ice water until fully chilled, stirring occasionally. Pour the mixture into an ice cream maker and freeze according to manufacturer's instructions. Transfer the sorbet to an airtight container and freeze until set, 1 to 2 hours, before serving.

To serve, let the sorbet sit on the counter for 15 to 20 minutes (or in the refrigerator for about 1 hour) before scooping it into small chilled dishes.

## KUMQUAT SORBET

**MAKES ABOUT 3 CUPS** / The kumquat is an interesting little member of the citrus family, with its edible tender rind that is deeply aromatic and flavorful. This sorbet would be ideal alongside the Fallen Dark Chocolate Soufflé (page 201, minus the peach soup).

$1/2$ pound kumquats, stemmed

$1^{1}/2$ cups water

$3/4$ cup sugar

1 tablespoon Grand Marnier or other orange liqueur

$1/2$ teaspoon freshly squeezed lemon juice

$1/4$ teaspoon orange flower water

Halve the kumquats lengthwise and put them in a saucepan. Add the water and sugar and bring to a boil over medium-high heat, stirring to help the sugar dissolve. Decrease the heat to medium, stir in the Grand Marnier, lemon juice, and orange flower water and simmer until the kumquats are tender, 15 to 20 minutes. Set the pan aside to cool slightly, then purée the mixture in a food processor or blender. Press the purée through a fine-mesh sieve into a bowl and set over a larger bowl of ice water until fully chilled, stirring occasionally. Pour the mixture into an ice cream maker and freeze according to the manufacturer's instructions. Transfer the sorbet to an airtight container and freeze until set, at least 2 hours.

To serve, let the sorbet sit on the counter for 15 to 20 minutes (or in the refrigerator for about 1 hour) before scooping into small chilled dishes.

## RED BEET SORBET

**MAKES ABOUT 1 CUP /** In addition to serving this as a palate cleanser, I've served this sorbet to accompany a cucumber salad with some fresh goat cheese along-side, a great way to start a meal in the heat of summer.

3 large beets (about $1^1/_2$ pounds), scrubbed

Leaves from 8 to 10 thyme sprigs

3 tablespoons sugar

2 tablespoons red wine vinegar

Peel the beets, cut them into large pieces, and extract their juice in a juicer (you should have about $1^1/_2$ cups of juice). Skim away and discard any froth from the beet juice, then put the juice in a small saucepan with the thyme leaves, sugar, and vinegar. Bring the juice to a boil over medium-high heat, stirring to help the sugar dissolve, then decrease the heat to medium-low and simmer, 3 to 5 minutes. Strain the liquid through a sieve into a bowl and set over a larger bowl of ice water until fully chilled, stirring occasionally. Pour the mixture into an ice cream maker and freeze according to the manufacturer's instructions. Transfer the sorbet to an airtight container and freeze until set, at least 2 hours.

To serve, let the sorbet sit on the counter for about 10 minutes (or in the refrigerator for 30 minutes) before scooping it into small chilled dishes.

# CELERY AND FENNEL SORBET

**MAKES ABOUT 3 CUPS** / This is a cool and refreshing sorbet to serve as a palate cleanser for a dinner party, although I have also served it as a garnish for fish tartare and salads. You'll need a good juicer to extract the juice from the fennel, celery, and parsley; it's a worthy addition to any kitchen.

1 fennel bulb

5 large celery stalks, trimmed and coarsely chopped

1/2 bunch curly parsley (about 2 1/2 ounces), trimmed

1/4 cup sugar

3 tablespoons Pastis or other anisette liqueur

Trim, core, and coarsely chop the fennel bulb, reserving some of the tender fennel fronds for garnish. Use a juicer to extract the juice from the celery, fennel, and parsley. You should have about 2 cups of juice in all.

Combine the juice with the sugar and Pastis in a saucepan and bring to a boil over medium-high heat, stirring to help the sugar dissolve. Decrease the heat to medium and simmer, 3 to 5 minutes. Transfer the mixture to a bowl and set over a larger bowl of ice water until fully chilled, stirring occasionally. Pour the mixture into an ice cream maker and freeze according to the manufacturer's instructions. Transfer the sorbet to an airtight container and freeze until set, at least 2 hours.

To serve, let the sorbet sit on the counter for 15 to 20 minutes (or in the refrigerator for about 1 hour) before scooping it into small chilled dishes.

# Desserts

# CHOCOLATE TERRINE

## with Candied Cranberries and Rum Crème Anglaise

**MAKES 8 TO 10 SERVINGS /** I use a long, narrow mold with a rounded bottom for this chocolate terrine, which when sliced creates a half-moon shape that makes a very attractive presentation. You could also make the terrine in a narrow terrine mold or standard loaf pan if you like. The terrine can be made up to 2 days in advance, unmolded, and glazed up to 6 hours ahead. It makes a great dinner party dessert, as all that remains to be done is to slice and serve. The final glaze is optional, for the terrine is glorious as is.

One of my favorite garnishes for this terrine is candied fresh cranberries, their vivid color and vibrant flavor a wonderful contrast to the rich chocolate terrine. Note that the candied cranberries must be prepared the day before serving, as their sugar coating needs to dry overnight.

Disznókö 1988 Tokaji Aszú Eszencia, Hungary

$^1/_2$ **pound top-quality bittersweet chocolate, finely chopped**

$1^1/_4$ **cups heavy cream**

$^1/_4$ **cup light corn syrup**

**4 tablespoons unsalted butter, cut into** $^1/_2$**-inch pieces**

**2 tablespoons Grand Marnier or other liqueur**

$1^1/_2$ **cups Crème Anglaise (page 221)**

**2 tablespoons dark rum**

**Candied Cranberries**

**1 cup sugar, or more if needed**

**2 cups cranberries**

**3 tablespoons cold water, or more if needed**

*For the candied cranberries,* put 1 cup of the sugar in a large bowl. Bring a saucepan of water to a rolling boil. Add the cranberries to the water and cook just until slightly softened, about 15 seconds. Drain the cranberries, tossing well to remove the excess water. Add the berries to the sugar, immediately tossing them to coat evenly with sugar. Gently lift out the cranberries and place on a rimmed baking sheet, spreading them out so they are touching as little as possible; reserve a few tablespoons of the sugar from the bowl for the cranberry coulis. Let the sugar-coated cranberries dry on the counter, uncovered, overnight. Once dried and firm, the cranberries can be stored in an airtight container.

Line a terrine mold with plastic wrap as neatly as possible.

Put the chocolate in a medium bowl. Combine the cream and corn syrup in a medium saucepan and bring to a boil over medium-high heat, stirring occasionally to help the syrup dissolve. When the mixture reaches a boil, slowly pour it over the chocolate, whisking gently until the chocolate melts and the mixture is very smooth. Add the butter a few pieces at a time, whisking after each addition until fully

**Glaze (optional)**

**10 ounces top-quality bittersweet or white chocolate, finely chopped**

**¹/₄ cup vegetable oil**

**2 tablespoons Grand Marnier or other liqueur**

incorporated before adding more. Whisk in the Grand Marnier and continue blending until very smooth. Pour the chocolate mixture into the prepared mold, then lightly tap the mold on the counter a few times to remove any air bubbles. Let cool to room temperature, then cover with plastic wrap and refrigerate until set, at least 6 hours.

*Two to 3 hours before serving, make the glaze,* if desired. Put the chocolate in a heatproof bowl and set over a pan of gently simmering, not boiling, water (the bottom of the bowl should not touch the water). Stir often with a wooden spoon until the chocolate is melted and smooth. Stirring constantly, slowly drizzle in the oil until fully incorporated and smooth. Slowly stir in the Grand Marnier until well blended. Set aside to cool.

Unmold the chocolate terrine onto a wire rack set over a rimmed baking sheet (to make slicing easier later, you may want to unmold the terrine onto a piece of foil-wrapped cardboard first and set it cardboard-side down on the rack). Working in an even motion from one end of the terrine to the other, slowly drizzle the glaze over the terrine to coat the top and sides fully and evenly with the chocolate. Refrigerate until the glaze has set, about 1 hour. Put the crème anglaise in a small bowl, stir in the rum, and refrigerate, covered, until ready to serve.

Put about half of the candied cranberries in a blender or food processor. Add the 3 tablespoons of cold water and 1 tablespoon of the reserved cranberry sugar; purée until smooth. If the purée is quite thick, add another drizzle of water. Pass the purée through a fine-mesh sieve into a small bowl to remove the tiny seeds, pressing with the back of a spoon to extract as much of the purée as possible. Taste the purée for sweetness, adding more sugar if needed.

To serve, warm a thin-bladed knife under warm running water, quickly dry the blade, and cut the terrine into ¹/₂-inch-thick slices, rewarming and wiping the knife blade as needed. Arrange 2 slices of the terrine in the center of each plate, slightly overlapping them. Spoon the rum crème anglaise around the slices, top the crème anglaise with dots or drizzles of cranberry purée, then scatter a few of the whole cranberries around the terrine. Serve right away.

# HONEY MOUSSE CHARLOTTE
## with Rhubarb Purée

**MAKES 8 SERVINGS /** This recipe is a good reason to use a special aromatic honey, which will yield more distinctive results than fireweed honey. One of my favorites is honeysuckle honey from Sicily, though I also like to use clover or huckleberry honey produced here in the Northwest. Rather than forming the dessert in a traditional charlotte mold—a round pan almost as tall as it is wide with gently sloping sides—you could instead spoon the honey mousse into large martini glasses, tumblers, or coffee mugs, and spoon the rhubarb purée on top just before serving. In that case, serve the ladyfingers alongside, use a few to line each glass, or simply omit them.

Château de Fesles 1999 Bonnezeaux, France

About 20 Ladyfingers (page 225)

4 gelatin sheets or 4 teaspoons
    unflavored gelatin powder

1/2 cup aromatic honey

2 large eggs

1 tablespoon sugar

2 tablespoons Grand Marnier

1 1/2 cups heavy cream

Line the base of a 2-quart charlotte mold with a round of parchment paper. Line the side of the mold with the ladyfingers, rounded sides facing out, then use a small knife to trim the tops of the ladyfingers even with the top of the mold. Trim one end of the remaining ladyfingers to a 45-degree point and arrange them in the base of the mold with the pointed ends meeting in the center, so they form a starburst pattern.

Break the gelatin sheets into pieces and soften in a bowl of cold water for 5 to 10 minutes, then drain. (If using powdered gelatin, sprinkle it over 1/3 cup of cold water in a small dish and set aside to soften, about 5 minutes.)

Warm the honey in a bowl set over a pan of simmering, not boiling, water. Add the softened gelatin to the warm honey, whisking until it is thoroughly melted. Set aside to cool to room temperature.

Combine the eggs and sugar in the bowl of a stand mixer fitted with the whisk attachment. Beat at medium speed until pale in color and lightened in texture, 2 to 3 minutes. Slowly add the cooled honey and the Grand Marnier, mixing to blend. Whip the cream in a large bowl until soft peaks form. Fold the cream into the honey mixture

**Rhubarb Purée**

**½ pound rhubarb (about 4 stalks)**

**3 cups water**

**1 cup sugar**

**Garnish**

**Orange segments (page 235)**

until well blended. Pour the honey mousse into the prepared charlotte mold, cover with plastic wrap, and refrigerate until set, at least 4 hours or up to overnight.

*For the rhubarb purée,* trim the rhubarb stalks and cut them into 4-inch lengths. Combine the water and sugar in a saucepan and bring just to a boil over medium-high heat, stirring to help the sugar dissolve. Add the rhubarb, decrease the heat to medium-low, and gently simmer until the rhubarb is tender, 8 to 10 minutes. With a slotted spoon, lift out the rhubarb and set aside on a plate to cool, reserving the poaching liquid in the pan.

Purée the cooled rhubarb in a blender or food processor until very smooth, adding 2 to 3 tablespoons of the poaching liquid to form a smooth, light purée. Refrigerate until ready to serve.

To serve, unmold the charlotte onto a cutting board; cut the charlotte into 8 wedges. Spoon the rhubarb purée in a pool to one side of each plate, place a charlotte wedge so it is partially on the purée, and arrange orange segments around the charlotte.

# PEAR AND APPLE FRANGIPANE TARTLETS

## with Caramel and Huckleberry Sauces

**MAKES 8 SERVINGS /** Frangipane is a classic element of the French pastry kitchen, a nutty cream made with almond paste. One traditional use is spreading it in tart shells before adding fruit, as I do here with fall's juicy pears. For a touch of extra elegance, I add some Calvados-spiked apple compote to the frangipane before baking. The tart can also be made with apple slices or plum or apricot halves.

Campbells Muscat Rutherglen, Australia

½ recipe Pâte Sucrée (page 223)

1 to 2 ripe Comice pears

1 tablespoon sugar

### Apple Compote

1 Granny Smith apple

2 tablespoons water

2 tablespoons sugar, or more to taste

2 tablespoons unsalted butter

2 tablespoons Calvados or brandy

### Frangipane

3 ounces almond paste

½ cup sugar

6 tablespoons unsalted butter, at room temperature

1 large egg

⅓ cup all-purpose flour, sifted

*For the apple compote,* peel, core, and chop the apple. Put it in a saucepan with the water and cook, covered, over medium heat until the apple has softened, 8 to 10 minutes. Purée the apple and any cooking liquid in a food processor until very smooth. Return the purée to the saucepan, add the sugar, butter, and Calvados and cook over medium-low heat, stirring often to help keep it from sticking on the bottom, until the compote has thickened, 12 to 15 minutes, adding more sugar to taste if needed. Set aside to cool completely.

*For the frangipane,* combine the almond paste and sugar in a clean food processor and pulse until the almond paste is in fine bits. Add the butter and egg and pulse until smooth, scraping down the side of the bowl as needed. Add the flour in 2 or 3 batches, pulsing just until it is fully incorporated. Transfer the frangipane to a bowl. Stir in the cooled apple compote, cover with plastic wrap, and refrigerate until needed.

*For the caramel sauce,* combine the sugar and water in a saucepan and bring to a boil over medium heat, stirring occasionally to help the sugar dissolve. Increase the heat to medium-high and cook, without stirring, until the mixture has a deep caramel color and aroma, 5 to 7 minutes. Have a small bowl of water and a heatproof pastry brush alongside and occasionally brush the damp (but not dripping wet) bristles around the inside edge of the pan, just above the sugar mixture, to help impede the formation of crystals, which will affect

**Caramel Sauce**

1 cup sugar

¹/₃ cup water

1 cup heavy cream

**Huckleberry Sauce**

¹/₂ pound huckleberries

¹/₄ cup sugar

¹/₄ cup water

¹/₄ cup tawny port

1 teaspoon freshly squeezed lemon juice

**Garnish**

Crème Anglaise (page 221)

the texture of the caramel. Remove the pan from the heat and slowly add the cream, whisking gently and taking care because the mixture will bubble up and steam will rise from the pan. When all of the cream has been added, set the pan back over medium heat and cook to thicken slightly, 1 to 2 minutes. Transfer the sauce to a bowl and set aside to cool.

*For the huckleberry sauce,* combine the berries, sugar, water, port, and lemon juice in a small saucepan and bring to a boil over medium-high heat, stirring to help the sugar dissolve. Decrease the heat to medium and simmer until the berries are tender, 8 to 10 minutes. Purée the mixture in a blender and press through a fine-mesh sieve into a bowl. Set aside to cool to room temperature.

Preheat the oven to 375°F.

Roll out the pastry on a lightly floured work surface to about ¹/₁₆ inch thick. Use the pastry to line eight 4-inch fluted tart pans and set them on a rimmed baking sheet for easier handling.

Spoon the apple-frangipane mixture into the tart shells, spreading it out evenly to about two-thirds full. Peel, core, and thinly slice the pear and arrange the slices, slightly overlapping, on top of the frangipane, trimming the slices as needed so they cover neatly. Sprinkle the sugar over the pear slices and bake the tartlets until the frangipane is set and the tops are lightly browned, 25 to 30 minutes. Transfer the tartlets to a wire rack to cool slightly before serving.

To serve, spoon a pool of the caramel sauce onto half of each plate and spoon the huckleberry sauce onto the other half. Draw the tip of a knife back and forth through both sauces to form a decorative pattern. Add dots of crème anglaise around the outer edge of the sauces. Carefully remove the tartlets from their pans and set a tartlet in the center of each plate.

# ORANGE PANNA COTTA

## with Pomegranate Sorbet

**MAKES 8 SERVINGS /** *Panna cotta* (Italian for "cooked cream") is a deliciously versatile recipe. Here, the dessert gets added aroma and flavor from fresh orange zest and exotic-tasting orange flower water, which is available in specialty food shops and in the pastry section of well-stocked grocery stores. Its "cousin," rose water, would also be delicious in this panna cotta, though use just $1/2$ teaspoon, as its flavor is more pronounced. The tuile cookies used for garnish should be baked in the classic round shape, then cooled over a rolling pin to create a curved shape in which a small quenelle of pomegranate sorbet is placed for serving.

Michel Chapoutier 1999 Muscat de Rivesaltes, France

2 cups whole milk

2 cups heavy cream

$3/4$ cup sugar

2 vanilla beans, split lengthwise

Finely grated zest of 2 oranges (about 2 tablespoons)

$3/4$ teaspoon orange flower water

3 gelatin sheets or 3 teaspoons unflavored gelatin powder

2 teaspoons Grand Marnier (optional)

**Pomegranate Sorbet**

$1/2$ cup sugar

$1/4$ cup water

2 cups pomegranate juice (page 235)

**Pomegranate Syrup**

$1/3$ cup sugar

3 tablespoons water

$1/2$ cup pomegranate juice (page 235)

Lightly oil eight $1/2$-cup ramekins, cups, or other small dishes with canola or other neutral oil.

Combine the milk, cream, sugar, and vanilla beans in a saucepan and bring to a boil over medium-high heat, stirring to help the sugar dissolve. Stir in the orange zest and orange flower water, remove the pan from the heat, and set aside and let the flavors infuse for 30 minutes.

Break the gelatin sheets into pieces and soften in a bowl of cold water for 5 to 10 minutes, then drain. (If using powdered gelatin, sprinkle it over $1/4$ cup of cold water in a small dish and set aside to soften, about 5 minutes.) Add the softened gelatin to the warm cream, stirring until it is thoroughly melted. Strain the cream mixture through a fine-mesh sieve into a bowl, then run the vanilla bean halves between your thumb and forefinger to remove as many of the tiny flavorful seeds as possible and add to the cream mixture. Stir in the Grand Marnier, if using, and ladle the mixture into the prepared ramekins. Let cool to room temperature, then cover each dish with plastic wrap and refrigerate until the panna cotta sets, at least 2 hours or up to overnight.

**Garnish**

**8 Tuile Cookies (page 222)**

**Crème Anglaise (page 221)**

**Pomegranate seeds**

*Meanwhile, make the pomegranate sorbet.* Combine the sugar and water in a small saucepan and bring just to a boil over medium-high heat, stirring to help the sugar dissolve. Add the pomegranate juice and transfer the mixture to a bowl. Set the bowl in a larger bowl of ice water to cool it quickly, then refrigerate until fully chilled. When cold, pour the mixture into an ice cream maker and freeze according to the manufacturer's instructions. Transfer the sorbet to an airtight container and freeze until ready to serve.

*For the pomegranate syrup*, combine the sugar and water in a small saucepan and bring just to a boil over medium-high heat, stirring occasionally to help the sugar dissolve. Add the pomegranate juice and simmer over medium heat until the syrup has reduced slightly, about 5 minutes. Remove from the heat and set aside to cool. Take the sorbet from the freezer and let it sit on the counter for 15 to 20 minutes (or in the refrigerator for about 1 hour) before serving.

To serve, warm the bottom of one of the ramekins with a dish towel warmed in hot water. Set the ramekin upside down on a chilled serving plate and shake it to help it unmold. Repeat with the remaining ramekins. Set a tuile cookie on top of each panna cotta, with rounded edges facing up, and form the pomegranate sorbet into 8 small quenelles (page 235), setting one in each tuile. Drizzle the pomegranate syrup and crème anglaise around the panna cottas, scatter a few pomegranate seeds over the sauce, and serve right away.

# BLACK AND WHITE CHOCOLATE MOUSSE

## with Illy Espresso Sauce

**MAKES 6 SERVINGS /** At Rover's, the portions for desserts such as this one are on the small side, since our "dessert symphony" includes a number of different bites for our guests. For forming this frozen layered mousse, we use special pastry strips of lightly coated cardboard to form cylindrical molds that are about $1^3/_4$ inches across. Rather than making individual portions, you could instead form the mousse layers in a plastic wrap-lined terrine, unmolding it directly onto a serving platter to thaw before slicing to serve (it will be easier to cut if still partly frozen, then allowed to continue thawing on individual plates before serving). The hazelnut cookies served alongside can be baked into any shape you like or even omitted. Coffee-lovers will revel in the deeply flavored sauce, for which the espresso beans should be very finely ground.

Ramos-Pinto 20-Year Tawny Port, Portugal

**Dark Chocolate Mousse**

$^1/_4$ **pound top-quality bittersweet chocolate, chopped**

**3 large egg yolks**

$^1/_4$ **cup sugar**

$^1/_4$ **cup warm water**

$^1/_2$ **cup heavy cream**

*For the dark chocolate mousse,* put the bittersweet chocolate in the top of a double boiler or bowl set over a pan of simmering, not boiling, water. Warm over medium heat, stirring occasionally, until melted. Remove the pan from the heat to cool slightly.

Put the egg yolks in the bowl of a stand mixer fitted with the whisk attachment. Add the sugar and beat at medium-high speed until it is very light, has about doubled in volume, and a ribbon of the mixture holds on the surface for a few seconds when the whisk is lifted, 3 to 4 minutes. Whisk in the warm water and continue beating until the mixture is light and fully blended. Decrease the mixer speed to medium-low, add the warm (not hot) melted chocolate, and beat until fully incorporated. Chill the chocolate mixture in the refrigerator for about 15 minutes, whisking occasionally so it cools evenly.

While the chocolate is cooling, prepare the molds (see box, page 187). Set the molds on a rimmed baking sheet with the tidiest, most even sides down (to help ensure the mousse doesn't seep out) and set aside.

*continued*

## White Chocolate Mousse

1 gelatin sheet or 1 teaspoon unflavored
gelatin powder

$^{1}/_{4}$ pound top-quality white chocolate,
chopped

4 tablespoons unsalted butter, cut into
pieces

3 large egg yolks

$^{3}/_{4}$ cup heavy cream

$2^{1}/_{2}$ tablespoons sugar

## Espresso Sauce

1 cup heavy cream

$^{1}/_{4}$ cup freshly ground espresso or other
dark-roast coffee beans

3 large egg yolks

$^{1}/_{3}$ cup sugar

2 tablespoons Kahlua

When the chocolate mixture is cool, whip the heavy cream to nearly stiff peaks and fold it into the chocolate. Half-fill the molds with the dark chocolate mousse and gently but firmly rap the baking sheet down on the counter a couple of times to remove any air pockets in the mousse and level the surface. Place the dark chocolate mousse in the freezer while making the white chocolate mousse (make sure the molds are sitting perfectly flat so they freeze evenly).

*For the white chocolate mousse,* break the gelatin sheet into pieces and soften in a bowl of cold water, 5 to 10 minutes, then drain. (If using powdered gelatin, sprinkle it over 2 tablespoons of cold water in a small dish and set aside to soften, about 5 minutes.)

Combine the white chocolate with the butter in the top of a double boiler or in a bowl set over a pan of simmering, not boiling, water. Warm over medium heat, stirring occasionally, until melted. Remove the pan from the heat and whisk in the softened gelatin until thoroughly melted and blended. Set aside to cool slightly.

Beat the egg yolks in an electric mixer fitted with the whisk attachment at medium-high speed until well blended. With the mixer running, slowly add the white chocolate mixture and continue beating until fully blended, smooth, and cooled to room temperature.

Whip the cream with the sugar to nearly stiff peaks. Fold into the cooled white chocolate mixture, then spoon the white chocolate mousse over the dark chocolate mousse in the molds. Again, gently rap the baking sheet on the counter to remove any air pockets and level the surface of the mousse. Freeze until fully set and firm, 2 to 3 hours.

*For the espresso sauce,* put the cream and ground espresso beans in a saucepan and bring just to a boil over medium-high heat. Remove the pan from the heat and set aside for 10 minutes.

**Garnish**

**6 Hazelnut Butter Cookies (page 226),** cut out slightly larger than the diameter of the mousse molds

Combine the egg yolks and sugar in a bowl, whisking until thoroughly blended and lightened in color. Slowly add the warm espresso cream, whisking constantly until blended. Return the mixture to the saucepan and cook over medium heat, stirring with a wooden spoon, until the mixture thickens enough to coat the back of the spoon (a path should remain clear when you run your finger across the back of the spoon), 8 to 10 minutes. Strain the sauce through a fine-mesh sieve into a small bowl and stir in the Kahlua. Set aside until cool, then refrigerate until ready to serve.

One to 2 hours before serving, remove the mousse from the freezer. Carefully unwrap the molds, discard the foil, and set each mousse on a hazelnut cookie. Place each mousse on a plate and let thaw gently in the refrigerator.

To serve, spoon the espresso sauce around the mousse and serve right away.

**TO MAKE FOIL MOLDS**—This technique can be used to make forms of different sizes and shapes, such as a square. They are a good stand-in for the ring molds I use for mousselike recipes.

Cut a piece of foil about 10 inches long. Carefully fold the foil lengthwise in half so the folded edge is even. Fold the foil lengthwise in half again, creating a 4-ply strip about 3 inches wide. (If the foil you're using is wider than the standard width, you should trim it lengthwise to a 12-inch width before starting.) Wrap the strip around a standard 14-ounce can (like a soup can) for a 3-inch mold, or use a rolling pin or smaller can for a smaller size. Overlap the ends very evenly and secure with a piece of tape.

# SAVORY STRAWBERRY SOUP

**MAKES 4 SERVINGS /** Not everyone enjoys a sweet finish to dinner, so this combination of fresh strawberries with herbs and Banyuls wine makes a great alternative. It has a kind of *sauvage* (wild) flavor that is something of a surprise at the end of a meal. Banyuls is a moderately sweet red wine from the south of France, made principally with the grenache grape. It is a rather one-of-a-kind ingredient with no direct substitute; the closest option would be a relatively light tawny port. The salted and peppered ricotta cheese, topped with chives, is reminiscent of *cervelle de canut*, a blend of fresh cheese and herbs from Lyon. The tuile cookies for garnish should be formed into slender triangles, 6 to 8 inches long and 2 inches wide at their base, then laid over the rounded bottom of a large bowl or similar object so they dry with a slight curve in their shape.

Tedeschi 1997 Recioto della Valpolicella "Monte Fontana," Veneto, Italy

3/4 pound fresh strawberries, rinsed and hulled

1 cup Banyuls wine

2 tablespoons clover honey

Freshly ground black pepper

1 clove garlic, halved

3 to 4 basil sprigs

1 teaspoon fresh thyme leaves

1/2 cup whole milk ricotta

1 to 2 tablespoons heavy cream

Sea salt

Halve the strawberries, then cut the halves across into 1/2-inch pieces. Put the wine in a bowl, add the honey, and stir until the honey dissolves. Add the strawberries and 5 grinds of pepper. Cut a piece of cheesecloth about 6 inches square. Put the garlic, half of the basil, and the thyme leaves in the cheesecloth and tie the packet securely with kitchen string. Add the seasoning packet to the strawberry mixture and refrigerate to marinate for 2 hours (not much longer or the infused flavors will become quite strong; if making the soup farther in advance, remove the seasoning packet after 2 hours).

Shortly before serving, put the ricotta in a bowl and stir with a whisk to soften slightly. Add 1 tablespoon of the cream and whip just to blend and form a smooth mixture. If your ricotta is quite dry, you might need another tablespoon of cream; the cheese should be smooth and malleable but still hold its shape. Season with a pinch each of salt and pepper.

**Garnish**

**4 large strawberries**

**4 Tuile Cookies (page 222)**

**Chopped fresh chives**

To serve, discard the seasoning packet from the strawberries. Mince the remaining basil and stir it into the soup. Hull the large strawberries for garnish, setting them hull-side down on the cutting board. Cut each strawberry into $1/8$ inch-thick slices, keeping the slices together as you go. Use your fingers to slide the slices gently away from one another to form a strip of partly overlapping slices 3 to 4 inches long. Set each sliced strawberry strip upright in an arc to one side of a chilled shallow soup bowl, then spoon the soup into the bowls. Form the ricotta into 4 quenelles (page 235) and set 1 in the center of each soup. Set a tuile cookie on top, so that its broad end rests on the quenelle and the tip extends over the side of the bowl. Sprinkle the quenelle with a pinch of chives.

# CHOCOLATE CARAMEL HAZELNUT CAKE

**MAKES 12 SERVINGS** / This is a decadent cake, no doubt about it: rich cake layers sandwiched with a layer of caramel, chocolate ganache, and hazelnuts. Another layer of ganache coats the top of the cake, making it sinfully good. The cake can be assembled up to a day in advance, a great choice as the finale to a luxurious dinner party. To make it easier to transfer the finished cake from the wire rack to a plate, I recommend that you cut a piece of sturdy cardboard into a 7½- by 11-inch rectangle and cover it with plastic wrap or foil. Set the bottom cake layer on the cardboard and place it on the wire rack for assembling the cake.

Columbia Crest 1998 Reserve Semillon Ice Wine, Washington State

## Chocolate Cake

6 ounces top-quality bittersweet chocolate, chopped

¼ cup water

1¼ cups all-purpose flour

½ teaspoon baking soda

¼ teaspoon sea salt

1 cup sugar

½ cup (1 stick) unsalted butter, at room temperature

2 large eggs, separated

½ cup buttermilk

## Ganache

½ pound top-quality bittersweet chocolate, chopped

1 cup heavy cream

2 tablespoons sugar

2 tablespoons unsalted butter

¾ cup very finely chopped toasted hazelnuts (page 234)

Preheat the oven to 350°F. Brush a half-sheet pan (12 inches by 18 inches) with melted butter and line it with parchment paper, lightly buttering the paper as well.

*For the cake,* combine the chocolate and water in a heatproof bowl set over a pan of simmering, not boiling, water. Stir occasionally until the chocolate melts and the mixture is smooth, 3 to 5 minutes. Set aside to cool to room temperature.

Sift the flour, baking soda, and salt together into a bowl and set aside. Combine the sugar, butter, and egg yolks in the bowl of a stand mixer fitted with the paddle attachment. Beat at medium speed until thoroughly combined. Add the cooled chocolate and blend at low speed to incorporate. Add the flour mixture to the chocolate mixture in 3 additions, alternating with the buttermilk, and beginning and ending with the flour mixture. Decrease the speed to medium-low and continue mixing until the batter is well blended, scraping down the side of the bowl as needed.

Whip the egg whites to soft peaks in a large bowl, then gently fold into the batter in 2 or 3 batches. Pour the batter onto the prepared baking pan and spread evenly. Bake until the cake springs back when gently pressed with a finger, 18 to 20 minutes. Run a small knife around the edges of the cake to loosen it from the pan and invert onto a parchment-lined wire rack. Peel away the parchment paper and let the cake cool completely.

**Caramel Sauce**

1¹/₂ cups sugar

¹/₂ cup water

1 cup heavy cream

3 tablespoons unsalted butter

2 tablespoons Frangelico

**Garnish**

Crème Anglaise (page 221) or Crème
  Fraîche, homemade (page 212) or
  store-bought

*For the ganache,* put the chocolate in a heatproof bowl. Combine the cream, sugar, and butter in a saucepan and bring just to a boil over medium-high heat, stirring to help the sugar dissolve. Pour the hot cream mixture over the chocolate and stir until it is melted and smooth. Transfer about one-third of the ganache to a small bowl and refrigerate until set but still spreadable, about 45 minutes; set the remaining ganache aside at room temperature.

*For the caramel sauce,* combine the sugar and water in a saucepan and bring to a boil over medium heat, stirring occasionally to help the sugar dissolve. Increase the heat to medium-high and cook, without stirring, until the mixture has a deep caramel color and aroma, 5 to 7 minutes. Have a small bowl of water and a heatproof pastry brush alongside and occasionally brush the damp (but not dripping wet) bristles around the inside edge of the pan, just above the sugar mixture, to help impede the formation of crystals, which will affect the texture of the caramel. Remove the pan from the heat and slowly add the cream, whisking gently and taking care to avoid the hot steam that rises from the pan. When all the cream has been added, set the pan back over medium heat and cook until thickened slightly, 1 to 2 minutes. Whisk in the butter and 1 tablespoon of the Frangelico, then transfer the sauce to a bowl and set aside to cool.

Cut the cooled cake crosswise in half into 2 rectangles about 7¹/₂ inches by 11 inches. Set one half of the cake on the wire rack (on a prepared piece of cardboard, if using) set over a rimmed baking sheet. Drizzle about ¹/₂ cup of the caramel over the cake and spread it out to a thin layer. Add ¹/₂ cup of the chopped hazelnuts to the chilled ganache (it should not be too firm; if it's too firm to spread, let it sit for a few minutes before using), stirring to mix evenly, then spread this mixture over the caramel. Drizzle another ¹/₂ cup of the caramel over the hazelnut ganache as evenly as you can. Set the other cake half on top, with the flattest, most even side facing up.

Pour the room-temperature ganache (if your kitchen is cool and the ganache has thickened some, gently soften it over a pan of warm water, stirring, until it is pourable but not very warm) over the top of the cake and carefully spread it with a narrow spatula, so it drips evenly over the sides of the cake. Refrigerate to allow the ganache to set, about 1 hour.

*continued*

Just before serving, trim the sides of the cake to make tidy, even edges, dipping the knife blade into warm water and quickly drying it off between cuts. Cut the cake lengthwise into thirds, then across into quarters to form 12 squares. Cut each piece diagonally in half to form 2 triangles.

To serve, set 2 cake triangles in the center of each plate, cut sides facing but not touching. Stir the remaining 1/4 cup of hazelnuts and 1 tablespoon of Frangelico into the remaining caramel sauce and spoon around the cakes. Top the caramel with drizzles of crème anglaise.

# RASPBERRY AND BLUEBERRY MILLEFEUILLE

MAKES 4 SERVINGS / The colors of red, white, and blue give this summertime dessert a festive Fourth of July look, though it could just as well be in honor of Bastille Day, which is celebrated in France on July 14, since the French flag has the same color scheme. Whidbeys loganberry liqueur is named for Whidbey Island, which is north of Seattle on the Puget Sound. It adds the ideal complement of berry flavor to the filling, though you could use Chambord, cassis, or another berry liqueur in its place.

The final topping for the millefeuille is a pastry-cream filling that is lightened with a small amount of whipped egg white (just a couple tablespoons), a light finish that gets browned with a blowtorch just before it is topped with fresh berries. You can omit that step, if you like, and simply top the layered pastry with berries.

Veuve Cliquot NV Champagne Demi-Sec, France

1/2 pound Pâte Feuilletée (page 224)

3/4 cup Crème Pâtissière (page 221)

1/4 cup heavy cream

1 tablespoon Whidbeys liqueur

1 large egg white

2 teaspoons sugar

6 ounces fresh raspberries

6 ounces fresh blueberries

Garnish

Raspberry Coulis (page 215)

Crème Anglaise (page 221)

Blueberry Coulis (see Raspberry Coulis, page 215)

Preheat the oven to 400°F. Line a rimmed baking sheet with a silicone baking mat or parchment paper.

Roll out the pâte feuilletée (puff pastry) on a lightly floured surface (preferably marble) to a rectangle that is 1/16 inch thick and measures about 12 inches wide and 15 inches long. Trim the dough to make 2 rectangles about 5 inches wide and 14 inches long. Refrigerate one of the strips, wrapped in plastic wrap, until ready to bake. Transfer the other pastry strip to the prepared baking sheet and set another silicone baking mat or sheet of parchment paper on top. Set another baking sheet on top of the baking mat and weight it down with a couple of bricks or a cast-iron skillet filled with rock salt. Bake the pastry for 20 minutes. Remove from the oven, carefully turn the pastry over with a large spatula, and restack the baking sheets. Bake until the pastry is evenly browned and crisp, about 10 minutes longer. Transfer the pastry to a wire rack to cool completely and repeat with the second pastry strip.

Put 1/2 cup of the crème pâtissière in a bowl and stir to soften it slightly. Whip the cream in another bowl until stiff peaks form, then whip in the Whidbeys liqueur. Whip about one-fourth of the whipped

*continued*

cream into the pastry cream to lighten it, then fold in the remaining cream. Refrigerate until set, at least 1 hour.

Put the remaining ¼ cup of crème pâtissière in a bowl and stir to soften slightly. Whip the egg white until frothy, then add the sugar and continue whipping until glossy medium-stiff peaks form. Gently fold 2 tablespoons of the beaten egg white into the pastry cream until evenly blended (discard the remaining egg white). Refrigerate until ready to use.

Shortly before serving, transfer the pastry strips to a cutting board and use a serrated knife to trim the strips into rectangles measuring about 12 inches by 4½ inches. Cut the strips across to make twelve 2-inch-wide rectangles. Set 4 of the rectangles on the work surface and spread half of the pastry cream–whipped cream mixture evenly over the rectangles. Top the cream with raspberries, reserving some for garnish; if the berries are large, halve them lengthwise first and set them, cut-side down, on the cream. Spread 4 more pastry rectangles with the remaining pastry cream–whipped cream mixture and set them on top of the raspberries. Top with an even layer of blueberries, reserving some for garnish.

Spread the pastry cream–egg white mixture over the remaining 4 pastry rectangles and caramelize with a blowtorch or under a broiler. Set the rectangles on top of the blueberries and garnish the tops with the reserved berries.

To serve, squeeze or neatly spoon the raspberry coulis in a strip about 1 inch wide and 3 inches long to one side of each plate. Add a strip of crème anglaise alongside, then a strip of blueberry coulis alongside the crème anglaise. Draw the tip of a knife through the sauces in alternating directions to make an attractive feather pattern. Transfer the berry millefeuille to the plates, just off center and partly over the sauces.

# CITRUS MERINGUE

## with Bing Cherries and Mascarpone

**MAKES 6 SERVINGS /** Although this recipe calls for fresh cherries, this is also one way we use the canned cherries we put up over the summer to add brightness to dessert offerings over the winter. You can also use top-quality canned cherries (which need no poaching, so use the canning liquid for the filling).

Pol Roger NV Champagne Rich Demi-Sec, France

½ pound fresh Bing cherries

3 cups water

1 cup granulated sugar

1 cup (½ pound) mascarpone cheese, at room temperature

¾ cup heavy cream

**Citrus Meringue**

5 egg whites

½ cup confectioners' sugar

½ cup granulated sugar

Grated zest of 1 orange (about 1 tablespoon)

Grated zest of 1 lemon (about 2 teaspoons)

**Garnish**

**Heavy cream**

Set 2 oven racks in the middle section of the oven. Preheat the oven to 200°F. Line 2 baking sheets with silicone baking mats or parchment paper.

*For the meringue,* put the egg whites in the bowl of a stand mixer fitted with the whisk attachment and beat at medium speed until frothy. Meanwhile, sift together the confectioners' sugar and granulated sugar onto a piece of parchment paper or waxed paper. Increase the mixer speed to medium-high and gradually add the sugar mixture to the egg whites. Continue beating until the egg whites are very fluffy, are glossy, and form stiff peaks, 2 to 3 minutes after all the sugar has been added. Fold the orange and lemon zests into the meringue until evenly blended. Put the meringue in a large pastry bag fitted with a medium plain tip. (If using parchment paper, put a tiny dab of the meringue under the corners of parchment paper on each baking sheet to hold it down securely.) Pipe 6 circles that are about 4 inches across onto one of the prepared baking sheets, then pipe 6 rings that have 2-inch holes in the centers on the other sheet. Any extra meringue can be piped into small 1-inch rounds to use for garnish.

Bake the meringues until very dry and firm (they will continue to crisp as they cool), 2½ to 3 hours. The meringues should not color; reduce the oven to 175°F if needed. Take the pans from the oven and let the meringues cool for a few minutes, then carefully peel the meringues away from the baking mats and let cool completely on a wire rack. Store them in an airtight container until ready to use.

While the meringues are baking, pit the cherries. Combine the water and $3/4$ cup of the sugar in a saucepan. Bring just to a boil over medium-high heat, stirring to help the sugar dissolve, then add the cherries. Decrease the heat to medium and gently poach the cherries until just barely softened, 3 to 5 minutes. With a slotted spoon, lift out the cherries and place on paper towels to drain and cool. Return the poaching liquid to a boil and boil until reduced by half, 10 to 12 minutes. Set aside to cool completely.

Put the mascarpone cheese in the bowl of a stand mixer fitted with the whisk attachment and blend at medium speed to soften. Add the cream, the remaining $1/4$ cup of sugar, and $1/4$ cup of the reduced poaching liquid. Begin blending at low speed until fully combined, then increase the speed to medium-high and continue blending until the mixture is fluffy and holds firm peaks. Cut three-fourths of the poached cherries into quarters and fold them into the mascarpone mixture. Refrigerate until well chilled, at least 45 minutes. Halve the remaining cherries.

To serve, set a meringue disk in the center of each plate. Spoon the cherry-mascarpone mixture on top in a neat circle about 1 inch thick. Top the mousse with a meringue ring and arrange the reserved cherry halves in the center of each ring, slightly overlapping them. Drizzle the remaining reduced poaching liquid around the meringues and top the reduction with a drizzle of cream. Garnish the plate with meringue dots, if you have them.

# APPLE AND HAZELNUT CHOUX
## with Pain d'Epice Caramel Sauce

**MAKES 4 SERVINGS** / This aromatic dessert, which features caramel and apple, includes the Northwest contribution of hazelnuts. An unexpected Burgundian addition here is the warm, aromatic flavor of some Pain d'Epice Spice Mix (page 212), a wonderful complement to the apples and hazelnuts.

The choux recipe makes more pastry puffs than you will need here, but the extras will keep well for a few days in the refrigerator, or freeze them in an airtight container for up to a few weeks. They can be filled with your favorite ice cream and topped with chocolate sauce for profiteroles, or fill them with a goat cheese–herb mixture for a tempting cocktail snack.

Cossart Gordon 1997 Malmsey Madeira

1 large Braeburn apple

2 tablespoons fireweed honey

2 tablespoons chopped toasted hazelnuts (page 234)

1 tablespoon Pain d'Epice Spice Mix (page 212)

1/2 cup Crème Pâtissière (page 221)

1 cup sugar

1/2 cup water

3/4 cup heavy cream

1/4 cup apple cider

1 tablespoon Calvados

Preheat the oven to 375°F.

Halve and core the apple and set it, cut-side up, in the center of a 12-inch piece of foil. Top the apple halves with the honey, hazelnuts, and 1/2 teaspoon of the pain d'épice spice mix. Loosely wrap the apple in the foil to enclose it. Bake until the apple is fully tender, about 1 hour. Carefully open the foil packet to avoid any steam and set aside to cool completely.

Scoop the tender flesh away from the apple skin and discard the skin. Purée the apple in a food processor with about 1 tablespoon of the cooking liquid in the packet until very smooth. Put the crème pâtissière into a bowl and stir a bit to soften. Stir in the apple purée until evenly blended and refrigerate until ready to serve.

Combine the sugar and water in a saucepan and cook over medium heat until the sugar dissolves, 3 to 5 minutes. Increase the heat to medium-high and continue cooking, without stirring, until the mixture turns a medium caramel color, about 12 minutes longer. Have a bowl of cold water and a pastry brush alongside and occasionally lightly brush down the side of the pan with water to keep the side clean and prevent crystallization; choose a bowl large enough that

*continued*

## Pâte à Choux

1 cup water

1/2 cup (1 stick) unsalted butter, cut into pieces

1/4 teaspoon sea salt

1 cup all-purpose flour, sifted

4 large eggs

## Garnish

Heavy cream

Chopped toasted hazelnuts

you will be able to set the bottom of the saucepan in it later to stop the cooking quickly. Add the remaining 2¹/2 teaspoons of the spice mixture to the caramel, stir to mix, then slowly drizzle in the cream, being careful to avoid the hot steam that rises from the pan as the cream bubbles up. Stir in the cider and Calvados to blend and cook for about 1 minute, then set the bottom of the pan in the bowl of cold water to stop the cooking and to chill it down quickly. When cool, transfer the caramel sauce to a bowl and set aside.

*For the pâte à choux,* combine the water, butter, and salt in a saucepan and heat over medium heat until the butter melts. Add the flour all at once, stirring briskly with a wooden spoon until it is fully blended and smooth. Continue stirring over the heat until the dough becomes cohesive and pulls away from the side of the pan, 1 to 2 minutes longer. Remove the pan from the heat and transfer the mixture to the bowl of a stand mixer fitted with the paddle attachment. Add one of the eggs and beat at medium-low speed until it is fully incorporated. Add the remaining eggs, one at a time, blending well after each addition. (Alternatively, you can blend the dough by hand. Remove the pan from the heat and use a wooden spoon to stir in 1 egg at a time.) Set the dough aside to cool slightly, about 10 minutes.

Preheat the oven to 400°F. Line 2 baking sheets with silicone baking mats or parchment paper.

Put the pâte à choux dough into a pastry bag fitted with a large plain tip. Pipe the dough into mounds about 1¹/2 inches across and ³/4 inch tall, leaving at least 1 inch between the mounds. When 1 baking sheet is filled, dip a pastry brush into water and shake it to remove the excess water. Lightly dab the top of each mound to round off any point left from the pastry tip. Bake the choux until they are puffed and browned, about 30 minutes. Transfer the choux pastries to a wire rack to cool completely and bake the remaining choux (you should have about 3 dozen in all).

To serve, use a small knife to cut off the top third of 12 of the choux puffs and set the tops aside. Fill the choux bottoms with the apple-purée mixture. Dip the choux tops into the caramel sauce and set them on top of the filling. Set 3 choux in the center of each plate. Drizzle the remaining caramel around the choux, drizzle cream over the caramel, and scatter chopped hazelnuts on top of the choux.

# CHILLED YAKIMA PEACH SOUP

## with Fallen Dark Chocolate Soufflé

**MAKES 4 SERVINGS /** This peach soup is the essence of late summer in a bowl. While the soup is delicious as is, one of my favorite elegant ways to serve it is with this fallen chocolate soufflé in the center, the bittersweet chocolate the ideal contrast to the nectarlike sweetness of the peaches. The soufflé, which is richly flavored—and surprisingly easy—can be served solo, finished with a drizzle of Raspberry Coulis (page 215).

The soufflé batter can be made up to 1 day before baking, then stored, covered, in the refrigerator. Let the batter come to room temperature before spooning it into the molds to bake. You can also bake the soufflés up to an hour before serving and serve them at room temperature, or gently reheat them in the oven.

Domaine Durban 2001 Muscat de Beaumes de Venise, France

4 cups water

1 cup sugar

2 ripe peaches, halved and pitted

**Fallen Dark Chocolate Soufflé**

3 ounces top-quality bittersweet
　chocolate, coarsely chopped

4 tablespoons unsalted butter, cut into
　pieces

1 tablespoon all-purpose flour, sifted

1 large egg

1 large egg yolk

3 tablespoons sugar

**Garnish**

Lavender blossoms or blue cornflower
　petals

Combine the water and sugar in a saucepan and bring just to a boil over medium-high heat, stirring to help the sugar dissolve. Decrease the heat to medium, add the peach halves, and lay a piece of parchment paper directly on the liquid. (This helps hold the peaches down so they will be completely submerged and not brown.) Poach the peaches until nearly tender, 3 to 5 minutes. With a slotted spoon, scoop out the peaches and set aside on a plate to cool. Pour the poaching liquid into a bowl. When the peaches are cool, peel away and discard the skins and quarter each half. Return the peach pieces to the poaching liquid and lay a piece of plastic wrap directly on the surface to prevent any discoloration. Refrigerate the peaches until fully chilled. (The peaches can be prepared up to a day ahead.)

Preheat the oven to 350°F. Butter four $^1/_2$-cup ramekins. Line the bottom of each ramekin with a parchment-paper circle and butter the paper as well. Coat the insides of the ramekins with a thin layer of sugar, tapping the ramekins upside down to remove the excess sugar. Set the molds on a small rimmed baking sheet.

*continued*

*For the soufflé,* combine the chocolate with the butter in the top of a double boiler or in a heat-proof bowl set over a pan of simmering, not boiling, water. Warm over medium heat, stirring occasionally, until melted and smooth. Remove the pan from the heat and stir in the flour until blended. Set aside to cool while preparing the eggs.

Combine the egg and egg yolk in the bowl of a stand mixer fitted with the whisk attachment. Add the sugar and beat at medium-high speed until the mixture is very light and a ribbon of the mixture holds on the surface for a few seconds when the whisk is lifted. Stir about one-fourth of the egg mixture into the cooled chocolate to lighten it, then gently fold in the remaining egg mixture until thoroughly blended. Spoon the batter into the prepared molds (it should come about two-thirds up the side of the dish) and bake until puffed and firm, about 15 minutes. Remove the baking sheet from the oven and let sit until the soufflés have fallen, about 10 minutes.

Meanwhile, purée the chilled peaches and 2 cups of the poaching liquid in a food processor or blender until very smooth.

To serve, unmold the soufflés into the centers of shallow soup bowls (discarding the parchment round) and ladle the soup around. Top the soup with a few lavender blossoms and serve right away.

# Foundation Recipes

# A Lesson in Stocks

There is no overestimating the importance of a good stock. Stock is so important in French cuisine that its name, *fond,* translates literally as "foundation." It is the foundation of many recipes. Shortcuts just won't do, at least not with the intended results. Here are some tips to help you make the most of your stock.

- If the veal bones are very large, ask your butcher to cut them into easy-to-handle pieces.

- When adding water to the roasted bones and vegetables, be sure to use only cold water. Don't be tempted to accelerate the boiling process by adding hot water. Starting with hot water draws impurities from the bones and infuses them into the water. The process of heating the cold water brings those impurities to the surface, creating that wonderful scum that is skimmed away as the stock simmers. Less impurities means less bitterness.

- It is important to let the water come to a boil and to skim away the scum before adding aromatic ingredients, such as peppercorns and herbs (particularly those that will float). If those ingredients were added earlier with the cold water, a good amount of their flavor contribution would be drawn to the surface with the scum and removed. Adding the aromatics later ensures that a maximum of their flavor will be contributed to the stock.

- Another way to avoid impurities in the final stock is to be sure that the stock doesn't cook at a rolling boil. It should come just to a boil at the beginning, then the heat should be lowered immediately so the stock simmers with a gentle rippling on the surface.

- Stocks are never seasoned with salt while they're being made, because a stock will often be reduced in later preparations. If the stock is salted too soon, it might become too salty in its more concentrated form.

- One example of kitchen efficiency is the use of parsley stems—not the leaves—for the making of stock. The leaves are saved for other recipes and garnishes, but the stems still hold plenty of flavor that is easily extracted in stocks. In fact, parsley leaves (and celery leaves) should not be used in stock making because they can become bitter after long cooking.

- When cutting vegetables to use in a stock, keep in mind how long the stock will be simmered. A vegetable stock simmers about 1 hour and a fish stock only 20 minutes, so the vegetables in these preparations should be diced or sliced to create a maximum amount of surface area exposed to the water. This allows as much flavor as possible to be drawn into the liquid during the short simmer time. A veal stock or game stock, which simmers for many hours, allows plenty of time for all the flavor to be drawn from vegetables that are simply quartered. The same is true for peppercorns, which are used whole in a veal stock, but cracked for a vegetable stock so that the flavor can be released more quickly.

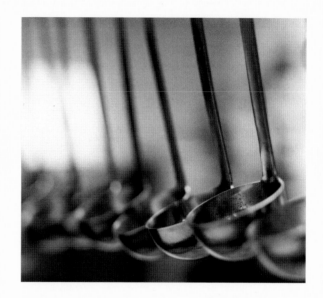

- If a stock will be heavily reduced later, it is best to take extra care when straining it to remove as many of the solids as possible, as they can make the reduction cloudy. After the stock is strained (as noted in the recipes) through a double thickness of cheesecloth, I recommend that you strain it again through a damp clean kitchen towel to remove any remaining impurities.

- It's a good idea to go ahead and make a large batch of stock—more than you will need for one use—and freeze the rest to have on hand for another time. You'll be thrilled when that "next time" comes along and you don't have to start from scratch to make more stock.

- If you're worried about freezer space, simply boil the strained stock to reduce it by at least half

before storing in an airtight container. You can reconstitute it later by adding water. Or you can reduce the stock to about one-eighth of its original quantity to make *glace de viande* (meat glaze), which can be poured into ice cube trays and frozen. When frozen, pop out the cubes and store them in a resealable freezer bag. One cube can be reconstituted to make about 1 cup of stock and used in recipes that call for veal stock. Or you can use the stock in its concentrated form to add robust flavor to a simple pan sauce.

- Lastly, it's best to freeze stock in portions of 1 to 2 cups each (or the reduced stock in ice cube trays) so you can defrost only what you'll need for a future use.

# VEAL STOCK

**MAKES ABOUT 2 QUARTS /** This aromatic stock is the backbone of many sauces and other preparations at Rover's. We go through so much that each batch we make begins with 40 pounds of veal bones, which makes enough stock to last a few days. This is a brown veal stock; the bones and vegetables are first roasted for added flavor and color before they are simmered in water.

Yes, this recipe does require at least 10 hours to prepare, and time is of the essence—literally. But without simmering for hours to draw out all the flavors from the bones and other ingredients, the resulting stock would lack depth of flavor and richness. You'll want to begin early in the morning so the stock will be finished in the afternoon, with time left to chill the stock thoroughly before refrigerating it. You won't be struck by lightening if you shorten the simmering time by an hour or two, but I would rather not know that you did! Be sure to read "A Lesson in Stocks" (page 204) before you begin.

2 tablespoons olive oil

5 pounds veal bones, preferably knuckle bones

2 onions, quartered

4 carrots, peeled and quartered

8 celery stalks, cut into 2-inch lengths

1 can (6 ounces) tomato paste

4 to 5 thyme sprigs

15 parsley stems

4 bay leaves, preferably fresh, partly torn

1 teaspoon whole coriander seeds

1 teaspoon black peppercorns

Preheat the oven to 450°F.

Put the olive oil in the bottom of a large heavy roasting pan and add the veal bones. Roast the bones until they are browned and aromatic, 45 minutes to 1 hour. Scatter the onions, carrots, and celery over the bones and continue roasting until the vegetables are well browned, about 45 minutes longer. Smear the tomato paste over the vegetables and bones and continue roasting for 20 minutes longer. (Roasting the tomato paste helps remove its acidity and also develops the tomato flavor.)

Using a large slotted spoon, transfer the bones and vegetables to a large stockpot. Discard the fat from the roasting pan and deglaze the pan with about 2 cups of water. Add this to the stockpot, then add enough cold water to cover the bones by about 2 inches. Bring the water to a boil, using a spoon to skim off the scum that rises to the surface. Add the thyme sprigs, parsley stems, bay leaves, coriander, and peppercorns, then decrease the heat to medium-low and gently simmer the stock until the liquid is richly flavored, about 8 hours. Continue to skim away the fat and impurities that rise to the top from time to time. Remove the pot from the heat and let cool slightly. Lift out and discard the large bone pieces, then carefully pour the stock through a sieve lined with a double layer of cheesecloth into a large bowl, discarding the bones and other solids. Fill the sink about one-fourth full with cold water and plenty of ice cubes, then set the bowl of stock in the ice water. This will help chill the stock quickly so it can be refrigerated as soon as possible. If there is any residual fat in the stock, it will rise to the surface and solidify as the stock cools, making it easy to remove and discard. The stock can be used right away or refrigerated to use within 3 to 5 days. For longer storage, freeze the stock in small containers for up to 2 months.

# POULTRY STOCK

**MAKES ABOUT 2 QUARTS /** Chicken bones are a good starting point for poultry stock, though for more richly flavored stock I prefer using duck bones and/or bones from the game birds we use at Rover's. To get the most flavor from them, we first roast the bones with the vegetables.

2 tablespoons canola oil

2 pounds poultry bones, rinsed well

1 onion, chopped

2 large carrots, peeled and chopped

2 leeks, white and green parts, split lengthwise, rinsed, and diced

4 celery stalks, diced

1 cup chopped tomato

3 to 4 thyme sprigs

10 parsley stems

2 bay leaves, preferably fresh, partly torn

1 teaspoon black peppercorns

Preheat the oven to 450°F.

Drizzle the oil over the bottom of a large heavy roasting pan and add the poultry bones. Roast in the oven for about 15 minutes, then take the pan from the oven and scatter the onion, carrots, leeks, and celery on top. Continue roasting until lightly browned and aromatic, about 30 minutes.

Using a large slotted spoon, transfer the bones and vegetables to a large stockpot. Spoon off and discard any remaining oil from the roasting pan. Deglaze the pan with about 2 cups of water. Add this to the stockpot with the tomato, then add enough cold water to cover the bones by about 2 inches. Bring the water to a boil over medium-high heat, using a spoon to skim off the scum that rises to the surface. Add the thyme sprigs, parsley stems, bay leaves, and peppercorns, then decrease the heat to medium-low and gently simmer the stock until it is richly flavored, about 3 hours.

Remove the pot from the heat and let cool slightly. Carefully pour the stock through a sieve lined with a double layer of cheesecloth into a large bowl, discarding the bones and other solids. Fill the sink about one-fourth full with cold water and plenty of ice cubes, then set the bowl of stock in the ice water. This will help chill the stock quickly so it can be refrigerated as soon as possible. If there is any residual fat in the stock, it will rise to the surface and solidify as the stock cools, making it easy to remove and discard. The stock can be used right away or refrigerated to use within 3 to 5 days. For longer storage, freeze in small containers for up to 2 months.

# FISH STOCK

**MAKES ABOUT 2 QUARTS** / When making stock, it's best to use saltwater—not freshwater—fish. Halibut is what I use most at Rover's because it's a local fish, though sole, cod, or other mild- to medium-flavored fish are good choices as well. Avoid salmon or other strongly flavored fish, unless the stock will be used in a recipe that will specifically benefit from that distinct flavor, such as the Salmon Gelée with Leeks and Smoked Salmon (page 64). It is important when making fish stock not to simmer the bones for too long, or they will impart a bitter flavor.

2 pounds fish bones

2 tablespoons unsalted butter

1 onion, diced

2 leeks, white and light green parts, split lengthwise, rinsed, and sliced

1 celery stalk, sliced

6 to 8 parsley sprigs

5 thyme sprigs

2 bay leaves, preferably fresh, partly torn

10 cracked white peppercorns

Rinse the fish bones well under cold running water, then drain and cut into 2-inch pieces.

Heat the butter in a stockpot over medium heat until melted and foamy white. Add the onion, leeks, celery, parsley sprigs, and thyme sprigs and cook, stirring occasionally, until the vegetables are tender and aromatic but not at all browned, 3 to 5 minutes. Add the fish bones and enough cold water to cover the bones by about 2 inches. Bring the water to a boil over medium-high heat, using a spoon to skim away the scum that rises to the surface. Decrease the heat to medium-low, add the bay leaves and peppercorns, and gently simmer the stock until it is flavorful, 25 to 30 minutes.

Remove the pot from the heat and let cool slightly. Carefully pour the liquid through a sieve lined with a double layer of cheesecloth into a large bowl, discarding the bones and other solids. Fill the sink about one-fourth full with cold water and plenty of ice cubes, then set the bowl of stock in the ice water. This will help chill the stock quickly so it can be refrigerated as soon as possible. The stock can be used right away or refrigerated to use within 3 to 5 days. For longer storage, freeze the stock in small containers for up to 2 months.

# LOBSTER STOCK

**MAKES ABOUT 2 QUARTS** / Lobster is a common ingredient on the menu at Rover's, so we always have plenty of shells for making stock. Rather than buying 4 lobsters just to make this aromatic stock, save the shells when cooking 1 or 2 lobsters for another dish, and freeze them in an airtight freezer bag until you have accumulated enough to make stock. If you have limited freezer space, first coarsely chop or crush the shells to make them less bulky. For an even more deep-flavored stock, ideal for rich dishes such as lobster bisque, we sometimes first roast the shells with the onion, celery, and fennel. You can do the same, if you like, by tossing the ingredients in a roasting pan and roasting at 375°F until aromatic, 15 to 20 minutes, before proceeding with the recipe. Another flavorful use for lobster shells is the Lobster Oil (page 219).

4 live lobsters (about 1½ pounds each)

1 fennel bulb

1 onion, diced

3 celery stalks, diced

4 to 5 thyme sprigs

4 to 5 parsley sprigs

2 bay leaves, preferably fresh, partly torn

½ teaspoon cracked black peppercorns

Cook the lobster and pick the meat from the shells (page 234); save the meat for another use. Split the head and clean it well under cold running water, discarding the head sac.

Trim the stalks from the fennel bulb and discard (or save to use in Vegetable Stock, page 210), reserving some of the tender fennel fronds for garnish. Halve the fennel bulbs lengthwise and cut out the tough core. Separate the layers of fennel, trimming away any tough or browned portions, then coarsely chop the fennel.

Coarsely crush the lobster shells by putting them in a large deep bowl and pounding them with the blunt end of a rolling pin or the bottom of a small pot. (Breaking up the shells before cooking allows a maximum of flavor to be extracted from them.) Put the shells in a large stockpot. Add the onion, celery, fennel and enough cold water to cover by about 2 inches. Bring the water to a boil over high heat, using a spoon to skim off the scum that rises to the surface. Add the thyme sprigs, parsley sprigs, bay leaves, and peppercorns, then decrease the heat to medium-low and gently simmer the stock until it is flavorful and quite aromatic, 45 minutes to 1 hour.

Remove the pot from the heat and let the stock cool slightly. Carefully pour the stock through a sieve lined with a double layer of cheesecloth into a large bowl, discarding the shells and other solids. Fill the sink about one-fourth full with cold water and plenty of ice cubes, then set the bowl of stock in the ice water. This will help chill the stock quickly it can be refrigerated as soon as possible. The stock can be used right away or refrigerated to use within 3 to 5 days. For longer storage, freeze it in small containers for up to 2 months.

# VEGETABLE STOCK

**MAKES ABOUT 2 QUARTS** / Light and aromatic, this stock is not only the foundation for many vegetarian dishes featured at Rover's, but it is also ideal in any lighter-style soups or sauces. If you have the trimmings from fennel or leeks left over from another recipe, use them in place of the whole leeks and fennel bulb.

1/4 cup olive oil

1 onion, diced

2 leeks, white and pale green parts, split lengthwise, rinsed, and sliced

1 carrot, peeled and diced

1 celery stalk, diced

1 fennel bulb, diced

4 to 5 thyme sprigs

10 parsley sprigs or stems

2 bay leaves, preferably fresh, partly torn

10 whole coriander seeds

1/2 teaspoon cracked black peppercorns

2 whole cloves

Heat a large stockpot over medium heat, then add the olive oil. Add the onion, leeks, carrot, celery, and fennel and cook, stirring often, until tender, 3 to 5 minutes. Add enough cold water to cover the vegetables by about 2 inches. Bring the water to a boil, using a spoon to skim off the scum that rises to the surface. Add the thyme sprigs, parsley sprigs, bay leaves, coriander seeds, peppercorns, and cloves, then decrease the heat to medium-low and gently simmer the stock until it is flavorful and aromatic, about 1 hour.

Remove the pot from the heat and let cool slightly. Carefully pour the stock through a strainer lined with a double layer of cheesecloth into a large bowl, discarding the vegetables and other solids. Fill the sink about one-fourth full with cold water and plenty of ice cubes, then set the bowl of stock in the ice water. This will help chill the stock quickly so it can be refrigerated as soon as possible. The stock can be used right away or refrigerated to use within 3 to 5 days. For longer storage, freeze the stock in small containers for up to 2 months.

# HOUSE-CURED SALMON

MAKES 1½ TO 2 POUNDS CURED SALMON / Cured salmon is a staple in my kitchen, an ingredient we use for a variety of dishes, or it can be thinly sliced and served simply with toasted bread or crackers. My recipe is similar to Scandinavian gravlax, though I use a variety of fresh herbs rather than the traditional dill. I also add some pain d'épice spice mix, which I find adds a depth of flavor and a hint of exotic aroma to the cured salmon. When preparing the herbs, it's important that they are very dry. Rinse the herb leaves quickly in cold water and dry thoroughly with paper towels before chopping. Lovage, a broad-leafed herb that has a bright celerylike flavor, is an old-fashioned herb not commonly available today. Look for it in gourmet groceries. If you are unable to find lovage, you can use celery leaves instead.

1 whole wild salmon fillet (2½ to 3 pounds),
   skin and pin bones removed

1 ounce lovage leaves (about 1 cup moderately packed)

1 ounce fresh flat-leaf parsley leaves
   (about 1 cup moderately packed)

1 ounce fresh rosemary leaves (about ½ cup
   moderately packed)

¾ ounce fennel fronds (about ½ cup
   moderately packed)

¾ ounce fresh sage leaves (about ½ cup
   moderately packed)

½ ounce fresh basil leaves (about ½ cup
   moderately packed)

1½ cups sugar

1 cup fine sea salt

¼ cup Pain d'Epice Spice Mix (see box page 212)

1 tablespoon olive oil

Trim off an inch or two of the thin, fatty belly meat from the salmon fillet, because it will not cure in the same amount of time as the leaner, thicker part of the flesh. (The belly meat can be saved for grilling or sautéing.) Also carefully trim away any dark gray flesh that lies just beneath the skin, so only the vivid orange salmon flesh remains.

Working with just a few handfuls of herbs at a time, coarsely chop them (avoid overchopping). Put the chopped herbs in a large bowl and add the sugar, salt, and Pain d'Epice Spice Mix, stirring to mix evenly.

Put one-fourth of the cure mixture in the bottom of a glass or ceramic 13- by 9-inch baking dish and set the salmon, skinned-side down, on top. Drizzle the olive oil evenly over the salmon. Pour the remaining herb-cure mixture evenly over and around the salmon fillet, using clean dry hands to press the mixture firmly onto the surface of the fish. Lay a piece of plastic wrap over the salmon to cover it and the surrounding cure fully, pressing it down into the dish (not pulled taut across the top edges of the dish). Set another smaller baking dish directly on top of the salmon. Place some heavy cans in the dish (8 to 10 pounds' worth), to weight down the salmon to help extract the excess liquid and ensure the salmon is evenly cured. Refrigerate for about 24 hours. (Don't cure it much longer or the salmon will become too salty.)

Scrape the cure away from the salmon, discarding the herbs and other seasonings. Thoroughly rinse the salmon under cold running water and pat dry with paper towels. Refrigerate, wrapped, until needed. The cured salmon will keep for up to a week in the refrigerator. To serve, use a sharp, thin-bladed knife to cut the salmon into thin slices, beginning a few inches in from the tail end and slicing at a deep angle.

# CRÈME FRAÎCHE

**MAKES ABOUT 1 QUART /** Crème fraîche adds a distinctive tangy richness to sauces, soups, and toppings that regular heavy cream can't. Although you can find crème fraîche in the dairy case of many well-stocked grocery stores, it is very easy to make at home and keeps well for a few weeks. You can halve this recipe if you like.

**1 quart heavy cream**

**1/4 cup buttermilk**

Heat the cream in a saucepan until it reaches 85°F on an instant-read thermometer. Remove the pan from the heat and stir in the buttermilk. Pour the mixture into a nonmetallic vessel, such as a glass or ceramic bowl. Cover the bowl with cheesecloth or a thin clean kitchen towel and let sit at room temperature (ideally in a warm spot in the kitchen, such as near the stove) until the crème fraîche is well thickened, about 24 hours. To see whether the crème fraîche has thickened sufficiently, plunge a spoon into the center; it should stand up on its own. If the kitchen is on the cool side, it might take up to 48 hours for the crème fraîche to thicken properly. Once it has set, skim away the thin skin that has formed on the surface and spoon most of the crème fraîche into a clean bowl, discarding the liquid whey at the bottom. Cover with plastic wrap and refrigerate until needed.

**PAIN D'EPICE SPICE MIX**—Pain d'épice is a culinary signature of Burgundy, along with mustard, snails, and cassis (black currant liqueur). This rather dense, darkly colored bread is lightly sweetened with aromatic warm spices, and sometimes dried fruit. It makes a great afternoon snack when served alongside a bracing espresso. I use a pre-blended spice mix from France, which is not easy to find in the United States. To make your own spice blend, stir together 2 tablespoons ground cinnamon, 1 1/2 tablespoons 5-spice powder, 1 teaspoon ground ginger, and 1/2 teaspoon ground cloves.

# DUCK CONFIT

**MAKES 5 TO 6 CUPS SHREDDED CONFIT /** This is the classic French bistro recipe of meltingly tender duck that is served still on the bone, often with sautéed potatoes (cooked in duck fat for added flavor!). At Rover's, we dress up confit by removing the meat from the bones to use in salads, as a garnish for consommé, and in amuses bouches, the tiny bites offered to guests before the meal begins, to whet their appetites. Confit must be prepared with pure duck fat, which you will likely need to order from your butcher or gourmet food outlets. D'Artagnan (page 228) is a good source of mail-order duck products, including duck fat and even prepared confit, a great shortcut. After the confit is made, the fat can be reserved for other uses. Strain the melted fat into a large bowl. Let the fat cool until it solidifies, then scoop it into an airtight container, leaving behind the duck liquid that settles to the bottom of the bowl.

6 whole duck legs (thighs and drumsticks,
    about 3/4 pound each)

About 5 cups coarse sea salt

6 bay leaves, preferably fresh, partly torn

12 thyme sprigs

1 tablespoon cracked black peppercorns

About 5 pounds duck fat

Rinse the duck legs well under cold running water and dry thoroughly with paper towels. Scatter about half of the salt in a baking dish just large enough to hold the duck legs comfortably in a single layer. Set the duck, skin-side down, on the salt and top each leg with 1 bay leaf and 2 thyme sprigs. Scatter the peppercorns evenly over the duck. Cover the legs with the remaining salt, wrap the dish in plastic wrap, and refrigerate for 24 hours.

The next day, remove the duck from the salt and rinse well under cold running water, then thoroughly dry the legs with paper towels (discard the salt and herbs). Wash out the baking dish and dry it well.

Meanwhile, preheat the oven to 300°F.

Place the duck legs in the baking dish, skin-side up, in a single layer. Melt the duck fat in a saucepan over medium heat. When fully melted, slowly pour the fat over the duck legs (the fat must completely cover the duck). Cover the dish with foil and bake until the meat is so tender that it easily slips from the bone, 3 to 3 1/2 hours.

To use the confit, remove the legs from the fat and let cool, then pull the meat from the bones. If not using the confit right away, let it cool in the dish; when cool, cover with plastic wrap and refrigerate for up to 2 weeks.

# COULIS

MAKES ABOUT 3/4 CUP / Anyone who has watched me in action knows that a squeeze bottle of coulis is never far from reach. Yes, coulis does add vibrant color for great visual appeal, but its key role is to add a touch of additional flavor to a finished dish. Extra coulis will keep for several days in the refrigerator; add it to soups, toss it with sautéed shrimp, or drizzle it over steamed green beans. A blender works best when making coulis because it purées vegetables more finely than a food processor can.

## RED OR YELLOW BELL PEPPER COULIS

2 tablespoons olive oil

2 large red or yellow bell peppers, cored, seeded, and cut into a large dice

1 shallot, minced

2 cloves garlic, minced

1/2 teaspoon fresh thyme leaves

3 tablespoons Vegetable Stock (page 210) or water, plus more if needed

1 tablespoon extra virgin olive oil

Sea salt and freshly ground white pepper

Heat a skillet over medium heat, then add the olive oil. Add the bell peppers, shallot, garlic, and thyme and cook until the garlic is aromatic, 1 to 2 minutes. Add the stock and continue cooking until the bell pepper is tender but still brightly colored, 7 to 10 minutes. Take care not to let the bell pepper brown; decrease the heat or add another tablespoon of stock if needed. Remove the skillet from the heat and let cool slightly.

Using a slotted spoon, transfer the bell pepper mixture to a blender; reserve any liquid that remains in the skillet. Purée the pepper mixture until very smooth. Transfer the coulis to a fine-mesh sieve set over a bowl and press it through to remove any bits of skin that might clog the squeeze bottle. Stir in the extra virgin olive oil and season the coulis to taste with salt and pepper. If the coulis is very thick, stir in a little of the reserved pan liquid or stock. Set the bowl over another bowl of ice water to chill it quickly, stirring occasionally. Pour the coulis into a clean squeeze bottle or other sealed container and refrigerate until needed, up to 3 days.

## BEET OR CARROT COULIS

**MAKES ABOUT 1½ CUPS /** I make the carrot version of the coulis with either orange and yellow carrots.

½ pound beets, scrubbed, or carrots, scrubbed

1 tablespoon olive oil

1 shallot, minced

2 cloves garlic, minced

½ teaspoon fresh thyme leaves

⅓ cup Vegetable Stock (page 210) or water, plus more if needed

1 tablespoon extra virgin olive oil

Sea salt and freshly ground white pepper

Put the beets or carrots in a saucepan of salted water and bring to a boil over high heat. Decrease the heat to medium and simmer until the vegetables are tender, 20 to 25 minutes for carrots, about 1¼ hours for beets. The beets should be fully covered with water as they cook; if needed, add more hot water to the saucepan. Drain well. When cool enough to handle, trim the beets or carrots, peel away the skin, and coarsely chop.

Heat a small skillet over medium heat, then add the (regular) olive oil. Add the shallot, garlic, and thyme and cook until the shallot is tender and the mixture is aromatic, 3 to 5 minutes. Combine the beets (or carrots) with the shallot mixture in a blender. Add the stock, extra virgin olive oil, and a pinch each of salt and pepper; blend until very smooth. If the coulis is quite thick, you can add another tablespoon or two of stock. Pour the coulis into a clean squeeze bottle or other sealed container and refrigerate until needed, up to 3 days.

## RASPBERRY COULIS

**MAKES ABOUT 1 CUP /** This technique can also be used with fresh huckleberries, blackberries, blueberries, or strawberries.

¼ cup water

2 tablespoons sugar, or to taste

½ pound fresh raspberries

½ teaspoon freshly squeezed lemon juice

Combine the water and sugar in a small saucepan and bring just to a boil over medium-high heat, stirring to help the sugar dissolve. Add the berries, decrease the heat to medium-low, and simmer just until the berries soften and give off their juice, about 5 minutes. Remove from the heat and set aside to cool slightly, then transfer the berries to a blender or food processor and purée until smooth. Pass the mixture through a fine-mesh sieve into a small bowl to remove the seeds, pressing on the mixture with a rubber spatula to extract as much purée as possible. Stir in the lemon juice and taste for sweetness, adding more sugar if needed. Refrigerate in a container for up to 4 days.

## FLAVORED OILS

Flavored oils are a great addition to dishes, imparting their own distinct flavor—from fairly mild turmeric to more pronounced beet—while complementing the other elements in the dish. We like to infuse oil with fresh herbs that are especially delicate, such as basil, which burn if overheated. The flavored oil is then used for finishing a dish rather than for cooking. We also like to flavor oil with lobster, tomato, or spices, such as turmeric or curry, to use both for finishing dishes and for cooking. For easy use, I store the oils in squeeze bottles. It's important to store all flavored oils in the refrigerator, because the infused essence requires chilling to stay fresh. Spice-infused oils keep longer but should still be used within a few weeks. It's a good idea to put a date on the bottle so you know when its time is up.

## BASIL OIL

**MAKES ABOUT 1½ CUPS /** This is a great use for basil that is starting to wilt a bit and no longer in prime form for garnishing a plate but still has plenty of flavor. We also make chive oil, following the same technique. Blanch the chives for just 15 seconds and chop them a little more finely before blending to prevent the chives from wrapping around the blender blades.

1 ounce fresh basil leaves (about 1⅓ cups loosely packed)

2 cups canola oil

Trim away the stems from the basil leaves. Bring a saucepan of salted water to a boil and prepare a bowl of ice water. Add the basil to the boiling water and blanch until tender but still bright green, 30 to 60 seconds. Drain well and plunge the basil into the ice water to chill it quickly and thoroughly. Drain again and pat dry with paper towels.

Coarsely chop the blanched basil and put in a blender with the canola oil. Blend at high speed until very thoroughly puréed, at least 10 minutes. If the base of the blender jar becomes warm, turn off the blender and place the base of the jar in a bowl of cool water to cool it down, then dry it off well and continue blending. The extended blending will give the oil the maximum basil flavor possible. At Rover's we blend for as long as 20 minutes.

Let the blended basil sit for at least 1 hour (or preferably overnight in the refrigerator), then drain through a fine-mesh sieve lined with cheesecloth into a bowl. Let the oil drain through slowly and naturally (it will take about 2 hours; don't press on the solids). The remaining basil pulp can be used for pesto or added to tomato sauce, though it won't be as boldly flavored as fresh basil. Transfer the oil to a clean squeeze bottle or other sealed container and refrigerate for up to 2 weeks.

# TOMATO OIL

**MAKES ABOUT 1¹/₂ CUPS /** This recipe requires 4 to 5 hours of roasting to infuse the oil with the flavor of the tomato and accompanying aromatics. The results are delicious, however, and leave you with very flavorful solids that can be puréed (pick out the herb sprigs) and used as a spread, as you would ketchup, or in pasta dishes or other recipes. When fresh tomatoes aren't at their best, you can use drained and chopped top-quality canned tomatoes.

2 tablespoons olive oil

1 large carrot, peeled and chopped

1 large celery stalk, chopped

¹/₂ onion, chopped

3 cloves garlic, minced

¹/₂ teaspoon black peppercorns

2¹/₂ cups chopped plum tomatoes
    (about 1¹/₄ pounds)

2 cans (6 ounces each) tomato paste

3 thyme sprigs

2 bay leaves, preferably fresh, partly torn

2 cups peanut or canola oil

Preheat the oven to 275°F.

Heat the olive oil in a large ovenproof sauté pan over medium heat. Add the carrot, celery, onion, garlic, and peppercorns. Sauté until the vegetables are tender, aromatic, and lightly browned, 5 to 7 minutes. Add the plum tomatoes, tomato paste, thyme sprigs, and bay leaves, stirring to combine, then carefully stir in the oil.

Transfer the sauté pan to the oven and roast the mixture, stirring occasionally, until it has a deep brick-red color and pronounced aroma, 4 to 5 hours. Transfer the mixture to a fine-mesh sieve lined with cheesecloth set over a bowl and let the oil drain through slowly and naturally (it will take about 2 hours; don't press on the solids). Transfer the oil to a clean squeeze bottle or other sealed container and refrigerate for up to 2 weeks.

## TURMERIC OIL

**MAKES ABOUT ³/₄ CUP /** Most of the flavored oils we use at Rover's are finishing oils meant to be tossed with ingredients or drizzled across a dish just before serving. In the case of turmeric oil, however, we also use it for sautéing. Because it needs to be heat tolerant, it's important to use peanut oil, which has a high smoke point and doesn't become bitter. If the turmeric in your cupboard is over a year old, now would be a good time to replace it with a fresh jar. This same technique can be used with curry powder to make curry oil.

1 tablespoon ground turmeric

1 cup peanut oil

Put the turmeric in a small saucepan and slowly drizzle in the oil, whisking constantly to blend. Warm the oil over medium heat, whisking often, until an instant-read thermometer reaches 95°F or so, which will take 3 to 5 minutes. Remove the pan from the heat and let sit for at least 1 hour, without stirring, so the solids settle to the bottom of the bowl. Pour the oil through a paper coffee filter into a bowl. (Or decant the oil by pouring it off into another bowl, leaving all the solids behind in the bottom of the first bowl.) If you find that some solids have collected in the bottom of the second bowl, repeat the decanting until the oil is completely clear. Transfer the oil to a clean squeeze bottle or other sealed container and refrigerate for up to 2 weeks.

## RED OR YELLOW BELL PEPPER OIL

**MAKES ABOUT 1 CUP**

1 red or yellow bell pepper, cored, seeded, and coarsely chopped

³/₄ cup extra virgin olive oil

Put the bell pepper in a small saucepan and add enough cold water to just cover. Bring the water to a boil over high heat, then decrease the heat to medium and cook until most of the water has evaporated, about 30 minutes. Set aside to cool, then transfer the bell pepper to a blender. Add the olive oil and blend until very smooth, 1 to 2 minutes. Drain the oil through a fine-mesh sieve lined with cheesecloth into a bowl, letting the oil drain through slowly and naturally (it will take about 2 hours; don't press on the solids). Transfer the oil to a clean squeeze bottle or other sealed container and refrigerate for up to 2 weeks.

## BEET OR CARROT OIL

**MAKES ABOUT 1 CUP**

1/2 pound beets, scrubbed, or carrots, scrubbed

1 cup olive oil

Put the beets or carrots in a saucepan of cold salted water and bring to a boil over high heat. Decrease the heat to medium and simmer until the vegetables are tender, about 1 1/4 hours for beets, 25 minutes for carrots. When cooked, drain the beets or carrots well and let cool until easy to handle. Slip off the skins, trim the vegetables, and coarsely chop. Purée the beets or carrots with the oil in a blender until very smooth, 3 to 5 minutes. Drain the oil through a fine-mesh sieve lined with cheesecloth into a bowl, letting the oil drain through slowly and naturally (it will take about 2 hours; don't press on the solids). Transfer the oil to a clean squeeze bottle or other sealed container and refrigerate for up to 2 weeks.

## LOBSTER OIL

**MAKES ABOUT 2 1/2 CUPS /** This oil is the ideal garnish for soup, for drizzling around the Corn Flan with Lobster (page 84), or for stirring into rich mashed potatoes just before serving. The meaty insides of the lobster heads can be used for Lobster Stock (page 209) if you like.

Shells from 2 to 3 lobsters (tails, claws, and carapace)

About 3 cups canola oil

Preheat the oven to 375°F.

Rinse and drain the lobster shells and put them in a baking dish. Roast the shells until they have a toasty aroma and are quite dry, 20 to 25 minutes. Transfer the shells to a saucepan and crush them with the back of a large ladle, the blunt end of a rolling pin, or the bottom of a small pot. Add enough canola oil to just cover the shells and warm the oil over medium heat until an instant-read thermometer reaches about 200°F, 2 to 3 minutes. Remove the pan from the heat and let sit at room temperature for at least 4 hours or up to overnight (refrigerated), covering the pan with its lid or a clean kitchen towel when the oil has cooled to room temperature. Strain the oil through a fine-mesh sieve lined with cheesecloth into a bowl. Transfer the oil to a clean squeeze bottle or other sealed container and refrigerate for up to 2 weeks.

# THYME BRIOCHE

**MAKES 1 LOAF /** This Rover's staple is used for a wide variety of dishes, including amuses bouches (topped with olive tapenade or smoked salmon), Terrine of Sonoma Valley Foie Gras with Sauternes Aspic and Thyme Brioche (page 60), and Dungeness Crab Salad with Garlic, Roasted Shallots, and Pomegranate Vinaigrette (page 33). The brioche also makes tasty crumbs when you have leftovers that are on the dry side. The secret to making a perfect loaf is in the proofing (rising time), which is a critical part of this recipe. If the dough is underproofed, it will be overly dense, while if it is overproofed, the brioche will have too light a texture and not be sturdy enough to work with.

We bake our brioche in a cylindrical form, so the finished loaf can be easily sliced into rounds for serving. You can instead bake the brioche in a traditional loaf pan, then slice the bread and cut it into rounds using a cookie cutter.

1/4 cup warm water (105° to 110°F)

2 envelopes (4 1/2 teaspoons) active dry yeast

3 large eggs plus 1 egg yolk

1 tablespoon sugar

1 1/2 teaspoons plus a pinch of sea salt

2 3/4 cups all-purpose flour, sifted

1/2 cup (1 stick) unsalted butter, cut into small cubes, at room temperature

2 tablespoons minced fresh thyme

2 teaspoons cold water

Put the warm water in a small bowl, sprinkle the yeast over, and set side until the yeast has dissolved and the mixture is frothy, about 5 minutes. Combine the 3 eggs, sugar, 1 1/2 teaspoons of the salt, and the yeast mixture in the bowl of a stand mixer fitted with the paddle attachment and mix at low speed until evenly blended. Gradually add the flour, switching to the dough hook when about half of the flour has been added. Continue beating at medium speed until the dough is perfectly smooth, very elastic, and pulls away from the side of the bowl, 20 to 25 minutes.

Gradually add the butter pieces to the dough, then the thyme, and continue beating until both are fully incorporated and the dough is satiny, 10 to 15 minutes longer, scraping the bowl a few times as needed. Transfer the dough to a lightly oiled ceramic or glass bowl, turning to coat evenly. Cover the bowl with a clean kitchen towel and set aside in a warm spot (such as near the stove) until doubled in bulk, about 45 minutes.

Lightly butter a 9- by 5-inch loaf pan or an 11- by 3-inch terrine mold. Punch down the dough and shape it into a cylinder the same length as the pan and of even thickness throughout (so it will rise and bake evenly); set it in the prepared pan. Cover and set aside in a warm spot until doubled in bulk, about 1 hour.

Meanwhile, preheat the oven to 350°F.

Bake the brioche for 25 minutes. Beat the egg yolk with the cold water and the remaining pinch of salt in a small bowl until blended, then brush over the top of the brioche. Continue baking until the bread has nicely browned, 5 to 10 minutes longer. Unmold the brioche onto a wire rack to cool completely (at least an hour) before slicing. Wrap well in plastic to store. The brioche will keep for a few days at room temperature, or freeze it for up to a few weeks.

## CRÈME ANGLAISE

MAKES ABOUT 1²/₃ CUPS

1 vanilla bean, split lengthwise

³/₄ cup whole milk

³/₄ cup heavy cream

¹/₃ cup sugar

3 large egg yolks

Scrape the tiny seeds from the vanilla bean by running the back of a knife blade down the length of each bean half. Combine the milk, cream, and vanilla bean and seeds in a heavy saucepan and bring just to a low boil over medium-high heat. Whisk the sugar and egg yolks together in a bowl until thoroughly blended and pale yellow. Slowly add the hot milk mixture, whisking constantly and starting with a thin drizzle, to warm the egg yolks gently, which helps avoid curdling.

Set the bowl over a pan of simmering, not boiling, water and cook, stirring with a wooden spoon, until the mixture thickens enough to coat the back of the spoon (a path should remain clear when you run your finger across the back of the spoon), 8 to 10 minutes. Strain the sauce through a fine-mesh sieve into a bowl; discard the vanilla bean. Prepare a larger bowl of ice water; set the bowl of crème anglaise in it so it cools quickly, stirring occasionally. When fully cooled, cover the crème anglaise with plastic wrap and refrigerate for up to 3 days.

## CRÈME PÂTISSIÈRE (PASTRY CREAM)

MAKES ABOUT 2¹/₂ CUPS

2 cups whole milk

¹/₂ vanilla bean, split lengthwise, or ¹/₂ teaspoon pure vanilla extract

¹/₂ cup sugar

4 large egg yolks

¹/₃ cup all-purpose flour, sifted

Combine the milk and vanilla bean (if using extract, it will be added later) in a small heavy saucepan and bring just to a boil over medium-high heat. Whisk the sugar and egg yolks together in a bowl until thoroughly blended and pale yellow. Whisk in the flour until well blended.

Slowly add the hot milk mixture to the egg yolk mixture, whisking constantly and starting with a thin drizzle, to warm the egg yolks gently, which helps avoid curdling. Return the mixture to the saucepan and cook over medium heat, whisking constantly, until it has thickened and there is no raw flour taste, 5 to 7 minutes. Transfer the pastry cream to a bowl. Remove the vanilla bean halves and run them between your thumb and forefinger to remove as many of the tiny flavorful seeds as possible and add to the pastry cream (or add the vanilla extract, if using). Set the pastry cream aside until fully cooled, then cover with plastic wrap and refrigerate for up to 3 days.

# TUILE COOKIES

**MAKES 3 TO 4 DOZEN COOKIES (DEPENDING ON THE SIZE AND SHAPE) /** Tuile cookies can be turned into a wide variety of shapes. After being baked into circles, they can be kept flat or formed into a curved shape reminiscent of the roof tiles for which the cookies were named. To do this, the still-warm cookie rounds are draped over a rolling pin until cool and set. You have to work quickly to accomplish this before the cookies harden. But if they do, a couple of minutes back in the oven will soften them up. You can also drape the warm cookies over upside-down small ramekins or custard cups, gently pressing the cookies against the sides of the dishes to shape them into softly ruffled cups. The cookie cups become elegant, edible dishes in which to serve mousse, ice cream, or fresh berries with a dab of whipped cream.

Cookie circles can be formed freehand. For more elaborate forms, such as stars, leaves, or crescents, it's easy to make a simple template. Use the large plastic top from a yogurt or other similar container (trim the outer rim from the lid), or a plastic sheet from an office supply store (just be sure to wash it before using). Use the tip of an Exacto knife or small scissors to cut out the desired shape carefully from the center of the plastic, then use a small offset spatula to spread the tuile batter thinly and evenly onto the template.

2 large egg whites

$1/2$ cup sugar

4 tablespoons unsalted butter, at room temperature

$1/2$ vanilla bean, split lengthwise

$1/2$ cup all-purpose flour, sifted

Whip the egg whites in a large bowl until frothy, then gradually add $1/4$ cup of the sugar and continue whisking until the sugar dissolves and the egg whites form soft peaks. Combine the butter and the remaining $1/4$ cup of sugar in the bowl of a stand mixer fitted with the paddle attachment and beat at medium speed until well blended. Run the back of a knife blade down the length of the vanilla-bean halves to scrape out the tiny vanilla seeds and add them to the butter mixture. Fold in the egg whites just until evenly blended, then fold in the flour. Refrigerate the tuile batter for at least 1 hour before baking.

Meanwhile, preheat the oven to 350°F. Line a heavy baking sheet with a silicone baking mat or parchment.

Using an offset spatula, spread the tuile batter into the desired shape on the prepared baking sheet with about 1 inch between them. Bake until the edges of the cookies are just beginning to turn brown and the centers are firm, 5 to 7 minutes. Using a metal spatula, immediately lift the cookies from the sheet and drape them over a rolling pin to cool (or transfer to a wire rack to cool flat). When the cookies are set, transfer them to a wire rack to cool completely. Repeat with the remaining batter. Store in an airtight container until ready to serve. Tuile cookies are at their best when baked just a few hours before serving, though the batter can be made a day in advance.

## PÂTE BRISÉE (PASTRY DOUGH)

**MAKES ABOUT 1¼ POUNDS DOUGH /** This recipe makes enough dough for two 9-inch tarts or about sixteen 3-inch tartlets. Any extra dough can be well wrapped in plastic wrap and frozen for up to 2 weeks; thaw in the refrigerator.

2 cups all-purpose flour, sifted

1 teaspoon sea salt

½ cup (1 stick) unsalted butter, cut into pieces and chilled

2 large egg yolks

6 tablespoons ice water, plus more if needed

Combine the flour and salt in a food processor and pulse once or twice to blend. Add the butter and pulse until the mixture has the texture of coarse sand, then add the egg yolks and pulse twice to incorporate. Gradually add the water, pulsing as you go. Pinch some of the dough between your fingers to check its texture; if still dry and dusty, add another 2 to 3 teaspoons of water. The dough should hold its shape when pinched. Be sure not to overmix the dough or it will become tough. Alternatively, you can make the dough by hand: Combine the flour and salt in a bowl. Add the butter and use a pastry blender or your fingers to work the butter into the flour until the mixture is well blended and has a crumbly texture. Stir in the egg yolks with a wooden spoon, followed by the water—1 tablespoon at a time—just until the dough is cohesive and no longer dry, but not sticky either. Turn the dough out onto a lightly floured work surface and gently press down on it with the heel of your hand to help fully blend in the ingredients. Shape the dough into a disk, wrap in plastic wrap, and refrigerate for at least 1 hour.

## PÂTE SUCRÉE (SWEET PASTRY DOUGH)

**MAKES ABOUT 1¼ POUNDS DOUGH /** This dough is supple and easy to work with. If your kitchen's quite warm, however, you might need to take extra care to keep the dough chilled while rolling it out. Be sure to refrigerate it until firm, then work quickly to roll it out. If the dough becomes too soft to work with, chill it for 10 or 15 minutes before continuing. You can also place a large rimmed baking sheet on the work surface and fill it with ice to chill down the surface before you roll out the dough. We roll dough out on a marble surface; it's a pastry chef's best tool for keeping cool, even in a warm kitchen. The dough makes enough for two 9-inch tarts or about sixteen 3-inch tartlets. Any extra dough can be well wrapped in plastic wrap and frozen for up to 2 weeks; thaw in the refrigerator.

½ cup (1 stick) unsalted butter, at room temperature

¾ cup confectioners' sugar, sifted

2 large eggs

2 cups all-purpose flour

Pinch of sea salt

Cream the butter and sugar together in the bowl of a stand mixer fitted with the paddle attachment. Add the eggs, one at a time, incorporating each one well before adding the next, and scraping down the side of the bowl as needed. Whisk the flour and salt together in a small bowl and add to the batter in 3 batches, decreasing the mixer speed to low to blend evenly. Cut the dough in half, shape each portion into a disk, and wrap in plastic wrap. Refrigerate for at least 1 hour before rolling out.

# PÂTE FEUILLETÉE
# (PUFF PASTRY)

**MAKES ABOUT 1 1/2 POUNDS DOUGH /** This dough is one of the hallmarks of French cuisine and is used to make the layered dessert known as *mille-feuille* ("a thousand leaves"). Puff pastry is wonderfully versatile; it can be cut into rounds, topped with fresh fruit (such as slices of apple or plum) and baked, or turned into the elegant dessert known as pithiviers, in which an almond-paste filling is encased in 2 rounds of the dough. The pastry also has savory uses. For a simple and delicious cocktail snack, cut the dough into 1/2-inch-wide strips, brush with an egg wash, and sprinkle with grated Parmesan or poppy seeds. Gently twist the strips to make spirals, bake at 400°F until puffed and crisp, and serve.

Puff pastry is not complicated to make. In fact, it is a rather simple dough that is layered with softened butter. More involved is the careful rolling technique that ensures the even layering of the dough and butter and a solid time commitment to achieve the "turns" that create the thousand leaves effect.

2 cups all-purpose flour, sifted

1 teaspoon sea salt

1 teaspoon sugar

1/2 cup cold water, plus more if needed

1 cup (2 sticks) cold unsalted butter, plus 2 teaspoons unsalted butter, melted

Combine the flour, salt, and sugar in the bowl of a stand mixer fitted with the paddle attachment. Blend at low speed just to mix, then add 1/2 cup of water and the melted butter and blend at medium-low speed just to form a smooth dough; avoid overmixing, which would develop the gluten in the dough and make it harder to roll out. Form the dough into a ball, wrap in plastic wrap, and refrigerate for 1 hour.

Roll out the dough on a lightly floured work surface into an 8-inch square. Gently pound the cold butter between 2 pieces of plastic wrap or waxed paper with a rolling pin to form a square about 5 inches across. Set the butter square in the center of the dough at a 90-degree angle to the sides of the dough (the corners of the butter square should be pointed at the sides, not the corners, of the dough). Fold the corners of the dough down and over the butter so the points meet in the center, completely enclosing the butter. Gently pinch the seams together to seal the dough edges.

Lightly flour the dough and roll it out into a rectangle about 3 times longer than it is wide. It's important to roll the dough only in an even forward motion, not side to side or at an angle, so the butter is evenly distributed within the dough. It is also important that the dough be lightly and consistently floured on the bottom and top to avoid sticking. Keep in mind, however, that too much flour will make the dough dry and heavy; brush away the excess before folding the dough. Fold the bottom third of the dough up and the top third down, just like you would fold a letter. This technique of rolling and folding the dough is called a "turn." Repeat another turn, rolling the dough out so it is 3 times longer than it is wide and then fold like a letter. Wrap the dough loosely in plastic and refrigerate for about 30 minutes. Give the dough 2 more turns and refrigerate again for 30 minutes. Follow with another 2 turns, and chill again for 30 minutes. Give the dough a seventh and final turn. At this point, the dough can be refrigerated for up to 4 days or frozen for up to 2 weeks.

# LADYFINGERS

**MAKES ABOUT 2 DOZEN** / Ladyfingers are a classic French pastry. These fingerlike strips are traditionally used to line charlotte molds to enclose a variety of fillings, such as in the Honey Mousse Charlotte with Rhubarb Purée (page 178). But sometimes I like to break with tradition and pipe the batter into squares or rounds to use for any number of layered desserts.

1/2 cup cornstarch

1/2 cup all-purpose flour

3 large eggs, separated

1/2 cup granulated sugar

1/4 teaspoon finely grated lemon zest

1/8 teaspoon freshly squeezed lemon juice

1 tablespoon confectioners' sugar

Set 2 oven racks in the middle of the oven and preheat the oven to 350°F. Line 2 baking sheets with parchment paper.

Sift the cornstarch and flour together into a bowl and set aside. Whip the egg yolks with 1/4 cup of the granulated sugar until thick and pale yellow, then whisk in the lemon zest and juice. In another bowl (or in a stand mixer fitted with the whip attachment), whip the egg whites until they are fluffy and very soft peaks form, then gradually sprinkle the remaining 1/4 cup of granulated sugar over, whisking constantly, until glossy and soft peaks form. Fold the beaten egg whites into the egg yolk mixture, then fold in the cornstarch-flour mixture, in 2 batches, until blended.

Transfer the batter to a large piping bag fitted with a large plain tip. Put a tiny dab of the batter under the corners of the parchment paper on each baking sheet to hold it down securely. Pipe the batter into fingers about 1 inch wide and 4 inches long, leaving about 2 inches between them. Put the confectioners' sugar in a small sieve and lightly dust the tops of the ladyfingers with the sugar. Bake the ladyfingers until they are puffed and lightly browned, 12 to 15 minutes, switching the positions of the pans halfway through the baking.

Let the ladyfingers cool on the baking sheets, then carefully peel them away from the parchment paper. Store in an airtight container for up to 2 days.

## BUTTER COOKIES

This trio of butter cookie variations—hazelnut, lemon, and chocolate—is delightfully versatile. The dough can be cut into any number of shapes or sizes to match the way they'll be served. The cookies can also have a functional role, serving as the base for delicate desserts such as the Black and White Chocolate Mousse (page 184). The cookies can also be served with coffee or as an afternoon snack. The dough can be frozen for up to 1 week if you want to save a portion for later use. Make sure the dough is well wrapped in a couple of layers of plastic wrap, and allow the dough to thaw in the refrigerator for a few hours before rolling it out.

## HAZELNUT BUTTER COOKIES

MAKES 2 TO 4 DOZEN (DEPENDING ON THE SIZE AND SHAPE) / You could also use toasted and ground almonds or pecans if you like.

1 cup finely ground toasted hazelnuts (page 234)

1/2 cup (1 stick) unsalted butter, at room temperature

1/3 cup sugar

1 1/4 cups all-purpose flour, sifted

Combine the nuts, butter, and sugar in the bowl of a mixer fitted with the paddle attachment and beat at medium speed until well blended. Decrease the mixer speed to medium-low and gradually add the flour, blending until the mixture forms a smooth dough.

Shape the dough into 2 disks and wrap each in plastic wrap. Refrigerate until firm, at least 30 minutes.

Preheat the oven to 350°F. Line 2 baking sheets with silicone baking mats or parchment paper.

Set one of the dough disks on a lightly floured work surface and let sit for a few minutes to soften slightly. Roll out the dough to a thickness of about 1/16 inch. Using a small knife or cookie cutters, cut the dough into the desired shape. Arrange the cookies on the prepared baking sheets, placing them about 1 inch apart. Bake until the cookies are firm and lightly browned around the edges, 8 to 10 minutes. Let the cookies sit on the baking sheets for a few minutes, then carefully transfer them to a wire rack to cool completely. Repeat with any remaining dough.

## CHOCOLATE BUTTER COOKIES

MAKES 2 TO 4 DOZEN (DEPENDING ON THE SIZE
AND SHAPE)

1 cup all-purpose flour

2 tablespoons unsweetened cocoa powder

$1/2$ vanilla bean, split lengthwise, or $1/8$ teaspoon pure
    vanilla extract

$1/2$ cup (1 stick) unsalted butter, at room temperature

$1/3$ cup confectioner' sugar, sifted

Sift the flour and cocoa powder together into a small
bowl and set aside. Scrape the tiny seeds from the
vanilla bean by running the back of a knife blade
down the length of each bean half. Combine the
butter, confectioners' sugar, and vanilla seeds in the
bowl of a stand mixer fitted with the paddle attachment and beat at medium speed until well blended.
Decrease the mixer speed to medium-low and gradually add the flour mixture, blending until the mixture
forms a smooth dough.

Shape the dough into 2 disks and wrap each in plastic
wrap. Refrigerate until firm, at least 30 minutes. Proceed as directed for the Hazelnut Butter Cookies.

## LEMON BUTTER COOKIES

MAKES 3 TO 5 DOZEN (DEPENDING ON THE SIZE
AND SHAPE)

1 cup confectioners' sugar, sifted

$3/4$ cup ($1 1/2$ sticks) unsalted butter,
    at room temperature

1 large egg

1 teaspoon finely grated lemon zest

1 tablespoon freshly squeezed lemon juice

$1/2$ teaspoon pure vanilla extract

$1/4$ teaspoon pure lemon extract (optional)

2 cups all-purpose flour, sifted

Combine the confectioners' sugar and butter in the
bowl of a stand mixer fitted with the paddle attachment and beat at medium speed until well blended.
Add the egg, lemon zest and juice, vanilla extract and
lemon extract, if using, and continue beating until
evenly mixed. Decrease the mixer speed to medium-
low and gradually add the flour, blending until the
mixture forms a smooth dough.

Shape the dough into 2 disks and wrap each in plastic
wrap. Refrigerate until firm, at least 30 minutes. Proceed as directed for the Hazelnut Butter Cookies.

# Resources & Techniques

## PURVEYORS

### ChefShop
Seattle, Washington
www.chefshop.com • (877) 337-2491

This is a great source for hard-to-find ingredients such as Pedro Ximenez noble sour, gourmet salts (including fleur de sel), interesting vinegars, snails, oils, honeys, jams, olives, nuts, dried beans, and lentils, as well as a huge list of other gourmet products.

### Corfini Gourmet
San Francisco, California
www.corfinigourmet.com • (415) 613-4572

Here is my source for Iranian saffron, Mighty Leaf teas, beautiful foie gras, wild game, and sweetbreads. They also carry a plethora of truffle products. Although they are primarily a wholesale supplier, Corfini is happy to take consumer calls and will do their best to accommodate your ordering needs.

### D'Artagnan
Newark, New Jersey
www.dartagnan.com • (800) 327-8246

D'Artagnan carries a huge selection of duck products, including foie gras, confit, fat, tongues, prosciutto, and breasts; other poultry, including Scottish wood pigeon, pheasant, squab, and quail; and other meats and game, including wild boar, organic bacon, caul fat (crépine), and frogs' legs. They also sell chestnuts, truffles, and wild mushrooms.

### Don and Joe's Meats
Seattle, Washington • (206) 682-7670

In addition to the more common cuts of beef, veal, lamb, pork, and chicken, this Pike Place Market butcher also carries (or can special order) less common items, such as lambs' tongues, kidneys, sweetbreads, oxtail, and pigs' feet, as well as duck, rabbit, quail, and goose.

### FrancVin
New York, New York
(212) 679-4674 or (888) 876-4300
www.amazon.com, then search on Gourmet Foods>FrancVin

They carry all sorts of wonderful vinegars, including honey thyme, champagne, red wine, marine cider, raspberry, cherry, and sherry; interesting spices such as the pain d'epice blend; French cold-pressed olive oils, sesame oil, and almond oil; Pedro Ximenez noble sour; and top-quality soy sauce. They do a little retail business out of their New York location; otherwise, your best bet is Amazon.com.

### Full Circle Farms
Carnation, Washington
www.fullcirclefarm.com • (425) 333-4677

One of my key sources for vegetables and herbs, this 100-plus acre certified organic farm is just northwest of Seattle. They offer a CSA (Community Supported Agriculture) program for local customers, sell produce at farmers' markets, and supply chefs in the area.

### Gerard & Dominique Seafood
Bothell, Washington
www.gourmetseafoods.com • (425) 488-4766

This is the salmon to use when my recipes call for cold-smoked (lox-style) salmon. I specifically purchase their smoked wild salmon; you should ask for that as well. They also make terrific hot-smoked salmon and other seafood products. Here in the Northwest, their seafood can be found at top-quality grocers, but you can order it online from their Web site, too.

### J. B. Prince
New York, New York
www.jbprince.com • (800) 473-0577

This is the place to go for all the wonderful professional chef's tools that help make food look beautiful. They carry an enormous selection of cutters, molds, and utensils, and they also have terrines, knives, and cookware.

### Klipsun
Red Mountain, Benton County, Washington
www.klipsun.com • (509) 967-3395

You can order Klipsun Vineyards verjus directly by e-mailing them at verjus@klipsun.com. Their verjus is sold in a few retail outlets around Seattle, Portland, Bellingham, Spokane, and Walla Walla, but they don't produce much of it, so it can be hard to find.

### Monteillet Cheese
Dayton, Washington • (509) 382-1917

Pierre-Louis and Joan Monteillet make fresh artisanal goat and sheep cheeses at their *fromagerie* in Eastern Washington. You can order by telephone, and they'll ship the cheese to you.

### Mustapha Gourmet Imports
Seattle, Washington
www.mustaphas.com • (800) 481-4590

I use a number of Mustapha's products, including their extra virgin olive oil, argan oil, and olive tapenade. They also carry preserved lemons, capers, harissa, and a huge variety of olives. You can order online, and some of their products are available in grocery stores.

### Mutual Fish
Seattle, Washington
www.mutualfish.com • (206) 322-4368

Owned and operated by three generations of the Yoshimura family since 1947, Mutual Fish carries the most incredible fresh seafood. They specialize in all types of Northwest seafood, both fish (halibut, salmon, sturgeon, tuna, yellow eye snapper) and shellfish (Penn Cove mussels, spot prawns, Alaskan scallops), but also source from the East Coast (turbot, wild striped sea bass, monkfish, lobster) and they ship overnight.

### Niman Ranch
Oakland, California
www.nimanranch.com • (866) 808-0340

Famous for their top-quality, hormone-free meats, Niman Ranch supplies me with bacon and pork belly. You can purchase beef (from cheeks to oxtails and every part in between), pork (including hams, shoulders, and tails), and lamb (racks and roasts, tongues, kidneys, and more) from their Web site.

### Penn Cove Organics
Whidbey Island, Washington • (360) 240-8125

Penn Cove Organics sells its produce primarily through an 80-member CSA (Community Supported Agriculture) program, but I am lucky enough to get some wonderful organic vegetables from them, including fava beans, lettuces, haricots verts, squash, and herbs. They also grow nuts, apples, and pears, and sell small quantities of chicken and duck eggs.

### Pike Place Market Creamery
Seattle, Washington • (206) 622-5029

This Pike Place Market institution carries lots of local organic dairy, including cream, milk, butter, crème fraîche, and yogurt, as well as farm-fresh eggs, including duck, chicken, and quail.

### Quillisascut Cheese

Rice, Washington

www.quillisascutcheese.com • (509) 738-2011

Their cheeses are available at PCC Natural Markets, Whole Foods, and other stores in the Seattle area with top-quality cheese selections. If you call, they can direct you to a retail location in your area, if available.

### Seattle Caviar

Seattle, Washington

www.caviar.com • (206) 323-3005

I'm fortunate to have a resource like Seattle Caviar so nearby. Owner Dale Sherrow delivers products to me, including the domestic white sturgeon caviar I use most, the occasional treat of some Iranian golden osetra caviar, and sometimes samples of other recently arrived caviars that he'd like me to taste. Customers can enjoy samples at their store. Seattle Caviar also sells foie gras (fresh lobes as well as cooked products) and truffles (winter white and black truffles from Europe), as well as accoutrements for such gourmet delights.

### Select Gourmet Foods

Kenmore, Washington

www.selectgourmetfoods.com • (206) 528-0332

A wonderful specialty food source that sells foie gras, quail, squab, pheasant, specialty oils, natural and organic beef, venison, and buffalo. They will ship anywhere in the U.S.

### Sosio's Produce

Seattle, Washington • (206) 622-1370

Located in the Pike Place Market, Sosio's carries all types of local, seasonal fruits and vegetables. I get the most wonderful peaches from them, lots of herbs, wild mushrooms, and, on occasion, such specialties as ramps (wild leeks). They'll even ship the best of our Northwest seasonal produce pretty much anywhere you happen to be.

### Sur La Table

www.surlatable.com • (800) 243-0852

Sur La Table carries everything you can think of for the kitchen. You can request a catalog, shop online, or visit one of their stores (which now criss-cross the country, though the original store is found in Seattle's own Pike Place Market).

### Uwajimaya

Seattle, Washington

www.uwajimaya.com • (206) 624-6248

A large Asian supermarket established in Seattle and now with a few outlets in the Northwest, Uwajimaya is a great source for otherwise hard-to-find ingredients, such as quail eggs, sea urchin roe, and sea beans. They also carry a wide variety of Northwest seafood, specialty meats, and every Asian ingredient you can think of.

### World Merchants Spice, Herb, and Tea House

Seattle, Washington

www.worldspice.com • (206) 682-7274

Tony Hill travels the world seeking out the best and most interesting spices, herbs, and teas, then brings them back to his shop just behind the Pike Place Market. Tony's recent book, *The Contemporary Encyclopedia of Herbs & Spices: Seasonings for the Global Kitchen*, is a great resource. When you're looking for hibiscus flowers and saffron, this is the place to go, in person or when ordering online.

# GLOSSARY OF INGREDIENTS AND TECHNIQUES

### Artichokes, *to prepare the bottoms*

Break the stem from the base by holding the artichoke firmly on its side on the work surface with one hand and pressing down hard on the stem with the heel of your other hand. Pull away and discard a few of the outer layers of leaves, taking care to avoid pricking your fingers with the thorns. Turn the artichoke upside down and, using a small sharp paring knife, begin trimming away the tough outer green parts, turning the artichoke as you go, and working from the bottom to the outer edges. When you get up to where the artichoke bottom gives way to the base of the tender leaves, stop and rub the exposed surface with the cut side of a lemon half. Holding the cone of remaining leaves in one hand, cut the leaves from the artichoke bottom about 1/4 inch up from where they meet. Rub the freshly cut surface of the artichoke bottom with lemon as well. Proceed as directed in the recipe.

### Bell Peppers, *to roast*

Roast the bell pepper(s) over a gas flame or on a rimmed baking sheet under the broiler until the skin blackens, turning occasionally to roast evenly, about 10 minutes total. Put the pepper in a large bowl, cover securely with plastic wrap, and set aside to cool. When cool enough to handle, peel away and discard the skin. Remove the core and seeds and proceed as directed in the recipe. Do not rinse the roasted peppers, as the oil on the surface contributes flavor.

### Butter, *to clarify*

Clarified butter—melted butter from which the milk solids have been removed—has a higher burning point than that of regular butter, making it a much better candidate for sautéing meats and other high-heat applications. I use two different methods, depending on how I plan to use the butter. It is easiest to make clarified butter in batches of 1 stick (1/2 cup) each, which will leave you with about 1/3 cup of clarified butter. Extra clarified butter can be refrigerated for up to 2 weeks.

Method #1. Melt the butter in a small saucepan over medium-low heat. When fully melted, use a small spoon to skim off the foamy white layer that forms on the surface. Slowly pour the melted butter into a small dish, leaving behind the solids that have collected in the bottom of the saucepan. This produces a neutral, mildly flavored clarified butter to use with vegetables, fish, and other mild foods.

Method #2. Melt the butter in a small saucepan over medium-low heat. When fully melted, use a small spoon to skim off the foamy white layer that forms on the surface. Continue to cook the melted butter over medium heat until the clarified butter takes on a slightly nutty color and aroma, 3 to 5 minutes longer. Slowly pour the melted butter into a small dish, leaving behind the solids that have collected in the bottom of the saucepan. This darker clarified butter is ideal for sautéing flavorful meats such as boar, venison, pork roast, lamb, or beef.

### Caviar

One elegant ingredient that is a mainstay at Rover's is caviar, the topping for our signature scrambled egg appetizer (page 89) and the final flourish for many other dishes. I've used different types of caviar over the years, but what I use most now is domestic white sturgeon caviar that is raised by Stolt Sea Farm outside Sacramento, California. This white sturgeon (*Acipenser transmontanus*), a prehistoric freshwater fish found along much of the West Coast, is a close cousin to the fish swimming in the Caspian Sea, source of the long-celebrated Russian and Iranian caviars. These traditional sources for caviar have become scarcer in recent years, due in part to over-fishing and leading to inconsistent quality and availability. The quality of the domestic caviar I use is so high that I'm able to offer my customers outstanding flavor and texture with a product that is more sustainable than the caviar from the Caspian Sea and that also supports a domestic producer. On occasion, I still buy some Iranian golden osetra caviar for an over-the-top extravagance.

The delicate, lightly salted eggs are at their best served simply, spooned onto a canapé or used to garnish a dish just before it is served, as is the case with the spot prawn martini (page 56). For caviar lovers like me, the ultimate is enjoying the roe on a delicate spoon made of mother of pearl, right from the container, which is perched on shaved ice. There is one recipe in the book in which the caviar is added to a rich champagne sabayon and used to top oysters (page 98), the roe infusing the sabayon with its distinctive character—simply exquisite!

### *Crépine* (caul fat)

*Crépine* is the lining of a pig stomach. It is a wonderful lacey film of fat that is used to enclose delicate foods to hold them together for cooking—traditional uses include wrapping pâtés and forming veal *paupiettes*. Much of the *crépine* melts away during cooking, so it also contributes moisture to the dish. You might need to special order *crépine* from your butcher or contact Select Gourmet Foods (page 230). There is no substitute for it in recipes.

### Dungeness Crab, *to cook and shell*

For all our dishes that include Dungeness crabmeat, I begin with live crabs and cook them just before needed. The flavor is sweeter and the texture more delicate than that of the bulk crabmeat available in stores, though that certainly is a convenient alternative. Bring a very large pot of generously salted water to a rolling boil. Add the whole live crab and boil 5 minutes for a 2-pound crab, 4 minutes for a

1½-pound crab. Drain and let the crab cool. Clean the crab by first pulling off and discarding the carapace (top shell). Scoop out and discard the soft innards and rinse the crab well under cold running water. Pinch off and discard the feathery gills. Pull off the legs, bending them backward, then cut the body in half. Use a small mallet or crab crackers to crack the leg shells lightly, then lift out the meat with a nut pick or small fork. To remove the meat from the large claws, it helps to first remove the smaller jointed half of the claw, which contains cartilage that extends into the larger section of the claw. Bend back the joint and pull gently to remove the cartilage. Pick the meat from the body portion, peeling away the thin white membrane from the individual sections. You should get about ½ pound of picked crabmeat from a 2-pound crab.

### Fava Beans

Fava beans are one of those late-spring treats that are often available into the summer as well. The large broad bean pods have a soft, cottony interior that protects the tender beans. Smaller favas beans are ideal, as they are less starchy than the larger, more mature beans. Pull away the tough string that runs down the length of the pod, separate the pod halves, and remove the beans. Each bean is covered with a pale green skin that must be removed before cooking and serving. My preferred method is to peel them raw, using a small knife to make a shallow slit in the skin and then peel it away. Another easier option is to blanch the beans in a large pan of salted water for about 30 seconds, then quickly cool them in ice water. Drain well, pat dry, then slip off the skin, which will be very easy to do.

Two pounds of whole pods will generally yield about 2 cups (about ½ pound) of peeled beans.

### Foie Gras

Foie gras is one of the undisputed pinnacles of French cuisine, an ingredient that is incredibly rich and delicious and brings elegance to any meal. It is a regular element on Rover's menus, a great way for me to share a decadent slice of French culinary culture with my guests.

There are a number of methods we use for cooking foie gras at Rover's. The terrine (page 60) is a classic; the livers first are lightly marinated, then packed into a terrine mold and gently baked to a silky firmness. Foie gras cooked *au torchon* (wrapped in a clean towel and gently simmered) is another French tradition; the raw liver is rolled very tightly in a dish towel, poached gently in game consommé, then chilled for a day before serving. I also sometimes roast foie gras whole, for which we pre-sear the lobe in a heavy pan, mound heated rock salt around it, and then bake in a hot oven for about 20 minutes.

But by far the most common technique we use is pan-searing, which takes no more than a couple of minutes to accomplish. We often present seared foie gras as a centerpiece for a small, rich course that is typically served as the transition between lighter seafood courses and heavier meat dishes. Seared Hudson Valley Foie Gras with Nectarine Chutney and Verjus Sauce (page 78) is such an example. We also sear smaller pieces of foie gras to use as a garnish for many dishes. In these cases, the seared liver serves to complement the texture and flavor components of the rest of the dish. Consider the Red Pot au Feu on page 136, where a small slice of seared foie gras adds richness and serves as a foil for the earthy flavors of the root vegetables and truffle and the sweetness of the lobster.

To do justice to the technique of pan-searing, it is very important that the slices of foie gras are added to the skillet only after it is thoroughly heated over high heat. This is not a good technique for most non-stick skillets, because the surface of the pan can be damaged by that level of heat. You don't have to worry about sticking, though, because the natural fat from the liver contributes more than enough to ensure it doesn't stick. Be sure to choose a heavy-bottomed skillet that will absorb the heat well and distribute it evenly. A cast-iron skillet is a great option.

In the restaurant kitchen, we heat small heavy stainless steel skillets over high heat for 3 or 4 minutes before adding the slices of foie gras—which are first lightly scored with the tip of a knife for even cooking, and then salted. If the skillet is properly preheated, the liver will produce a good amount of smoke on contact. We have a very large hood over the burners that easily draws away all the smoke. (Although she is a devout fan of foie gras in all forms, my coauthor Cynthia found it a little challenging to match our Rover's technique in her home kitchen, since the volume of smoke produced overwhelmed her stove's hood.)

At home, you can put a lid on the skillet right after you add the foie gras slices, which will help temper the amount of smoke, though not eliminate it. Make sure you have good ventilation from a hood. Most down-draft ventilation systems won't be able to keep up, though, so my best recommendation would be to cook the foie gras outdoors, if at all possible. On some occasions, when cooking at a friend's house or in a customer's home, I will cook the foie gras in a preheated cast-iron skillet on an outdoor gas grill. The only possible remaining concern, perhaps, is the neighbors inviting themselves over for dinner.

Foie gras from New York's Hudson Valley is my favorite foie gras to pan-sear. These livers are quite densely and evenly fatty, which makes them an ideal candidate for cooking with high, direct heat. The fat immediately begins to melt away when in contact with the heat, which creates a richly browned crust on the surface, while the center remains tender and succulent.

We also use foie gras from California, Canada, and France, which are best for moist and gentle cooking techniques, such as poaching, cooking in terrines, and cooking *au torchon*. The texture of these products is a little softer and less dense, so the foie gras responds well to these cooking methods.

## Lobster, *to cook and shell*

Bring a very large pot of generously salted water to a boil. Add the lobster(s) and boil for $3^{1}/_{2}$- minutes. Drain the lobster and set aside until cool enough to handle. It is important to have a pot that is large enough to accommodate generously the number of lobsters you are cooking. If your pot is not very large, you may want to cook one lobster at a time.

Hold the cooled lobster tail in one hand and the body in the other and twist to separate them. Use kitchen shears to cut down along the membrane on the underside of the tail, then peel the shell back to remove the meat. Use a small mallet or crab crackers to crack gently the shell of the lobster claw and knuckle. We also use the back of a heavy kitchen knife to crack the shells, but whatever method you use, take care to crack the shells carefully without crushing the shell into the delicate meat; remove the meat from the shells with a nut pick or small fork. To remove the meat from the large claw section, it helps to first remove the smaller jointed half of the claw, which has cartilage that extends into the larger section of the claw. Bend back the joint and break it off, then pull gently to remove the long, narrow piece of cartilage. Reserve the shells, if you like, for Lobster Stock, (page 209) or Lobster Oil (page 219).

## Meat, *resting*

It's very important for roasted and seared meats to rest for a minimum of 10 minutes after being cooked. This prevents the meat's juices from seeping out when cut. The resting also allows the juices, which have been drawn into the center during cooking, to redistribute throughout the meat, making the meat more tender and moist. The larger the piece of meat, the longer the resting time; a large roast should rest for 20 to 25 minutes.

## Mussels and Clams

Both mussels and clams must be alive when cooked. The shells naturally gape a little when alive, but a gentle squeezing or tapping of the shells against the counter should make them close tightly. If it doesn't, the shellfish is dead and should be discarded, not cooked. Also discard any shells that are cracked or crushed.

Using the back of a small knife or a small stiff brush, scrub the mussel shells and cut away the threadlike beard that often protrudes from the shell (mussels use the beards to attach themselves to rocks, ropes, and pilings). Remove the beards at the last minute, however, because the mussels will begin to expire when the beard is removed.

About an hour before cooking fresh clams, fill a large bowl with cold water, add the clams, and let sit for about 5 minutes. Swish the clams around in the bowl with your hands and transfer them to a colander. Discard the water and any sand in the bowl and repeat once or twice until the water is no longer sandy.

## Nuts, *to toast*

Preheat the oven to 350°F. Scatter the nuts in a baking pan and toast until browned and aromatic, 5 to 7 minutes for pine nuts or walnuts, 12 to 15 minutes for large or dense nuts, such as hazelnuts or almonds. Gently shake the pan once or twice to help the nuts toast evenly.

To remove the skins from hazelnuts, transfer the hot toasted nuts to a clean kitchen towel, fold up the ends over the nuts, and let sit for a few minutes to cool slightly. Rub the nuts inside the towel to remove as much of the papery skins as you can before using.

When finely chopping or grinding nuts in a food processor, it is important to avoid overprocessing, as the nuts can turn from ground to "peanut butter" quickly. One helpful solution is to avoid chopping the nuts while still warm. It also helps to add a tablespoon or two of the flour (or sugar, though flour is best) from the recipe to the food processor to grind with the nuts to help keep the nuts from turning into a paste.

**Oranges and other citrus fruit,** *to segment*

Cut both ends off the orange (or other citrus), just to the flesh. Set the orange upright on a cutting board and use the knife to cut away the peel and pith, following the curve of the fruit. (Try not to cut away too much of the flesh with the peel.) Working over a bowl to catch the juice, hold the peeled orange in your hand and slide the knife down along each side of the membranes to release the sections, letting them fall into the bowl. (Pick out and discard any seeds as you go.) Squeeze the juice from the membrane core into the bowl.

**Pepper**

The Rover's kitchen has two different pepper grinders that get a good amount of use. Pepper is always freshly ground in my kitchen, and it should be in yours, too. Black pepper has a wonderful bold flavor that we use on all our meats and most of the poultry, while in stock, we like to use whole black peppercorns. Slightly milder white pepper is ideal with fish and vegetables, as well as in pale foods and delicate sauces where specks of black pepper would be unwelcome.

**Pomegranates,** *to juice*

Gently but firmly roll the pomegranate over the counter to help break up many of the tiny, juicy seed pockets inside. Using a small knife, cut a $1/2$-inch hole in the top (blossom end) of the fruit, then gently squeeze the fruit over a bowl to extract the juice through the hole. (Avoid squeezing too hard or the fruit will break apart.) Keep in mind that pomegranate juice really stains, so wipe up any spills right away. If you want to extract the maximum of juice from the fruit, break the pomegranate into quarters and remove the seeds into a heavy-duty strainer or sieve. Set the strainer over a large bowl and press on the seeds with the back of a large wooden spoon to extract the juice. You should be able to get about $1/2$ cup of juice from 1 large pomegranate. You could

instead use purchased 100% pomegranate juice, such as the POM brand.

**Quail Eggs**

There are always quail eggs in my kitchen; I use the tiny little eggs—often fried but also hard-boiled—when I want a striking, flavorful garnish for a variety of dishes. The small eggs are often sold in specialty food stores and butcher shops, though you might want to call ahead to check the availability. The thin shell is quite fragile, so rather than cracking the egg against a hard surface, I use a small knife to tap gently the side of the egg nearer the broad end, then separate the halves.

**Quenelles,** *how to form*

In classic French cooking, quenelles are a mousseline mixture made with *brochet* (pike), egg white, and cream, as with *quenelle nantua*, a classic dish from the Lyon region. The mixture is formed into small football-like shapes using 2 spoons, and then poached. Over the years, the word "quenelle" has come to be shorthand for the shape in which mousseline is classically shaped, rather than the recipe itself. For a fancy presentation, mousse, sorbet, ice cream, and other soft mixtures are often shaped into quenelles, and it's rather easy to do.

To form a quenelle, choose 2 spoons of the same size and shape. Scoop some of the mixture you are using into one of the spoons, enough so that it mounds generously. Place the second spoon over the mixture, facing in the opposite direction, and gently smooth the top of the mixture with the bowl of the second spoon. Slide a long edge of the second spoon under the mixture to scoop it neatly into the second spoon. Repeat the smoothing and scooping with the spoons 4 or 5 times, until a nice tidy football shape has been formed.

Depending on how thick or sticky the mixture is, you may want to lightly oil the spoons first—for savory mousses or goat cheese—or dip them into cold water—for ice cream or sorbet—before starting the shaping process.

## Salt

The primary salt I use for cooking is fine sea salt. There's a dish of it always within reach on the counter or alongside the stove. I use this for all stages of cooking, from initial seasoning of meats and fish to final seasoning of sauces.

For finishing dishes, I often use coarse sea salt. The best salt of this type is called *fleur de sel* (flower of salt), flaky crystals of salt that are carefully removed from the prime top layer of seaside salt beds. Brittany is famous for its fleur de sel, though my favorite comes from Mauritius, a small island in the Indian Ocean off the coast of Madagascar. It is whiter than French sea salts, and I find the Mauritius salt to have a more pronounced, purer salt flavor. A sprinkle of fleur de sel over a dish just before serving adds a distinct boost of flavor, not to mention the wonderful crunch that the salt provides. Even a simple tomato slice, fresh from the garden, topped with a pinch of fleur de sel is made magnificent.

I also use a gray rock sea salt from Noirmoutier (an island close to my hometown on the coast of Vendée). Gray sea salt is one layer below the fleur de sel, and we commonly use it for blanching vegetables and for poaching meat and seafood. From time to time I also use black smoked sea salt from Iran and pink salt from one of the oldest mines in the world in Pakistan. These special salts are also used for finishing dishes just before serving.

## Truffles

Truffles are a wonderful underground fungi that have a robust, earthy flavor and add elegance to a wide range of dishes. They can be thinly shaved, grated, sliced, julienned, diced, and prepared in any number of ways. But unlike their near-kin wild mushrooms, truffles don't require cooking. They can be added to soups or sauces at the last minute or simply used as a garnish.

The king of all truffles, in my opinion, is the winter Périgord black truffle *(Tuber melanosporum)* from France, and the queen is the Italian white truffle *(Tuber magnatum)* that comes from the Piedmont region, which is also at its best in early winter. In summer, I am lucky enough to get summer black truffles *(Tuber aestivum)* from France, Spain, and Italy. These truffles are a bit lighter in color and aroma. Winter truffles don't lose their character when cooked, so they are more versatile; summer truffles are best used raw or added to a dish just before serving.

I store truffles whole, embedded in raw rice in an airtight container. They can be stored this way in the refrigerator for up to a week, so it's best not to buy more truffle than you plan to use up quickly. The rice will absorb some of the excess moisture from the truffle, which helps avoid spoilage. Luckily, the rice absorbs some aroma and flavor from the truffle as well, so once you use the truffle, cook up the rice for a special treat. Some people also store truffles in an airtight container with whole eggs. Egg shells are slightly porous, so they absorb some of the flavor and aroma of the truffle, particularly white truffles, which are very aromatic.

When you buy truffles, they should be quite firm, evenly colored on the outside, and with no soft spots or mold. First scrub the truffle well under cold running water, then dry very well with paper towels. I will even pop the truffle into a 350°F oven for just a minute or two to help ensure they are fully dry before being stored.

## Wild Mushrooms, *to clean*

I am so fortunate in the Northwest to have access to dozens of varieties of wild mushrooms. The greatest assortment—including chanterelle, cèpe (also known as porcini or king bolete), lobster, coral, cauliflower, hedgehog, yellowfoot, matsutake, hen of the woods, honey mushroom, black trumpet, oyster mushrooms—show up in fall and early winter. Spring brings morel mushrooms, and over the summer I often see early chanterelle and lobster mushrooms.

Use a pastry brush to remove any pine needles, dirt, or other debris. Some mushrooms, such as morels, have indentations and crevasses that cleverly hide dirt and debris. For these mushrooms, I fill a large bowl with cold water, add the mushrooms, and gently toss them around. I let the mushrooms sit for 30 to 60 seconds, then lift them out, gently shake them, and spread them out on paper towels to drain, patting the tops with more paper towels to remove the excess water as quickly as possible. It's best to do this a couple of hours ahead so they are very dry. Mushrooms absorb water, which they release when cooked, but it is still a good idea to keep their contact with water to a minimum.

We dry some of the season's mushrooms—such as morels, cèpes, and chanterelles—in our dehydrator to use later in the season. I reconstitute the dried mushrooms in cold water or vegetable stock for 3 to 4 hours before using them. The bonus with dried mushrooms is that you will be left with a flavorful and aromatic soaking liquid, which makes a tasty addition to sauces and soups.

## COOKING WITH VINEGAR

As you read through the recipes in this book, you'll notice that I like to cook with vinegar. There are always a dozen or so types on hand in the Rover's kitchen, including classic balsamic, red wine, sherry, and rice wine, as well as the less common thyme vinegar, cherry vinegar, walnut vinegar, and marine cider vinegar (based on apple cider, with the addition of seaweed).

Vinegar, with its bright, sharp flavor, is an ideal complement to recipes that are rich and/or sweet, easily perking up a sauce with its distinctive character. And vinegar naturally tempers the sweetness or richness of other ingredients, such as beets or foie gras.

As a simple example, take olive oil. A good olive oil has amazing flavor on its own. But add a touch of Champagne vinegar and its flavor is completely changed due to the richness of the oil. Vinegar adds a huge amount of personality to recipes, but don't overdo it. Vinegar's strong acidity can quickly take over a dish if used with a heavy hand, so it's important to add vinegar judiciously. I often reduce vinegar before using it; it helps accentuate its sugary qualities while toning down its sharpness.

We also make vinegar at the restaurant, which is very easy to do. In fact, vinegar (*vinaigre* in French) is simply wine *(vin)* that has gone sour *(aigre)*. If you were to keep a bottle of wine open on the counter, it would eventually turn to vinegar. Though we buy wine specifically for making vinegar at Rover's, you can store your leftover red wine in a vinegar crock or barrel (kitchen shops sell small countertop barrels just for this purpose) covered with cheesecloth. The first batch will take 4 to 6 months to sour, but after that you can continue adding small amounts of leftover or inexpensive wine and the red wine vinegar will continue maturing and developing over the course of many years. I've also made flavored vinegars as well, including raspberry, mixed berry, and rosemary. There have also been some experiments. Okay...so the lavender vinegar didn't work out too well.

## THIERRY'S ACKNOWLEDGMENTS

My deepest thanks to everyone who makes it possible for me to live out my passions at Rover's, the story of which is told in these pages:

To my parents for teaching me about those simple things in life, like tilling, planting, picking, cooking, and eating. They also taught me the pleasure of sitting together around the table for every meal, be it a dinner for four or a special party for fifteen. It is my hope to encourage readers to experience a bit of that same camaraderie around their own dinner tables.

To all our great customers who have consistently supported me through the years; some of them have become valued friends. I could not have done it without you.

To all the chef friends I have made through the years; these peers have kept me on my toes and inspired me along the way.

To all the foragers, farmers, growers, and suppliers who follow their passions every day; I am proud and privileged to be a recipient of their great work.

To my dedicated sous-chef, Adam Hoffman, who I am sure does not always love me but who always goes to bat for me.

To my longtime friend, manager, and sommelier extraordinaire, Cyril Fréchier, who I am very glad to have by my side in this endeavor.

To all the past and present employees who have truly made Rover's what it is today.

To Cynthia, my cowriter, for putting up with me while we worked on this book (which was not easy), for having the patience it needed, and for keeping her cool in the kitchen when things got hot.

To my wife, Kathy, for being such a great mom and for creating the gorgeous weekly flower arrangements that make Rover's look so good.

## CYNTHIA'S ACKNOWLEDGMENTS

I would like to thank Leora Bloom for all her assistance on this project, particularly with the recipe testing and copyediting. She said it was awfully hard to feel satisfied by a peanut butter sandwich when hunger hit while reading these recipes. Oh, I do know what she means!

# ROVER'S STAFF

### Cyril Fréchier, Sommelier and General Manager

A friend from my early Chicago days, Cyril and I met six months after I arrived in the United States some 25 years ago. With his slower and more thoughtful approach to decision making, Cyril has been a wonderful collaborator and confidant over the years. With the growth of the restaurant came the growth of the wine cellar and Cyril's increasing admiration for wines. Today he oversees a cellar with more than 500 selections, as well as managing the daily operation of the dining room; there is no room for boredom in his busy day! We moved from Chicago to Los Angeles together and were best man at each other's weddings. Eighteen years ago, Kathy and I made the decision to move to Seattle after a visit with Cyril and his wife, Carolyn. He has been at Rover's for more than 15 years, and the restaurant just wouldn't be the same without him.

### Adam Hoffman, Sous-Chef

Adam works very hard every day to accomplish what I want the way I want it, and he also makes sure that the kitchen runs smoothly. He has been my right hand in the kitchen for more than three years and began as a lead cook three years before that. He is an awesome cook. He also is a genuinely nice guy (a particularly pleasant attribute for any busy restaurant kitchen), and eager to try any new creation, crazy or not (both mine and his own). I am very fortunate to have someone like Adam in my kitchen.

# INDEX